Brief Review in
PHYSICS

Atomic
44 - 46

by
SAMUEL A. MARANTZ
James Madison High School
New York City

STANDARD PUBLISHING
104 5th Avenue • New York, N. Y. 10011

733

1 3 5 7 9 10 8 6 4 2

ABOUT THIS BOOK

BRIEF REVIEW IN PHYSICS is a concise text and review aid for the New York State Syllabus in Physics and a means of preparing for the Regents Examination in this subject. The following features of its content and organization will be of special interest to teachers and students.

1. Concise explanations of all understandings and fundamental concepts included in the syllabus.

2. An organization that closely follows the sequence of topics in the syllabus.

3. All the formulas and mathematical relationships that the student needs to know and use.

4. Sample problems illustrating the basic types of calculations the student should be able to perform.

5. Hundreds of practice questions of Regents type, conveniently divided into topical groupings.

6. A special Appendix that reviews basic mathematical skills required for physics problems.

7. The *Physics Reference Tables* that are needed for answering many of the Regents Examination questions.

8. Several of the most recent Regents Examinations.

CONTENTS

MECHANICS

WAVE PHENOMENA

ELECTRICITY

ATOMIC AND NUCLEAR PHYSICS

REGENTS EXAMINATIONS

MECHANICS

1. KINEMATICS

Mechanics is the study of forces and motion. We begin the study of mechanics with a mathematical description of motion itself, without regard to the forces that produce motion. This description is called *kinematics.*

Distance and Displacement

When an object moves from one point to another, its change in position may be described either by indicating the total distance it moves, or by indicating its straight-line distance from the starting point. The first is called *distance*; the second is called *displacement.* For example, if a baseball player runs the 90 ft from home plate to first base, then over-runs 10 ft and finally returns to first base, the *distance* that he has travelled is 110 ft, but his *displacement* from the starting point is 90 ft.

The distance is indicated simply by a numerical measurement of length, but the displacement must include the *direction* from starting to stopping point. Such measurements as distance, which include a number and unit quantity, are called *scalar* quantities; they are added and subtracted according to the rules of arithmetic. Such measurements as displacement, which also include an indication of direction, are called *vector* quantities. Geometric methods are often used in adding and subtracting vectors.

Velocity and Speed

Fundamentally, motion consists of both the distance an object moves and the time during which it moves. Rate of motion, or *speed*, is therefore expressed in terms of length per unit time. In the metric (MKS) system, the unit of length is the meter (m) and the unit of time is the second (sec). For example, if a car moves 150 m in 10 sec, its speed is $\dfrac{150 \text{ m}}{10 \text{ sec}} = 15$ m/sec. If the rate of motion of an object does not change, the object is said to be in *uniform motion.* If the rate does change, then the motion is non-uniform, and the speed given for the object is an average over the given distance. The equation for average speed is

$$\overline{v} = \frac{s}{t} \tag{1}$$

where $\overline{v}$ is average speed, s is distance and t is time.

Speed (or average speed) is a scalar quantity. If a direction is added to the description of the motion (for example, if the motion of a car is given as 15 m/sec northward), it becomes a measure of displacement per unit time. This is called the *velocity* (or *average velocity*, if the motion is non-uniform) and is a vector, since it includes a magnitude or number, "15"; a unit, "meters/second"; and

1

a direction, "northward." The average speed in this example is also the scalar quantity which represents the magnitude of the vector velocity.

Usually, a series of separate or successive displacements is shown by graphs in which the horizontal axis is time (because time is independent of the motion of any particular object), and the vertical axis is displacement. Such graphs clearly reveal the differences in various kinds of motion. A sloping straight line indicates that the speed is constant throughout the time interval; a curved line indicates that the speed is changing; a horizontal line indicates that the object is motionless. The steepness of the slope is a measure of the speed; the algebraic sign of the slope shows the direction of travel. A positive slope shows travel in a forward direction; a negative slope shows travel in the opposite direction. The graphs in Figure 1 represent these types of motion.

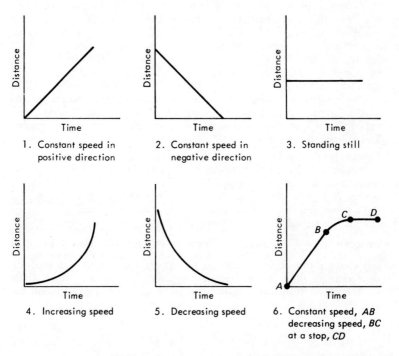

Figure 1. Graphs of linear motion.

Acceleration

Change of speed per unit time is called *acceleration*. The speed of a boy coasting downhill on roller skates may increase from 4 m/sec to 10 m/sec during a time of 3 sec. His change of speed, Δv (which is found by subtracting the initial speed, v_i, from the final speed, v_f) is 6 m/sec. The elapsed time, Δt, is 3 sec. The acceleration, a, is

$$a = \frac{\Delta v}{\Delta t} \tag{2}$$

$$= \frac{6 \text{ m/sec}}{3 \text{ sec}} = 2 \text{ m/sec per sec} = 2 \text{ m/sec}^2$$

This acceleration is shown graphically in Figure 2, where speed is plotted against time. The slope of the line shows the acceleration, as calculated from $\Delta v/\Delta t$. As mentioned above, acceleration is a scalar quantity. If a direction is associated with this acceleration magnitude, such as 2 m/sec² southwest, then the acceleration is a vector quantity like displacement or velocity.

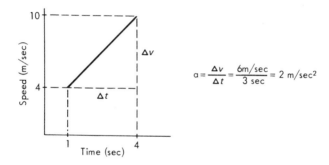

Figure 2. Graph on speed–time axes of boy accelerating at 2 m/sec².

Accelerated motion of various kinds can be shown on speed-time graphs (Figure 3). For example, a horizontal line shows constant speed (no acceleration); a line with positive slope shows increasing speed; and one with negative slope shows decreasing speed (negative acceleration or deceleration). A line which crosses the time axis is interpreted as a change of direction, whereas a curved line indicates that the acceleration itself is not constant.

QUESTIONS

1. **Which graph represents the motion of an object that is moving with constant velocity?**

2. **Which is a vector quantity?** (1) speed (2) time (3) velocity (4) distance

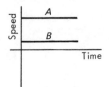

1. Both *A* and *B* are moving at constant speed; acceleration is zero; *A* is travelling faster than *B*.

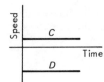

2. *C* and *D* have zero acceleration, constant speed. *D* is moving faster than *C*, but in the opposite direction.

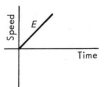

3. *E* is accelerating uniformly.

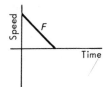

4. *F* is decreasing speed, and is accelerating (negative acceleration).

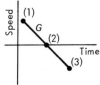

5. *G* is decreasing speed from (1) to (2), is motionless at (2), and increases speed in the opposite direction from (2) to (3). Slope and acceleration are negative at all times. (An object thrown upward would have this curve.)

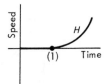

6. *H* is at rest up to time (1), and has non-uniform acceleration after that time.

Figure 3.   Graphs of various types of motion in a straight path, drawn on speed-time axes.

3-7. Questions 3 through 7 are based on the graph at right, which represents the trip of a cart along a straight line. The total trip takes 12 sec and starts at *t* = 0.

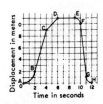

3. The part of the trip during which the cart was at rest is represented by line (1) *AB* (2) *BC* (3) *DE* (4) *GH*
4. What was the total *distance* covered by the cart during the trip (*AH*)? (1) 6 m (2) 11 m (3) 12 m (4) 22 m
5. What is the average speed of the cart during the part of the trip labeled *CD*? (1) 1 m/sec (2) 2 m/sec (3) 10 m/sec (4) 11 m/sec
6. Of the following, the part of the trip during which the cart was moving with constant speed is represented by line (1) *AB* (2) *BC* (3) *EF* (4) *GH*
7. Of the following, one part of the trip during which the speed was *not* constant is represented by line (1) *AB* (2) *BC* (3) *DE* (4) *FG*

Distance Travelled During Acceleration

The distance travelled by a uniformly accelerating object can be calculated from the formula

$$s = \bar{v}t \tag{3}$$

Since the speed is constantly changing, the average speed must be determined before this distance formula is used. The average speed, $\bar{v}$, is always one-half the difference between the initial speed v_i and the final speed v_f, if the acceleration is uniform:

$$\bar{v} = \frac{v_f + v_i}{2} \tag{4}$$

If the object starts from rest, $v_i = 0$ and $\bar{v} = \frac{v_f}{2}$. Rearranging terms in formula 2 gives the following formula for the final speed v_f after t sec of an object accelerating uniformly from rest $(v_i = 0)$:

$$v = at \tag{5}$$

By combining formulas 3, 4, and 5, we obtain the formula for the distance travelled by an object accelerating uniformly from rest:

$$s = \tfrac{1}{2}at^2 \tag{6}$$

When an object accelerates uniformly from rest, the distance it travels is proportional to the square of the time. Formula 6 must therefore be used to find this distance. For example, if the travel time is doubled, the distance covered is increased fourfold.

EXAMPLE

A plane increases its speed uniformly, starting from rest and reaching a speed of 50 m/sec after 10 sec. Find (a) the average speed of the plane, (b) the acceleration, and (c) the distance travelled during 10 sec.

Solution: (a) The average speed is, from formula 4:

$$\bar{v} = \frac{v}{2} = \frac{50 \text{ m/sec}}{2} = 25 \text{ m/sec}$$

(b) The acceleration is defined in formula 2 as

$$a = \frac{\Delta v}{\Delta t} \text{ or } \frac{v}{t} = \frac{50 \text{ m/sec}}{10 \text{ sec}} = 5 \text{ m/sec}^2$$

(c) The distance travelled is given by formula 6:

$$s = \tfrac{1}{2}at^2 = \tfrac{1}{2}(5 \text{ m/sec}^2)(10 \text{ sec})^2$$
$$= \tfrac{1}{2} \times 5 \text{ m} \times 100 = 250 \text{ m}$$

(The acceleration of the plane is graphed in Figure 4.)

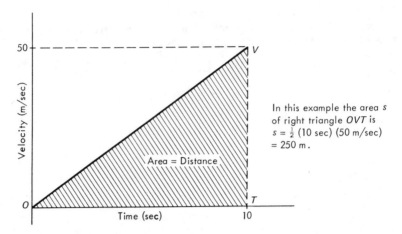

In this example the area s of right triangle OVT is
$s = \frac{1}{2}$ (10 sec) (50 m/sec)
= 250 m.

Figure 4.   Distance calculation from velocity-time graph.

The relations between time, acceleration, and distance can be shown as a graph. This is illustrated in Figure 4, where the initial speed $v(0)$ and the final speed, v, of the plane after t seconds are used to draw the graph. The distance s travelled by the plane may be calculated from the area of the shaded triangle OVT. The area of a triangle is one-half the base multiplied by the altitude. In this problem, the base is the time, 10 sec, and the altitude is the speed, 50 m/sec.

Figure 5 indicates how distances travelled at various speeds may be calculated and compared.

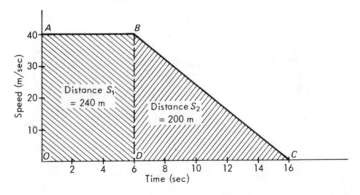

Figure 5.   From A to B, an object travels 240m, calculated from area $OABD$. From B to C, object travels 200m, calculated from area BDC.

Freely Falling Objects

An object falling in vacuum is said to be in "free fall." Experiment shows that such an object accelerates at the rate of 9.8 meters per second for each second (9.8 m/sec²). This acceleration is given the symbol g. After t seconds, the velocity of an object in free fall is

$$v = gt \qquad (7)$$

Similarly, the distance it travels is

$$s = \tfrac{1}{2}gt^2 \qquad (8)$$

The following table shows the changes in distance and velocity of an object during its first five seconds of free fall.

Time of fall (sec)	0	1	2	3	4	5
Velocity (m/sec)	0	9.8	19.6	29.4	39.2	49
Distance travelled (m)	0	4.9	19.6	44.1	78.4	122.5

QUESTIONS

1. The graph at right shows the speed of an object plotted against time. The total distance travelled by the object during the first 4 sec is (1) 0.5 m (2) 2 m (3) 8 m (4) 4 m

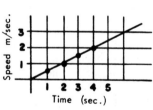

2. How far will a freely falling object, initially at rest, fall in 3 sec? (1) 14.7 m (2) 29.4 m (3) 44.1 m (4) 88.2 m

3. An object originally at rest is uniformly accelerated along a straight-line path to a speed of 8.0 m/sec in 2.0 sec. What was the acceleration of the object? (1) 0.25 m/sec² (2) 10 m/sec² (3) 16 m/sec² (4) 4.0 m/sec²

4. The time rate of change of displacement is (1) acceleration (2) distance (3) velocity (4) speed

5. A body falls freely from rest near the surface of the earth. The distance the object falls in 2 sec is (1) 4.9 m (2) 9.8 m (3) 19.6 m (4) 39.2 m

6. Which graph describes the motion of a freely falling object near the surface of the earth?

7. In order to have a change in velocity, there *must* be (1) an increase in speed (2) a decrease in speed (3) a change in either speed or direction (4) a change in both speed and direction

8. The motions of cars *A, B,* and *C* in a straight path are represented by the graph at right. During the time interval from t_1 to t_2, the three cars travel (1) the same distance (2) with the same velocity only (3) with the same acceleration only (4) with both the same velocity and acceleration

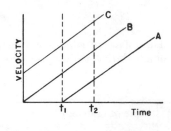

9. An object is accelerated from rest to a speed of 25 m/sec in 10 sec. The acceleration of the object is (1) 1.0 m/sec² (2) 2.0 m/sec² (3) 1.5 m/sec² (4) 2.5 m/sec²

10. How many meters will a 2.00-kg mass starting from rest fall freely in 1.00 sec? (1) 4.90 (2) 2.00 (3) 9.80 (4) 19.6

11. As the time required to accelerate an object from rest to a speed of 4 m/sec decreases, the acceleration of the object (1) decreases (2) increases (3) remains the same

12. As an object falls freely near the earth, its acceleration (1) decreases (2) increases (3) remains the same

13. The graph at right represents the velocity versus time relationship for a ball thrown vertically upward. Time zero represents the time of release. During the time interval between 1.0 sec and 2.0 sec, the displacement of the ball from the point where it was released (1) decreases (2) increases (3) remains the same

14-18. Base your answers to Questions 14 through 18 on the graph at right, which represents the changing speed of an object during an interval of 20 sec.

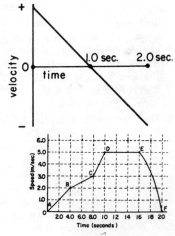

14. What is the distance covered in interval *AB*? (1) 1.0 m (2) 2.0 m
    (3) 8.0 m (4) 4.0 m
15. In which of the following intervals is the magnitude of acceleration
    greatest? (1) *AB* (2) *BC* (3) *CD* (4) *DE*
16. During interval *BC*, the magnitude of the acceleration is (1) 1.0
    m/sec² (2) 0.25 m/sec² (3) 0.50 m/sec² (4) 4.0 m/sec²
17. The average speed for interval *CD* is (1) 15 m/sec (2) 2.0 m/sec
    (3) 7.5 m/sec (4) 4.0 m/sec
18. In which interval is the acceleration changing? (1) *BC* (2) *CD*
    (3) *DE* (4) *EF*

19-23. Base your answers to Questions 19 through 23 on the graph at right, which represents velocity versus time for an object in linear motion. The object has a velocity of 20 m/sec at *t* = 0.

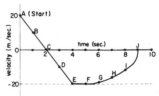

19. During which interval is the magnitude of the acceleration
    greatest? (1) *EF* (2) *FG* (3) *GH* (4) *IJ*
20. The acceleration of the object at point *D* on the curve is (1)
    0 m/sec² (2) 5 m/sec² (3) −10 m/sec² (4) −20 m/sec²
21. During what interval does the object have zero acceleration?
    (1) *BC* (2) *EF* (3) *GH* (4) *HI*
22. At what point is the distance from the start zero? (1) *C*
    (2) *E* (3) *F* (4) *J*
23. At what point is the distance from start a maximum? (1) *C*
    (2) *E* (3) *G* (4) *J*

24-28. Graph *ABCDE* represents the motion of an object. Velocity is plotted against time. For Questions 24 through 28, write the *number* preceding the word or expression that, of those given, best answers each question.

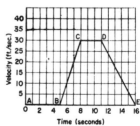

24. In which section of the graph is the shortest distance covered?
    (1) *AB* (2) *BC* (3) *CD* (4) *DE*
25. In which section of the graph is the average velocity the greatest?
    (1) *AB* (2) *BC* (3) *CD* (4) *DE*
26. In which section of the graph is the greatest distance covered?
    (1) *AB* (2) *BC* (3) *CD* (4) *DE*
27. In which section of the graph is the acceleration (positive or
    negative) the greatest? (1) *AB* (2) *BC* (3) *CD* (4) *DE*
28. In how many sections of the graph is the acceleration zero?
    (1) 1 (2) 2 (3) 3 (4) 4

2. FORCE

Any straight-line push or pull is a force. The amount of the push or pull is usually expressed in pounds (lb) in the English system, and in newtons (nt) in the metric system. Force is a vector quantity because it is always associated with a direction. If two forces act on the same object at the same time, their effect will be the same as the effect of a single force that combines both the magnitude and the direction of the original forces. For example, a 20 nt force and a 15 nt force may combine to act like a single 35 nt force, if they act in the same direction, or like a single 5 nt force, if they act in opposite directions.

Composition of Forces

Two or more forces that act on the same body at the same time are called *concurrent* forces. The single force that is equivalent to the combined effect of these concurrent forces is called the *resultant* force. The mathematical process of combining the magnitude and direction of concurrent forces to find their resultant is called *composition of forces*. The same mathematical process, vector addition, is used to find the resultant of any pair of vector quantities, such as resultant velocity, resultant displacement, or resultant acceleration.

Obviously, if two forces act in the same direction (at an angle of 0° to each other), their magnitudes are simply added to give the magnitude of the resultant force, which acts in the same direction as the two component forces. If the component forces act in opposite directions (at an angle of 180° to each other), the resultant force is equal in magnitude to the difference between the forces, and its direction is the same as that of the larger force. For example, a force F_1 of 8 nt and a force F_2 of 6 nt, both acting on the same body toward the north, will yield a resultant, R, equal to 14 nt north. But if F_1 is 8 nt north and F_2 is 6 nt south, then the resultant, R, is 2 nt north. Regardless of the angle at which a pair of forces act, the magnitude of their resultant cannot be larger than their sum or smaller than their difference.

The resultant, c, of two forces, a and b, acting at right angles (90°) to each other can be calculated from the theorem of Pythagoras, $c^2 = a^2 + b^2$. For example, if forces of 8 nt and 6 nt are acting at right angles on an object, the resultant force, R, is $R = \sqrt{(8 \text{ nt})^2 + (6 \text{ nt})^2} = \sqrt{100 \text{ nt}^2} = 10$ nt. This can be represented graphically by drawing each force vector to scale in the given direction, preferably on graph paper. The two vectors are positioned head-to-tail to form the sides of a right triangle. The third side of the triangle, drawn from the tail end of the first vector to the arrowhead of the second vector, represents the resultant force vector. Measuring the length of this resultant will give the magnitude of the force, and the angle that this resultant makes with the x-axis of the graph is the direction of the resultant. This graphical method of finding a resultant works for pairs of vectors acting at any angle. Figure 6 illustrates the resultant of a force of 8 nt north

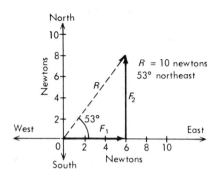

R is the resultant vector, obtained by drawing a vector from the tail of vector F_1 to the arrowhead of vector F_2. The magnitude is measured according to the scale, and the angle is found by protractor.

Figure 6. Determination of the resultant.

acting concurrently with a force of 6 nt east. By scale measurement of the resultant, the magnitude is found to be 10 nt, while a protractor measurement shows that the direction is 53° northeast.

Resolution of Forces

A single force can be treated as the resultant of two component forces. The process of finding the magnitude and direction of such component forces is known as *resolution* and is the reverse of composition of forces. The component forces are generally given specified directions, usually east-west and north-south to match the x and y axes of a graph. This method of force resolution is illustrated in Figure 7, which shows a force of 50 nt 37° northeast that has been

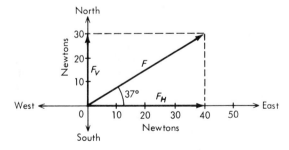

Figure 7. Resolution of forces. A force vector, F, of 50 nt directed 37° northeast is shown to be resolved into two forces, F_V and F_H, which are the vertical and horizontal components obtained by drawing perpendiculars to the axes. They measure 30 nt and 40 nt respectively, drawn to scale.

graphically resolved into two component forces at an angle of 90°
to each other. One force, F_1, is along the east-west axis, and the
other force, F_2, is along the north-south axis. The magnitude of each
force is found by drawing perpendiculars to each axis from the head
end of the given vector. The line drawn from the origin, O, to the
intersections will determine the magnitude of each vector. The components are thus found to be: $F_1 = 40$ nt east, $F_2 = 30$ nt north.

QUESTIONS

1. An object is displaced 3 m to the west and then 4 m to the
   south. Which vector represents the resultant displacement of
   the block?

2. Four forces act on a point as
   shown. The resultant of the
   four forces is (1) 0 nt (2) 5 nt
   (3) 14 nt (4) 20 nt

3. A 5 nt force directed north and a 5 nt force directed west both
   act on the same point. The resultant of these two forces is
   approximately (1) 5 nt northwest (2) 7 nt northwest (3) 5 nt
   southwest (4) 7 nt southwest

4. The resultant of a 12 nt force and a 7 nt force is 5 nt. The angle
   between the forces is (1) 0° (2) 45° (3) 90° (4) 180°

5. Two concurrent forces of 30 nt each act to produce a resultant
   whose magnitude is 60 nt. The angle between these two forces
   must be (1) 0° (2) 60° (3) 90° (4) 120°

6. Concurrent forces of 10 nt east and 10 nt south act on an
   object. The resultant force is (1) 0 nt (2) 5.0 nt southeast
   (3) 14 nt southeast (4) 20 nt southeast

7. Which pair of concurrent forces may have a resultant of 20 nt?
   (1) 5.0 nt and 10 nt (2) 20 nt and 20 nt (3) 20 nt and 50 nt
   (4) 30 nt and 5.0 nt

8. The magnitude of the resultant force produced by a 9.0 nt
   force acting west and a 12 nt force acting south is (1) 30 nt
   (2) 25 nt (3) 3.0 nt (4) 15 nt

9. Which vector best represents the resultant of forces F_1 and F_2 acting on point P?

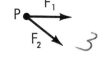

 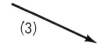

(1) (2) (3) (4)

10. The resultant of two forces acting on the same point is a maximum when the angle between the two forces is (1) 0° (2) 45° (3) 90° (4) 180°

11. The vector which best represents the resultant of the forces F_1 and F_2 shown acting on point P is

(1) (2) (3) (4)

12. What is the magnitude of the vertical or y-component of vector OB in the diagram? (1) 9 (2) 6 (3) 3 (4) 0

13. Which force could act concurrently with force A to produce force B as a resultant?

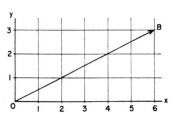

(1) (2) (3) (4)

14. Three forces act concurrently on an object in equilibrium. These forces are 10 nt, 8 nt, and 6 nt. The resultant of the 6 nt and 8 nt forces is (1) 0 (2) between 0 and 10 nt (3) 10 nt (4) greater than 10 nt

15. As the angle between two concurrent forces increases, the magnitude of their resultant (1) decreases (2) increases (3) remains the same

16. As the angle between two concurrent forces is increased from 10° to 75°, the magnitude of the resultant force (1) decreases (2) increases (3) remains the same

3. DYNAMICS

The study of how the forces acting on an object affect its motion is the subject matter of *dynamics*. The foundations of this branch of physics were developed by Galileo Galilei and Isaac Newton about 300 years ago.

The Relationship Between Force and Motion

Newton's First Law of Motion. When the resultant of all the forces acting on an object is 0, that is, all the forces are balanced, the object is said to be in a state of *equilibrium*. Newton's first law of motion, sometimes called the law of inertia, states that an object will *remain* in a state of equilibrium as long as all the forces acting on it remain in balance. The object will remain at rest, or, if in motion, will maintain a uniform (straight-line) velocity, unless it is acted upon by an unbalanced force. In effect, this law says that an unbalanced force will always produce a *change* in velocity—an acceleration—by changing either the speed of the object, or its direction of motion, or both.

For example, a car parked on a level road (velocity = 0) will not start moving (accelerating) unless a force is applied to it by the motor or by other means. Since the car is in a state of equilibrium, the forces that are acting on it, although at first glance not readily recognized, must be in balance. The same is true of an airplane moving at constant speed in one direction (constant velocity). Its velocity will not change unless an unbalanced force acts upon it.

Newton's Second Law of Motion. When an unbalanced force acts on an object, the object is accelerated in the direction in which the force acts. Obviously, for a given object, the larger the force, the greater the resulting acceleration. Acceleration is therefore directly proportional to force. Experience also shows that the more matter an object contains, the less a given force will accelerate it. For example, the same force will give less acceleration to a loaded cart than to an empty cart. The word *mass* is commonly used to mean the quantity of matter in an object. Acceleration is therefore inversely proportional to mass. Combining these proportionalities gives Newton's second law, which states that the force, F, applied to an object is equal to its mass, m, multiplied by the acceleration, a, produced by the force. In equation form,

$$F = ma \qquad\qquad (9)$$

Written in the form $a = F/m$, the equation shows that acceleration is directly proportional to force and inversely proportional to mass. In the form $m = F/a$, the equation defines the *inertial mass* of an object as the ratio between the force acting on it and the resulting acceleration. In the MKS system, the mass is given in kilograms (kg) and the acceleration in meters per second per second (m/sec^2).

Fundamental Units. By international agreement among scientists, the meter, kilogram, and second, which form the MKS system, are selected as fundamental units, and are not expressed in terms of other units. Other units, however, can be expressed in terms of these units of length, mass, and time. From Newton's second law, the unit of force is the product of the kilogram and the meter per second^2 (kg-m/sec^2). This unit is given the name newton (nt). One newton of force will accelerate a mass of 1 kg at the rate of 1 m/sec^2.

Newton's Third Law of Motion. According to Newton's third law of motion, whenever one object exerts a force on a second object, the second object exerts an equal force on the first object, but in the opposite direction. In Newton's words, "To every action there is always an equal and opposite reaction." The law states that a single force cannot be produced in nature; when one force is generated, another force of equal magnitude and opposite direction must also be generated. For example, when a person pushes against a wall with a 20 nt force, the wall pushes back on him with an identical 20 nt force. When a baseball receives a 50 nt force from a bat, the bat at the same time receives a 50 nt force from the ball in the opposite direction. Remember that each member of a pair of forces acts on a different mass: one force acts on the ball and another on the bat. If no other forces are present, each will be accelerated in opposite directions as long as force is applied.

QUESTIONS

1. What force is necessary to give a 2.0-kg mass initially at rest an acceleration of 5.0 m/sec^2? (1) 0.4 nt (2) 2.5 nt (3) 10 nt (4) 20 nt

2. A force of 10 nt applied to mass m accelerates it at 2.0 m/sec^2. The same force applied to a mass of 2 m would produce an acceleration of (1) 1.0 m/sec^2 (2) 2.0 m/sec^2 (3) 0.5 m/sec^2 (4) 4.0 m/sec^2

3. Which is a derived unit? (1) second (2) meter (3) kilogram (4) newton

4. A 2-nt force acts on a 3-kg mass for 6 sec. The change of velocity of the mass is (1) 18 m/sec (2) 2 m/sec (3) 36 m/sec (4) 4 m/sec

5. If a force of 50 nt will accelerate an object at 20 m/sec^2, then the mass of the object is (1) 0.4 kg (2) 2.5 kg (3) 70 kg (4) 1000 kg

6. The force required to accelerate a 2.0-kg mass at 4.0 m/sec^2 is (1) 6.0 nt (2) 2.0 nt (3) 8.0 nt (4) 16 nt

7. A 30-kg boy exerts a force of 100 nt on a 50-kg object. The force that the object exerts on the boy is (1) 0 nt (2) 100 nt (3) 980 nt (4) 1500 nt

8. A car whose mass is 2000 kg is accelerated uniformly on a level highway from rest to a speed of 15 m/sec in 10 sec. The net

2   force accelerating the car is (1) 2000 nt (2) 3000 nt (3) 20,000 nt (4) 30,000 nt

4 9. A certain net force causes a 10-kg mass to accelerate at 20 m/sec². The same force will cause a 5.0-kg mass to accelerate at (1) 9.8 m/sec² (2) 10 m/sec² (3) 25 m/sec² (4) 40 m/sec²

2 10. A car is travelling on a level highway at a speed of 15 m/sec. A braking force of 3000 nt brings the car to a stop in 10 sec. The mass of the car is (1) 1500 kg (2) 2000 kg (3) 2500 kg (4) 3000 kg

2 11. In the graph at right, the acceleration of an object is plotted against the unbalanced force on the object. The mass of the body is (1) 1.0 kg (2) 2.0 kg (3) 0.5 kg (4) 8.0 kg

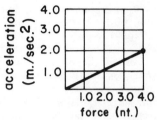

12. Which graph best represents the motion of an object on which the net force is zero?

1

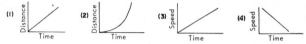

4 13. What is the net force on the block shown at right? (1) 0 nt (2) 9.8 nt (3) 10 nt (4) 20 nt

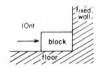

3 14. If the net force applied in the direction of motion to a certain mass on a horizontal frictionless surface is doubled, the acceleration of the body is (1) halved (2) unchanged (3) doubled (4) quadrupled

2 15. A 10-kg mass rests on a horizontal frictionless table. How much force is needed to give it a speed of 20 m/sec after 4 sec? (1) 40 nt (2) 50 nt (3) 200 nt (4) 800 nt

1 16. If the mass of an object is decreased, its inertia (1) decreases (2) increases (3) remains the same

3 17. If the sum of all the forces acting on a car is zero, the speed of the car always (1) decreases (2) increases (3) remains the same

2 18. As a constant unbalanced force acts on an object in the direction of motion, the object's speed (1) decreases (2) increases (3) remains the same

1 19. As the vector sum of all the forces acting on an object decreases, the acceleration of the object (1) decreases (2) increases (3) remains the same

20-24. Base your answers to Questions 20 through 24 on the following information.

A 2-kg mass starts to move to the *right* along a straight path, as shown by the accompanying velocity vs. time graph.

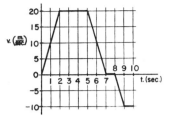

20. The mass has an acceleration of $+ 10$ m/sec^2 during the time interval (1) $t = 0$ sec to $t = 2$ sec (2) $t = 2$ sec to $t = 5$ sec (3) $t = 5$ sec to $t = 7$ sec (4) $t = 8$ sec to $t = 9$ sec

21. For the time interval $t = 0$ sec to $t = 2$ sec, how many meters will the 2-kg mass travel? (1) 10 (2) 20 (3) 30 (4) 40

22. The net force on the 2-kg mass is zero for the time interval (1) $t = 0$ sec to $t = 1$ sec (2) $t = 2$ sec to $t = 5$ sec (3) $t = 5$ sec to $t = 7$ sec (4) $t = 8$ sec to $t = 9$ sec

23. The 2-kg mass is at rest for the time interval (1) $t = 0$ sec to $t = 1$ sec (2) $t = 2$ sec to $t = 5$ sec (3) $t = 7$ sec to $t = 8$ sec (4) $t = 8$ sec to $t = 10$ sec

24. There is a net force toward the left on the 2-kg mass for the time interval (1) $t = 0$ sec to $t = 2$ sec (2) $t = 2$ sec to $t = 5$ sec (3) $t = 5$ sec to $t = 7$ sec (4) $t = 9$ sec to $t = 10$ sec

Newton's Law of Universal Gravitation

All objects appear to exert a force of attraction on each other, even when separated by large distances. This force is called gravity, or *gravitational force,* and is assumed to act throughout the universe. The relationship of this force to mass and distance was discovered by Newton. He found that any two masses attract one another with a force that is directly proportional to the product of the two masses and inversely proportional to the distance between them. In mathematical form,

$$F = \frac{GMm}{r^2} \qquad (10)$$

In the MKS system, F is the gravitational force in newtons between two objects, M and m are the masses of the objects in kilograms, r is in meters, and G is a proportionality constant equal to 6.67×10^{-11} nt-m^2/kg^2. The law holds for "point" masses, that is, masses whose sizes are small compared to the distance between them, and for spherical masses of uniform density. For hollow spheres, r is measured from the centers of the spheres.

Since r^2 appears in the denominator, if distance is doubled or tripled, the forces diminish to 1/4 or 1/9, respectively. If either mass is doubled or tripled, the forces increase only by a factor of 2 or 3, respectively. If both masses increase, for example, if one is doubled and the other is tripled, the force will increase by the product of these factors, that is, by 6 times.

Weight. The gravitational force acting on an object near the earth is called the *weight* of the object. If M is the mass of the earth and r is the distance from the center of the earth, it can be seen from Equation 10 that the weight w of a body at the earth's surface is directly proportional to its mass m, since all the other quantities are constant. Note, however, that w is a force and m is a mass, so that they are measured in different units. Also, the weight of a body will change if its distance r from the center of the earth changes.

EXAMPLE

An object of 10 kg mass is located 10^4 m from the center of an object of 10^9 kg mass in interstellar space. What is the gravitational force of attraction between the objects?

Solution:

The force of attraction is given by Newton's law of gravitation: $F = \dfrac{GMm}{r^2}$. The G constant everywhere in space is $G = 6.67 \times 10^{-11}$ nt-m^2/kg^2. Substituting the given values:

$$F = \frac{6.67 \times 10^{-11} \text{ nt-m}^2 \times 10^9 \text{ kg} \times 10^1 \text{ kg}}{\text{kg}^2 \times (10^4 \text{ m})^2}$$

$$= \frac{6.67 \times 10^{-11} \times 10^9 \times 10^1}{10^8} \text{ nt}$$

$$= 6.67 \times 10^{-9} \text{ nt}$$

The acceleration of a freely falling body is the result of the force of gravitation acting upon it. This force is its weight w, and we have seen that the acceleration near the earth's surface is g, a constant with a value of 9.8 m/sec^2 for all objects. We can therefore substitute the weight w for F and the acceleration g for a in Equation 9 (Newton's second law), and obtain

$$w = mg \tag{11}$$

In this formula, the weight w is a force expressed in newtons, the mass m is in kilograms, and the acceleration g is 9.8 m/sec^2. Therefore, *the weight of any object in newtons is 9.8 times its mass in kilograms.*

The weight of an object is always directed vertically downward. If the object is on an incline, the weight can be resolved into two components, one parallel to the incline, tending to make the object slide downward, and one perpendicular to the incline, tending to bend or break the surface. As the angle of inclination increases, the downhill component of the force (weight) increases and the incline-breaking component decreases.

Fields. In physics, the region in which some condition exists is called the *field* of that condition. For example, the region in which a force is observed to act is called the field of that force. Around every object there exists a *gravitational field* in which gravitational force acts on other objects. Similarly, surrounding magnetized objects, there is a *magnetic field* which affects other magnetic objects. The concept of fields is often used in physics to simplify the description of forces.

QUESTIONS

1. If the distance between two masses is tripled, the gravitational force between them becomes (1) 1/9 as great (2) 1/3 as great (3) 3 times as great (4) 9 times as great

2. A rocket weighs 10,000 nt at the earth's surface. If it rises to a height equal to the earth's radius, its weight will be (1) 2500 nt (2) 5000 nt (3) 10,000 nt (4) 40,000 nt

3. If the distance between two objects of constant mass is doubled, the gravitational force of attraction between them is (1) quartered (2) halved (3) doubled (4) quadrupled

4. If the mass of an object were doubled, its weight would be (1) halved (2) doubled (3) quadrupled (4) unchanged

5. An object weighing 20 nt at the earth's surface is moved to a distance where its weight is 10 nt. The acceleration due to gravity at this location would be (1) 2.4 m/sec^2 (2) 4.9 m/sec^2 (3) 9.8 m/sec^2 (4) 19.6 m/sec^2

6. If the weight of an object of mass m is mg, then the weight of an object of mass 3 m will be (1) $mg/3$ (2) mg (3) 3 mg (4) 9 mg

7. A block with a mass of 2.00 kg rests on a horizontal table. The force exerted by the table upon the mass is (1) 0.00 nt (2) 2.00 nt (3) 9.80 nt (4) 19.6 nt

8. A block with a mass of 2 kg rests on a horizontal table. The horizontal component of its weight is (1) 0 nt (2) 2 nt (3) 9.8 nt (4) 19.6 nt

9. A 10-kg iron ball and a 5-kg iron ball have the same acceleration when dropped from the same height because (1) action equals reaction (2) both are made of iron (3) the ratio of force to mass is the same for both (4) the gravitational force is the same for both

10. As the distance between two masses increases, the gravitational force of attraction between them (1) decreases (2) increases (3) remains the same

11. As a satellite moves farther away from the earth, the weight of the satellite with respect to the earth (1) decreases (2) increases (3) remains the same

12. Three equal masses A, B, and C are arranged as shown in the diagram. If the gravitational force between A and B is 3 nt, then the gravitational force between A and C is (1) 1 nt (2) 9 nt (3) 3 nt (4) 27 nt

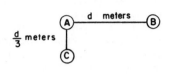

13. A man weighing 800 nt is standing in an elevator. If the elevator rises with an acceleration of 9.8 m/sec^2, the force exerted by the elevator on the man will be (1) 400 nt (2) 800 nt (3) 1600 nt (4) 2000 nt

14. A 2.00-kg mass is at rest on a horizontal surface. The force exerted by the surface on the mass is approximately (1) 0 nt (2) 2.00 nt (3) 9.80 nt (4) 19.6 nt

15. A block weighing 10 nt is held motionless on a frictionless inclined plane which makes an angle of 30° with the horizontal. The force parallel to the incline needed to hold the block in position is (1) 0 nt (2) 5 nt (3) 10 nt (4) 20 nt

16. A 10-kg rocket fragment falling toward the earth has net downward acceleration of 5 m/sec^2. The net downward force acting on the fragment is (1) 5 nt (2) 10 nt (3) 50 nt (4) 98 nt

17. A block with a mass of 2 kg rests on a horizontal table. The horizontal component of its weight is (1) 0 nt (2) 2 nt (3) 9.8 nt (4) 19.6 nt

18. Neglecting friction, as the initial speed of a bullet fired horizontally increases, the time required for it to fall a distance of 1 m (1) decreases (2) increases (3) remains the same

19. Neglecting air resistance, as a projectile fired from a cannon begins to fall, the horizontal component of its velocity (1) decreases (2) increases (3) remains the same

20. A box rests on a plank which is inclined to the horizontal. As the angle between the plank and the horizontal increases, the component of the weight of the box parallel to the plank (1) decreases (2) increases (3) remains the same

21. As an object moves away from the earth's surface, its inertia (1) decreases (2) increases (3) remains the same

22. Object A with a mass of 2 kg and object B with a mass of 4 kg are dropped simultaneously from rest near the surface of the earth. At the end of 3 sec, what is the ratio of the speed of object A to that of object B? (Neglect air resistance.) (1) 1:1 (2) 2:1 (3) 1:2 (4) 1:4

Uniform Circular Motion—Optional Topic

If a force is applied to an object moving at constant velocity, the velocity will change. If the force is applied in the direction of motion, the *magnitude* of the velocity will change; if it is applied perpendicular to the direction of motion, the *direction* of the velocity will change. Both changes are called acceleration. If the force is constant and always acts perpendicular to the direction of the velocity, the object will move in a circular path at uniform speed (uniform circular motion). Since the force vector and the acceleration vector are both directed at the center of the circle, they are called *centripetal* ("center-seeking").

The magnitude of the acceleration in non-linear travel depends on the speed of the body and on the size (radius) of the circle along which the body moves. The formula for *centripetal* acceleration is

$$a = \frac{v^2}{r} \tag{12}$$

When the speed v is measured in m/sec and the radius r in meters, the unit of acceleration is $\frac{(m/sec)^2}{m} = m/sec^2$.

The magnitude of the centripetal force is derived from $F = ma$ by substituting the acceleration $a = v^2/r$,

$$F_c = \frac{mv^2}{r} \tag{13}$$

EXAMPLE

An object of 1 kg mass moves in a circular path of 10 m radius at a constant speed of 20 m/sec.
(a) What is the centripetal acceleration?
(b) What is the centripetal force?

Solution:
(a) Centripetal acceleration

$$a = \frac{v^2}{r} = \frac{(20 \text{ m/sec})^2}{10 \text{ m}} = 40 \text{ m/sec}^2$$

(b) Centripetal force

$$F_c = \frac{mv^2}{r} = 1 \text{ kg} \times 40 \text{ m/sec}^2$$

$$= 40 \text{ kg-m/sec}^2 = 40 \text{ nt}$$

Momentum

The force needed to stop a moving object depends on both the object's mass and its velocity. The product of mass and velocity of a moving object is a vector quantity called *momentum*.

Impulse. If force is applied to an object, the product of the force F and the time t during which the force is applied, Ft, is called the *impulse*. The relationship between the momentum, mv, of a moving object and the impulse, Ft, applied to the object can be derived from Newton's second law of motion. Since acceleration is defined as $a = \Delta v/\Delta t$, this may be substituted in the second law, $F = ma$, producing the new equation

$$F = \frac{m\Delta v}{\Delta t} \tag{14}$$

This may be written as

$$F\Delta t = m\Delta v \tag{15}$$

If the mass starts moving from rest at a time $t = 0$, then this becomes

$$Ft = mv \tag{16}$$

This equation states that when a body is set into motion by a force, the impulse given to the body, Ft, is equal to the momentum, mv, attained by the body. Both momentum and impulse are vector quantities, since each is associated with both a magnitude and a direction. The momentum vector always has the same direction as the velocity vector, and the impulse vector has the same direction as the force vector.

Change in Momentum. The change in a quantity, ΔQ, is usually calculated by subtracting the initial value of the quantity, Q_i, from the final value, Q_f: $Q_f - Q_i = \Delta Q$. Accordingly, change in momentum is equal to final momentum minus initial momentum: $mv_2 - mv_1 = m\Delta v$ (sometimes written Δmv), where the mass, m, does not change, but the velocity changes from v_1 to v_2. The change in impulse, $F\Delta t$, is always equal to the change in momentum.

EXAMPLE

A mass m of 5 kg moving with a velocity v_1 of 8 m/sec east has a momentum mv_1 = 5 kg $\times$ 8 m/sec east = 40 kg-m/sec east. If an impulse is applied in the same direction, producing a velocity v_2 of 20 m/sec east, then the final momentum is mv_2 = 5 kg $\times$ 20 m/sec east = 100 kg-m/sec east. Without knowing the magnitude of the force or the time during which it was applied, we know that the impulse must be equal to the change in momentum. This change in momentum is

$\Delta mv = mv_2 - mv_1$

= (100 kg-m/sec east) − (40 kg-m/sec east) = 60 kg-m/sec east

The impulse is consequently also 60 kg-m/sec east, or its equivalent, 60 nt-sec east.

However, if the final velocity v_2 is decreased from 8 m/sec east to 2 m/sec east, then the change in momentum is

$$mv_2 - mv_1 = (5 \text{ kg}) \times (2 \text{ m/sec east}) - (5 \text{ kg}) \times (8 \text{ m/sec east})$$
$$= (10 \text{ kg-m/sec east}) - (40 \text{ kg-m/sec east})$$
$$= -30 \text{ kg-m/sec east}$$

The negative sign indicates that the force (and therefore the impulse) was applied in the direction opposite to the object's motion. Therefore, the impulse is 30 nt-sec *west* and the change in momentum is also +30 kg-m/sec west.

If the time is known to have been 3 sec, then the force acting must have been

$$F = \frac{Ft}{t} = \frac{30 \text{ nt-sec west}}{3 \text{ sec}} = 10 \text{ nt west}$$

Law of Conservation of Momentum. A group of objects removed from influence of external forces is called an isolated system. For objects in such a system there is a law, derived from Newton's laws of motion, which states that the sum of the momentums of the masses in an isolated system is always constant, even if the masses collide, changing their individual momentums. This law is called the *law of conservation of momentum.*

If there is a system consisting of two masses, m_1 and m_2, having respective velocities v_1 and v_2 at one time, then at a later time, in spite of collisions that may occur producing new respective velocities v'_1 and v'_2, it is always true that

$$m_1 v_1 + m_2 v_2 = m'_1 v'_1 + m'_2 v'_2 \qquad (17)$$

In applying this law in the form of equation 17, due regard must be taken of the vector nature of velocity and momentum. Thus if one direction, north for example, is taken as the positive direction, then south must be taken as the negative direction, and appropriate algebraic signs must be used. An example illustrates the use of the momentum conservation law.

EXAMPLE

A 2-kg cart, m_1, at rest on a frictionless air track is struck by a 5-kg cart, m_2, moving on the same track with velocity v_2, 6 m/sec north. After the collision, the 2-kg cart moves with a velocity v'_1, 10 m/sec north. What is the velocity v'_2 of the 5-kg cart?

Solution: The following data are given:

$$m_1 = 2 \text{ kg} \qquad v_2 = 6 \text{ m/sec north}$$
$$m_2 = 5 \text{ kg} \qquad v'_1 = 10 \text{ m/sec north}$$
$$v_1 = 0 \qquad v'_2 = ?$$

$$m_1 v_1 + m_2 v_2 = m_1 v'_1 + m_2 v'_2$$

(2 kg) $\times$ (0) + (5 kg) $\times$ (6 m/sec north) =
(2 kg) $\times$ (10 m/sec north) + (5 kg) $\times$ (v'_2)

0 + 30 kg-m/sec north = 20 kg-m/sec north + 5 kg $\times$ v'_2

10 kg-m/sec north = 5 kg $\times$ v'_2

$v'_2 = \dfrac{10 \text{ kg-m/sec north}}{5 \text{ kg}} = 2$ m/sec north

QUESTIONS

1. A 10-kg mass moving at a speed of 5 m/sec on a frictionless surface collides with a stationary 10-kg mass. If the two masses remain joined after the collision, their speed will be (1) 0 m/sec (2) 2.5 m/sec (3) 5.0 m/sec (4) 10.0 m/sec

2. A 1.0-kg object falls freely from rest. The magnitude of its momentum after one second of fall is (1) 1.0 kg-m/sec (2) 4.9 kg-m/sec (3) 9.8 kg-m/sec (4) 20 kg-m/sec

3. A 10-kg gun recoils with a speed of 0.1 m/sec as it fires a 0.001-kg bullet. What is the speed of the bullet as it leaves the gun? (Neglect friction.) (1) 10 m/sec (2) 100 m/sec (3) 1000 m/sec (4) 10,000 m/sec

4. Which is a scalar quantity? (1) speed (2) displacement (3) force (4) momentum

5. A mass with a momentum of 40 kg-m/sec receives an impulse of 30 nt-sec in the direction of its motion. The final momentum of the mass is (1) 1.3 kg-m/sec (2) 10 kg-m/sec (3) 70 kg-m/sec (4) 1200 kg-m/sec

6. A mass of 2.0 kg that undergoes a momentum change of 50 kg-m/sec must have received an impulse of (1) 25 nt-sec (2) 2.0 nt-sec (3) 50 nt-sec (4) 100 nt-sec

7. A mass undergoes a change of momentum of 35 kg-m/sec in 10 sec. What is the magnitude of the average force causing this change? (1) 3.5 nt (2) 35 nt (3) 45 nt (4) 350 nt

8. A 2.0-kg mass moves with a constant speed of 20 m/sec. The magnitude of its momentum is (1) 8.0 kg-m/sec (2) 10 kg-m/sec (3) 40 kg-m/sec (4) 160 kg-m/sec

9. A 1-kg ball of putty hits a wall perpendicularly with a speed of 5 m/sec and sticks to it. The ball undergoes a change of momentum of (1) 1 kg-m/sec (2) 5 kg-m/sec (3) 10 kg-m/sec (4) 0 kg-m/sec ·

10. A 1-kg ball hits a surface perpendicularly with a speed of 3 m/sec and bounces back with a speed of 2 m/sec. The ball undergoes a change in momentum of (1) 1 kg-m/sec (2) 5 kg-m/sec (3) 3 kg-m/sec (4) 6 kg-m/sec

11. An unbalanced force of 30 nt acts on a 2.0-kg mass for 3.0 sec. The mass undergoes a change in momentum of (1) 10 nt-sec (2) 15 m/sec (3) 6.0 kg-nt (4) 90 kg-m/sec

12. As an object falls freely toward the earth, the momentum of the object-earth system (1) decreases (2) increases (3) remains the same

13. As the momentum of a moving mass increases, the magnitude of the impulse required to stop the mass (1) decreases (2) increases (3) remains the same

14. When two stationary objects are suddenly pushed apart by a compressed spring between them, the total momentum of the system (1) increases (2) decreases (3) remains the same

15. As a freely falling object approaches the earth's surface, the impulse required to stop it (1) decreases (2) increases (3) remains the same

16-19. Base your answers to Questions 16 through 19 on the following information.

Block *A* moves with a velocity of 2 m/sec to the right, as shown in the diagram, and then collides elastically with block *B*, which is at rest. Block *A* stops moving, and block *B* moves to the right after the collision.

Frictionless Surface

16. What is the combined momentum of blocks *A* and *B* before the collision? (1) 0 kg-m/sec (2) 10 kg-m/sec (3) 20 kg-m/sec (4) 40 kg-m/sec

17. What is the total change in momentum of blocks *A* and *B*? (1) 0 kg-m/sec (2) 20 kg-m/sec (3) 40 kg-m/sec (4) 200 kg-m/sec

18. If block *A* is stopped in 0.1 sec, the average force acting on block *A* is (1) 50 nt .(2) 100 nt (3) 200 nt (4) 400 nt

19. If the blocks had remained together after collision, their velocity would have been (1) 1 m/sec (2) 2 m/sec (3) 0 m/sec (4) 0.5 m/sec

20-23. Base your answers to Questions 20 through 23 on the following information.

A horizontal force is applied to a 5.0-kg object resting on a horizontal surface. The force is always applied in the same direction but its magnitude varies with time according to the graph. (Neglect friction.)

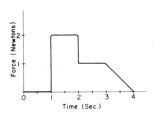

20. What is the acceleration of the object at time $t = 2.5$ sec? (1) 1.0 m/sec² (2) 0.2 m/sec² (3) 5.0 m/sec² (4) 9.8 m/sec²

21. During which time interval did the object have a constant velocity? (1) 0 sec to 1 sec (2) 1 sec to 2 sec (3) 2 sec to 3 sec (4) 3 sec to 4 sec

22. The greatest change in the momentum of the object occurred during the time interval from (1) 0 sec to 1 sec (2) 1 sec to 2 sec (3) 2 sec to 3 sec (4) 3 sec to 4 sec

23. If another 5-kg mass is added to the original mass at the time $t = 2.5$ sec, the acceleration will (1) decrease (2) increase (3) remain the same

24-28. Base your answers to Questions 24 through 28 on the following information.

A compressed spring is "exploded" between two carts initially at rest, as shown. The mass of cart *B* is twice that of cart *A*. The magnitude of the impulse acting on cart *B* is 8 nt-sec. (Neglect friction.)

24. The magnitude of the impulse acting on cart *A* is (1) 8 nt-sec (2) 2 nt-sec (3) 16 nt-sec (4) 4 nt-sec

25. If the time for the spring to explode is 0.1 sec, the average force on cart *B* is (1) 0.8 nt (2) 8 nt (3) 40 nt (4) 80 nt

26. If the total momentum of the carts before the explosion is 0, the total momentum after the explosion is (1) 0 kg-m/sec (2) 8 kg-m/sec (3) 16 kg-m/sec (4) 4 kg-m/sec

27. The ratio of the change in the magnitude of the momentum of cart *A* to the change in the magnitude of the momentum of cart *B* is (1) 1/1 (2) 1/2 (3) 2/1 (4) 8/1

28. Compared with the increase in kinetic energy of cart *B*, the increase in kinetic energy of cart *A* is (1) one-half as great (2) twice as great (3) the same (4) 4 times as great

29-32. Base your answers to Questions 29 through 32 on the accompanying graph, which shows the velocity of a 1500-kg car during a 20-sec time interval.

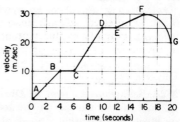

29. *No* unbalanced force is acting on the car during time interval (1) *BC* (2) *CD* (3) *EF* (4) *FG*

30. The acceleration of the car during time interval *AB* is (1) 0.40 m/sec² (2) 2.5 m/sec² (3) 10 m/sec² (4) 40 m/sec²

31. During time interval *CD*, the average velocity of the car is (1) 7.5 m/sec (2) 17.5 m/sec (3) 15 m/sec (4) 35 m/sec

32. The impulse applied to the car during time interval *AB* is (1) 9.0×10^2 nt-sec (2) 4.5×10^3 nt-sec (3) 6.0×10^3 nt-sec (4) 1.5×10^4 nt-sec

33. A constant unbalanced force acts on an object initially at rest. As the time the force acts increases, the momentum of the object (1) decreases (2) increases (3) remains the same

4. WORK AND ENERGY

Work

When a force is applied to a mass which consequently moves in the direction of the force, we say that *work* has been done on the mass. The amount of work done, W, is equal to the product of the force F, in newtons, and the displacement, s, in meters. The defining equation for work is therefore

$$W = Fs \qquad (18)$$

For example, a 10-nt force is doing work when it acts on a mass while the mass moves 5 m in the direction of the force.

$$W = (10 \text{ nt}) \times (5 \text{ m}) = 50 \text{ nt-m}$$

The unit of work is the *newton-meter* (nt-m), which because of its importance has been given the name *joule*. A force of one newton which moves a mass through one meter has done one joule of work.

If the resultant force on a body is zero, then no work is being done. This occurs when a body is at rest or moving with constant velocity. When a force is applied to a mass, but no motion occurs $(s = 0)$, again no work is done. This occurs, for example, when a person is holding an object, however heavy it may be, at a constant height above the ground. He might be expending much effort, but he is doing no work in the sense of the physical definition.

Another case in which force is applied without work being done occurs when a force applied to a mass moves it at constant speed in a circular path. In this case the force is applied along the radius (centripetal force) and is therefore *perpendicular* to the displacement, which is directed at each instant along a tangent to the circular path. An example of this type of motion is the orbiting of satellites in circular paths around the earth.

Energy

When one system can do work on another system, we say that the first system has *energy* relative to the second system. Commonly speaking, energy is the ability of a system to do work of any kind. When one system does work on another, the second system gains an amount of energy equal to the amount of work done on it. This process is called *transfer of energy*. Energy is a scalar quantity. In all its forms it is measured in joules.

Potential Energy. If the energy possessed by an object is due to its position relative to another object, the first object is said to possess *potential energy* relative to the second object. For example, when an object is removed from the earth's surface to a position above it, the object has acquired potential energy relative to the earth's surface and is able to do work by falling. Thus, a mass of 1000 kg of water falling from a 2 m height can do such work as turning water wheels to run machinery. When the water is above sea level, its energy (ability to do work) is due to its position and is therefore potential energy. Because potential energy in this case is the result of the earth's gravitational attraction, it is called *gravitational potential energy*. The amount of energy the water has is measured by the quantity of work that may be performed in its fall. In formula 18, the quantity of work is $W = Fs$. Since F is the weight of the water, mg (from formula 11), and s is equal to the height of fall, h, the equation for potential energy is

$$PE = mgh \qquad\qquad (19)$$

EXAMPLE

1000 kg of water is held at a height of 2 m above ground level. What is its potential energy relative to the ground?

Solution: PE = (1000 kg) $\times$ (9.8 m/sec^2) $\times$ 2 m

= 19,600 (kg-m/sec^2) $\times$ (m)

= 19,600 nt-m = 19,600 joules

Kinetic Energy. A moving object has energy because it is capable of doing work on other objects. Since this energy is due partly to motion, it is called *kinetic* ("moving") energy. If a mass, m, has speed v, then its kinetic energy is given by the formula

$$KE = \tfrac{1}{2}mv^2 \qquad\qquad (20)$$

If work done on a mass puts it into motion, the mass has acquired kinetic energy equivalent to the work done on it. Consequently, its kinetic energy may be measured either by the work required to bring it up to a given speed, or by the work required to bring it to rest.

Equation 20 is derived from the definition of work, $W = Fs$, and from Newton's second law, $F = ma$. Where a is constant, $W = mas$. From the relations of kinematics, since $a = v/t$, and $s = \bar{v}t$,

$$mas = (m) \times (v/t) \times (\bar{v}t)$$

Since the average speed $\bar{v}$ is $v/2$, this becomes

$$\text{work} = Fs = mas = (m) \times (v/t) \times (vt/2) = \tfrac{1}{2} mv^2$$

Power

The work performed by a source depends only on the product of the force and displacement. The time required to perform a quantity of work, or its equivalent, the rate at which work is done, is called *power*. It is a scalar quantity and is measured in units of work per unit time.

$$P = \frac{W}{t} \qquad\qquad (21)$$

EXAMPLE

(a) If 50 joules of work are performed in 5 sec, how much power is used?

(b) If the time required to do the work increases to 10 sec, what is the power?

Solution:

(a) $P = \dfrac{W}{t} = \dfrac{50 \text{ joules}}{5 \text{ sec}} = 10 \text{ joules/sec} = 10 \text{ watts}$

(b) $P = \dfrac{W}{t} = \dfrac{50 \text{ joules}}{10 \text{ sec}} = 5 \text{ joules/sec} = 5 \text{ watts}$

From the units for work and time, the unit of power is the joule per second. This unit is given a special name, the *watt*.

Since power is inversely proportional to time, the less time taken to perform a given quantity of work, the greater the power. Since $W = Fs$ and $s = v/t$, these equivalents may be substituted in equation 21:

$$P = \frac{W}{t} = \frac{Fs}{t} = Fv \qquad (22)$$

EXAMPLE

A force of 40 nt is exerted on a mass, causing it to move with a speed of 5 m/sec. What power is used?

Solution:

$P = (40 \text{ nt}) \times (5 \text{ m/sec}) = 200 \text{ nt-m/sec} = 200 \text{ joules/sec} = 200 \text{ watts}$

---

5. CONSERVATION OF ENERGY

All observations of energy transfer in an isolated system lead to the conclusion that the sum of the energies, potential and kinetic, in an isolated system is always constant. The energy may take various forms and may be interchanged among the components of the system, but there is never any net gain or net loss of energy by the system as a whole. This conclusion is called the *law of conservation of energy*. For example, an object of mass m at a height h above the ground has potential energy $PE = mgh$. If the object falls, its potential energy decreases, becoming zero at the moment the object touches the ground. According to the energy conservation law, however, this energy has not vanished but has taken another form. In this case, it is converted to kinetic energy, $KE = \frac{1}{2} mv^2$, which increases from zero, when the object begins to fall, to a maximum when the object touches the ground. Since $\Delta PE = -\Delta KE$,

$$mgh = -\frac{1}{2}mv^2 \tag{23}$$

Simplified by various substitutions, this equation becomes

$$v^2 = -2gh \tag{24}$$

From this equation, since g is constant, the speed may be determined if the height is known, or if the speed at which the mass strikes the ground is known, the height from which it has fallen may be calculated.

Friction

When two objects are in contact and moving relative to one another, as when a book slides along a table, there is always a force opposing the motion. This force is called *friction*. Its direction is always opposite to the direction of motion of the moving object. The effect of this force is to convert some or all of the kinetic energy of the moving object into potential or kinetic energy of the component particles of the object. The energy of these particles is called the *internal energy* of the object. The increase of internal energy usually appears as an increase in temperature of the objects in contact.

Since friction performs work on objects in motion, tending to increase their internal energy at the expense of their kinetic energy, this amount of work must be taken into account in applying the law of conservation of energy. For example, a boy and sled weighing 500 nt atop a hill 10 m above level ground have a potential energy of (500 nt) $\times$ (10 m) = 5000 joules. When they slide down to the bottom of the hill, their maximum calculated KE is 5000 joules, but their measured KE would be less because the force of friction opposes their motion. The difference between the actual energy and the calculated kinetic energy is due to the frictional work.

QUESTIONS

1. What is the work required to raise a 10-kg box from the surface of the earth to a height of 5.0 m? (1) **50 joules** (2) **100 joules** (3) **200 joules** (4) **490 joules**

2. The work done in accelerating an object along a frictionless horizontal surface is equal to the object's change in (1) momentum (2) velocity (3) potential energy (4) kinetic energy

3. Two unequal masses falling freely from the same point above the earth's surface would experience the same (1) acceleration (2) decrease in potential energy (3) increase in kinetic energy (4) increase in momentum

4. A 20-kg object is moved a distance of 6.0 m by a net force of 50 nt. The total work done is (1) 120 joules (2) 300 joules (3) 420 joules (4) 1000 joules

5. A 2-kg mass is thrown vertically upward from the earth's surface with an initial kinetic energy of 400 joules. The mass will rise to a height of approximately (1) 10 m (2) 20 m (3) 400 m (4) 800 m

6. Which is a scalar quantity? (1) acceleration (2) momentum (3) force (4) energy

7. A simple pendulum whose mass is 1.00 kg swings to a height of 0.200 m above its lowest point. Neglecting friction, the kinetic energy of the pendulum bob at the lowest point in its swing is (1) 0.980 joules (2) 1.96 joules (3) 9.80 joules (4) 19.6 joules

8. A box is sliding down an inclined plane as shown. The force of friction is directed toward point (1) *A* (2) *B* (3) *C* (4) *D*

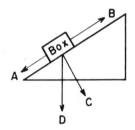

9. A bullet fired from a rifle emerges with a kinetic energy of 2400 joules. If the barrel of the rifle is 0.50 m long, then the average force on the bullet in the barrel is approximately (1) 600 nt (2) 1200 nt (3) 2400 nt (4) 4800 nt

10. Which is a vector quantity? (1) power (2) weight (3) energy (4) mass

11. The work required to lift a 50-nt box a vertical distance of 5 m is (1) 10 joules (2) 45 joules (3) 55 joules (4) 250 joules

12. If an object weighing 1 nt falls a vertical distance of 4 m, its loss in potential energy is (1) 1 joule (2) 9.8 joules (3) 39.2 joules (4) 4 joules

13. What is the amount of work done when a force of 5 nt moves a 10-kg mass a horizontal distance of 4 m? (1) 5 joules (2) 20 joules (3) 40 joules (4) 50 joules

14. A 2-kg mass that is 15 m above the ground has a potential energy of 294 joules. After falling 5 m, its potential energy, with respect to the ground, will be (1) 49 joules (2) 98 joules (3) 196 joules (4) 245 joules

15. Which is a unit of power?

    (1) joule (2) $\dfrac{\text{joule}}{\text{second}}$ (3) $\dfrac{\text{kilogram-meter}}{\text{second}}$ (4) $\dfrac{\text{newton-meter}^2}{\text{second}}$

16. At a height of 10 m above the earth's surface, the potential energy of a 2-kg mass is 196 joules. After the mass, which starts from rest, has fallen 5 m, its kinetic energy will be (1) 196 joules (2) 147 joules (3) 98 joules (4) 49 joules

17. If the kinetic energy of an object is 16 joules when its speed is 4.0 m/sec, then the mass of the object is (1) 0.5 kg (2) 2.0 kg (3) 8.0 kg (4) 19.6 kg

18. A 10-kg mass rests on a horizontal frictionless table. How much energy is needed to accelerate the mass from rest to a speed of 5 m/sec? (1) 25 joules (2) 125 joules (3) 3125 joules (4) 6250 joules

19. A force of 10 nt is required to move an object at a constant speed of 5 m/sec. The power used is (1) 0.5 watt (2) 2 watts (3) 5 watts (4) 50 watts

20. Which is a vector quantity? (1) velocity (2) speed (3) time (4) work

21. A net force of 9.0 nt acts through a distance of 3.0 m. The work done is (1) 81 joules (2) 27 joules (3) 98 joules (4) 120 joules

22. A 5.0-kg mass is raised 2.0 m above a laboratory table. The potential energy of the mass with respect to the table is (1) 10 joules (2) 50 joules (3) 98 joules (4) 120 joules

23. A mass of 2.0 kg dropped from a height of 10 m will strike the ground with a kinetic energy of approximately (1) 1.0×10^1 joules (2) 2.0×10^1 joules (3) 1.0×10^2 joules (4) 2.0×10^2 joules

24. A stone is thrown vertically upward. As it rises, there is an increase in its (1) weight (2) kinetic energy (3) potential energy (4) total energy

25. A wooden box is dragged along a horizontal floor toward the east. The direction of friction on the box is (1) up (2) down (3) east (4) west

26. One kg-m²/sec² is equivalent to one (1) newton (2) joule (3) watt (4) ampere

27. A box whose mass is 2 kg is pushed across a frictionless horizontal floor a distance of 3 m with a force of 10 nt. The increase in the potential energy of the box is (1) 0 joules (2) 2 joules (3) 6 joules (4) 20 joules

28. An elevator weighing 2.5×10^4 nt is raised to a height of 10 m. Neglecting friction, the work done is
    (1) 2.5×10^4 joules   (2) 2.5×10^5 joules
    (3) 2.5×10^3 joules   (4) 7.5×10^4 joules

29. As a ball falls freely toward the earth, its kinetic energy (1) decreases (2) increases (3) remains the same

30. As the time required for a person to run up a flight of stairs increases, the power developed by the person (1) decreases (2) increases (3) remains the same

31. As a satellite in orbit moves from a distance of 300 km to a distance of 160 km above the earth, the kinetic energy of the satellite (1) decreases (2) increases (3) remains the same

32. A pendulum is set into motion to oscillate freely. As the pendulum's displacement from its rest position increases, its potential energy with respect to the earth (1) decreases (2) increases (3) remains the same

33. As a bullet shot vertically upward rises, the kinetic energy of the bullet (1) decreases (2) increases (3) remains the same

34. As the time required to lift a 60-kg object 6 m increases, the work required to lift the body (1) decreases (2) increases (3) remains the same

35. A ball is thrown vertically upward. As the ball rises, its total energy (neglecting friction) (1) decreases (2) increases (3) remains the same

36. As the kinetic energy of an electron increases, its momentum (1) decreases (2) increases (3) remains the same

37. As the time required for accomplishing a given amount of work decreases, the rate at which energy is expended (1) decreases (2) increases (3) remains the same

38. As a mass falls freely in a uniform gravitational field, the total mechanical energy of the mass (1) decreases (2) increases (3) remains the same

39-43. Base your answers to Questions 39 through 43 on the following information.

As shown in the diagram, a 2.0-kg mass is moved at a constant speed from point A to point B on a horizontal surface. The distance from A to B is 5.0 m. The applied force F is 7.0 nt

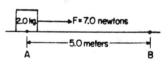

39. The force of friction acting on the mass is (1) 0 nt (2) 1.4 nt (3) 7.0 nt (4) 12.6 nt

40. When the mass moves from A to B, the increase in kinetic energy is (1) 0 joules (2) 10 joules (3) 14 joules (4) 35 joules

41. If energy is dissipated at the rate of 15 watts, the work done during 1 sec is (1) 7.5 joules (2) 15 joules (3) 30 joules (4) 35 joules

42. If no phase change occurs when the block is moved from A to B, the molecules of the block and surface will (1) increase in kinetic energy only (2) decrease in potential energy only (3) decrease in both kinetic energy and potential energy (4) increase in both kinetic energy and potential energy

43. If the surface were frictionless, the 7.0-nt force would produce an acceleration of (1) 2.5 m/sec^2 (2) 3.5 m/sec^2 (3) 10 m/sec^2 (4) 14 m/sec^2

44-48. Base your answers to Questions 44 through 48 on the following information.

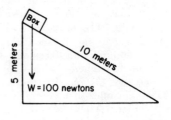

An inclined plane is 10 m long and is elevated 5 m on one end as shown in the diagram. Starting from rest at the top of the incline, a box weighing 100 nt accelerates at a rate of 2.5 m/sec².

44. The potential energy of the box at the top of the incline was approximately (1) 1000 joules (2) 500 joules (3) 50 joules (4) 0 joules

45. How many seconds will it take the box to reach the bottom of the incline? (1) 2.8 (2) 2.0 (3) 4.6 (4) 4.0

46. What is the approximate mass of the box? (1) 400 kg (2) 100 kg (3) 40 kg (4) 10 kg

47. If there is no friction as the box slides down the incline, the sum of its potential and kinetic energies will (1) decrease (2) increase (3) remain the same

48. As the box slides down the incline, its momentum will (1) decrease (2) increase (3) remain the same

49-53. Base your answers to Questions 49 through 53 on the following information.

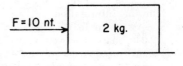

A horizontal force of 10 nt accelerates a 2-kg block from rest along a level table, as shown, at a rate of 4 m/sec².

49. The work done in moving the block 8 m is (1) 8 joules (2) 20 joules (3) 80 joules (4) 800 joules

50. When the speed of the block is 8 m/sec, its kinetic energy is (1) 8 joules (2) 16 joules (3) 64 joules (4) 80 joules

51. The number of seconds required for the block to attain a speed of 20 m/sec is (1) 1 (2) 2 (3) 5 (4) 4

52. What is the frictional force that is retarding the forward motion of the block? (1) 8 nt (2) 2 nt (3) 10 nt (4) 19.6 nt

53. If there were no friction between the block and the table, then the acceleration of the block would be (1) 20 m/sec² (2) 9.8 m/sec² (3) 5 m/sec² (4) 4 m/sec²

54-58. Base your answers to Questions 54 through 58 on the information below.

A 6.0-kg object falls freely from rest for 5.0 m and strikes the ground.

54. Which graph best describes the motion of the falling object?

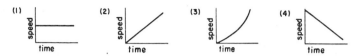

55. The speed of the object just before it strikes the ground is closest to (1) 140 m/sec (2) 30 m/sec (3) 10 m/sec (4) 5.0 m/sec

56. The number of seconds that the object fell is closest to (1) 0.10 (2) 1.0 (3) 10 (4) 15

57. The kinetic energy of the mass just before it strikes the ground is closest to (1) 1.0 joules (2) 30 joules (3) 50 joules (4) 300 joules

58. The weight of the object is closest to (1) 1.0 nt (2) 6.0 nt (3) 30 nt (4) 60 nt

59-63. Base your answers to Questions 59 through 63 on the statement below.

A 2-kg rock that was originally resting on the edge of a cliff 100 m high falls to the base of the cliff.

59. Before the rock fell, what was its potential energy with respect to the base of the cliff? (1) 50 joules (2) 980 joules (3) 1960 joules (4) 6400 joules

60. What is the kinetic energy of the rock 50 m above the base of the cliff? (1) 25 joules (2) 490 joules (3) 980 joules (4) 3200 joules

61. What is the momentum of the rock when its speed is 10 m/sec? (1) 10 kg-m/sec (2) 20 kg-m/sec (3) 50 kg-m/sec (4) 100 kg-m/sec

62. The speed of the rock an instant before it hits the base of the cliff is approximately (1) 22 m/sec (2) 31 m/sec (3) 44 m/sec (4) 62 m/sec

63. At the moment the rock begins to fall from the cliff, its total energy is equal to (1) its potential energy minus its kinetic energy (2) its kinetic energy minus its potential energy (3) the product of its kinetic and potential energies (4) the sum of its potential and kinetic energies

64-66. Base your answers to Questions 64 through 66 on the diagram, which shows a 1-kg aluminum sphere and a 3-kg brass sphere, both having the same diameter and both at the same height above the ground. Both spheres are allowed to fall freely. (Neglect air resistance.)

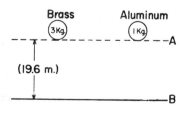

64. Both spheres are released at the same instant. They will reach the ground at (1) the same time but with different speeds (2) the same time with the same speeds (3) different times but with the same speeds (4) different times and with different speeds

65. If the spheres are 19.6 m above the ground, the time required for the aluminum sphere to reach the ground is (1) 1 sec (2) 2 sec (3) 8 sec (4) 4 sec

66. Which graph shows the relationship between the potential energy and height for each sphere?

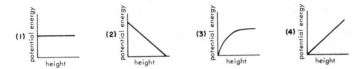

67-71 Base your answers to Questions 67 through 71 on the following information.

As shown in the diagrams, object *A* has a mass of 5 kg and a velocity of 10 m/sec at the foot of a frictionless hill. Object *B* has a mass of 10 kg and a velocity of 5 m/sec at the foot of an identical hill.

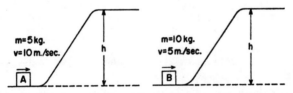

67. In the positions shown in the diagrams, how does the kinetic energy of object *A* compare with the kinetic energy of object *B*? (1) It is one-fourth as great. (2) It is one-half as great. (3) It is the same. (4) It is twice as great.

68. In the positions shown in the diagrams, how does the momentum of object *A* compare with the momentum of object *B*? (1) It is one-fourth as great. (2) It is one-half as great. (3) It is the same. (4) It is twice as great.

69. Which graph best represents the relationship between height and kinetic energy for each of the masses?

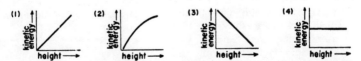

70. At the top of the hill, the force of gravity on *A*, compared with that on *B*, will be (1) greater (2) less (3) the same

71. At the top of the hill, the potential energy of *A*, compared with that of *B*, will be (1) greater (2) less (3) the same

72-75. Base your answers to Questions 72 through 75 on the following information.

A pendulum with a 10-kg bob is released at point A and allowed to swing without friction, as shown in the diagram.

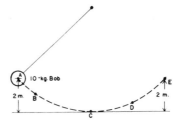

72. What is the weight of the bob? (1) 0.1 nt (2) 0.98 nt (3) 10 nt (4) 98 nt

73. The force of the string on the bob is greatest at point (1) A (2) B (3) C (4) D

74. What is the velocity of the bob at point E? (1) 0 m/sec (2) 2 m/sec (3) 6.3 m/sec (4) 9.8 m/sec

75. The centripetal acceleration of the bob is greatest at point (1) E (2) B (3) C (4) D

76-78. Base your answers to Questions 76 through 78 on the following information.

A car is travelling around the track at a constant speed of 20 m/sec. AG and CF are the diameters of the semicircular ends of the track.

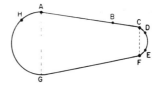

76. If the total length of the track is 700 m, the time required for the car to make a complete trip is (1) 17.5 sec (2) 35 sec (3) 7000 sec (4) 14,000 sec

77. The acceleration of the car is zero at point (1) E (2) B (3) H (4) D

78. As the car travels from point C to point D, the centripetal force on the car is (1) constant in magnitude but changing in direction (2) constant in both magnitude and direction (3) changing in magnitude but constant in direction (4) changing in both magnitude and direction

79-83. Base your answers to Questions 79 through 83 on the following information.

The diagram represents a flat (unbanked) circular race-track whose radius is 250 m. Racing car R is moving around the track at a uniform speed of 40.0 m/sec. The mass of the car is 2.00×10^3 kg.

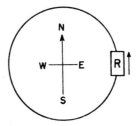

79. At the instant shown in the diagram, the car's acceleration is directed toward the (1) north (2) south (3) east (4) west

80. The magnitude of the car's acceleration is (1) 0.025 m/sec² (2) 1.60 m/sec² (3) 6.40 m/sec² (4) 12.8 m/sec²

81. The centripetal force necessary to keep the car in its circular path is provided by (1) the engine (2) the brakes (3) friction (4) the stability of the car

82. The kinetic energy of the car is (1) 2.50×10^5 joules (2) 1.60×10^6 joules (3) 6.40×10^6 joules (4) 1.30×10^7 joules

83. If the speed of the car were 50.0 m/sec the magnitude of the centripetal force would be (1) 4.00×10^2 nt (2) 1.00×10^1 nt (3) 2.00×10^4 nt (4) 4.00×10^4 nt

84-88. Base your answers to Questions 84 through 88 on the diagram, which represents a satellite orbiting the earth. The satellite's distance from the center of the earth equals 4 earth radii.

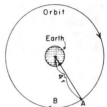

84. Which vector best represents the velocity of the satellite at B?

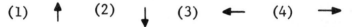

85. The original satellite is replaced by one with twice the mass, but the orbit speed and radius are unchanged. Compared to the magnitude of the acceleration of the original satellite, the magnitude of the acceleration of the new satellite is (1) one-half as great (2) the same (3) twice as great (4) four times as great

86. Which vector best represents the acceleration of the satellite at point *A* in its orbit?

87. As the satellite moves from point *A* to point *B*, its potential energy with respect to the earth will (1) decrease (2) increase (3) remain the same

88. If the satellite's distance from the center of the earth were increased to 5 earth radii, the centripetal force on the satellite would (1) decrease (2) increase (3) remain the same

6. INTERNAL ENERGY AND HEAT

The internal energy of an object is defined as the sum of kinetic and potential energies possessed by the molecules of the object due to their motions or positions relative to each other; it does not include the energy that the object itself possesses relative to other objects. The heat and temperature of an object depend on the kinetic energy of its molecules.

Mechanical Equivalent of Heat

The relationship between work and heat was known even to primitive men, who used the work of rubbing sticks together to produce fire. In the 18th century, observations of temperature change produced by cannon-boring machinery led scientists to measure the energy transfer by measuring temperature change.

When one kg of water increases in temperature one degree Celsius, then, by definition, it has absorbed a quantity of energy called one kilocalorie (kcal). The energy transferred because of differences in temperature between the objects involved is called *heat energy*. The effect of a transfer of heat energy is to increase kinetic and potential energy of the molecules of an object. It is only during this kind of energy transfer from one object to another do we speak of gain or loss of heat energy.

Since mechanical energy, both kinetic and potential, and heat energy are all varieties of energy, their units, the joule and the kcal, are convertible into one another. One kcal is equivalent to 4200 joules (4185 to 4 significant figures). For example, a mass weighing 420 nt falling 10 m will have 4200 joules of kinetic energy. If this were completely converted to heat energy only, it would raise the temperature of 1 kg of water by 1 Celsius degree, or would raise the temperature of ½ kg of water by 2 Celsius degrees. The *mechanical equivalent of heat* is given by the conversion equation

$$1 \text{ kcal} = 4200 \text{ joules} \qquad (25)$$

Temperature and Temperature Scales

The fact that some things are hot and others are cold is recognized very readily by the senses. In order to measure the difference in these conditions, which we call the *temperature,* several types of thermometers and scales have been invented. Scientists use the Celsius scale most often in laboratory work and the Kelvin scale in theoretical work. On the Celsius scale, the freezing point of water is 0° C and its boiling point is 100° C, at normal pressures. The one hundred equal divisions between these temperatures, together with those above and below these fixed points, complete the temperature scale. The Kelvin scale is used in many procedures because the average kinetic energy of the molecules of an object is directly proportional to its Kelvin temperature. The relation between the two scales is given by the conversion

$$°K = 273 + °C \qquad (26)$$

The temperature 0° K is called the *absolute zero* temperature and is equivalent to $-273°C$. At this temperature, atomic motion and internal energy of a mass is at a minimum, but is not equal to zero. Heat energy consequently cannot be transferred from a substance that is at absolute zero.

Internal Energy Transfer—Optional Topic

In an isolated system of masses, the total internal energy of the masses is constant, if no other form of energy is interchanged. This follows from the law of energy conservation and implies that any heat removed from one mass must appear as heat absorbed by other masses. For example, if a container of hot water loses 10 kcal to a container of cold water, then the cold container must gain 10 kcal of energy. The exchange will result in internal changes of average molecular kinetic energy, a loss for the hot water and a gain for the previously colder water.

Specific Heat. When 1 kg of water is raised 1 Celsius degree, then, by definition, it has absorbed 1 kcal of heat energy. When the same temperature rise is observed in 1 kg of ethyl alcohol it is found that only 0.58 kcal is required. The ratio of these quantities of heat energy, using water as a standard, is called the *specific heat, c,* of the substance. Thus the specific heat of ethyl alcohol is $c = 0.58$ kcal per kg per degree C. It follows therefore, that the heat energy, Q, required to raise a substance several degrees in temperature depends on the mass of the substance, m, the temperature rise ΔT and the specific heat, c, of the substance. This is summarized in the formula

$$Q = mc\Delta t \qquad (27)$$

Q is measured in kcal, m in kg, c is a numerical ratio, and ΔT is the temperature change. If the final temperature is less than the initial temperature, then heat energy has been transferred out of the body.

EXAMPLE

Given the specific heat of copper as 0.09 kcal/kg/°C, what quantity of heat energy is required to raise the temperature of 5 kg of copper from 40°C to 120°C?

Solution: m = 5 kg

c = 0.09 kcal/kg/°C

ΔT = 120° − 40° = 80°C

$Q = mc\Delta T = (5 \text{ kg}) \times \dfrac{0.09 \text{ kcal}}{\text{kg-°C}} \times (80°C)$

= 36 kcal

Change of Phase. Ordinarily, matter exists in one of three forms or phases: solid, liquid or gas. A change from one phase into another is accomplished by supplying or removing heat energy. At a given pressure the phase of a substance is determined by its temperature. As with water, at a given pressure there is only one temperature at which the solid and liquid phase of a substance may exist together. This temperature is called both the *melting point* and the *freezing point* of the substance.

(a) *Heat of Fusion.* If heat energy is supplied to a mixture of solid and liquid phases of a given substance at its melting point, there will be no rise in the temperature until all of the solid phase has been converted to liquid. Similarly, if heat energy is removed, the temperature will remain constant until all of the liquid phase has become solid. The number of kcal that must be added to melt 1 kg of a substance (or that must be removed to freeze 1 kg) at its melting temperature is called the *heat of fusion.* The heat of fusion of water is 80 kcal/kg at 0°C. If more than 1 kg is being melted or frozen, the total heat energy required is given by

$$Q = mH_f \qquad (28)$$

where Q is in kcal, m is in kg, and H_f is the heat of fusion in kcal/kg.

(b) *Heat of Vaporization.* There is also a specific temperature for each substance at which it changes phase from liquid to gas. At this temperature, the *boiling point,* there will be no rise in temperature as heat energy is added or removed from a mixture of the two phases. The temperature changes only when a single phase is present. The number of kcal that must be added to change one kg of a substance from liquid to gas phase (or removed to condense one kg from gas to liquid) is called the *heat of vaporization.* The heat of vaporization of water is 540 kcal/kg at 100°C. As with heat of fusion, the heat of vaporization of more than 1 kg of a substance can be calculated from the formula

$$Q = mH_v \qquad (29)$$

where Q is in kcal, m in kg, and H_v is heat of vaporization in kcal/kg.

7. THE KINETIC THEORY OF GASES—OPTIONAL TOPIC

Observation of the behavior of gases has revealed regular relationships between their temperature, pressure, and volume. These relationships are called the gas laws, and are given below. In order to explain these relationships scientists have developed a model of gases called the *kinetic-molecular* theory. The principal features of this model are:

1. Gases are composed of large numbers of small particles (molecules).
2. These molecules are in constant, random motion.
3. In gases at ordinary pressures the molecules are separated by distances that are large relative to their size. (This means that the total volume of the molecules themselves is much less than the total volume occupied by the gas.)
4. Collisions between molecules transfer energy without loss.

5. In gases at ordinary pressures, the force of attraction between molecules is negligible.

6. The average kinetic energy of gas molecules is proportional to the absolute temperature, and the pressure exerted by gases is accounted for by the large number of collisions per unit time between gas molecules and the walls of a container.

Gas Laws

The kinetic theory has enabled scientists to account successfully for the observed regularities of gas behavior mentioned above. These regularities, the gas laws, are:

1. At constant temperature, the pressure in a confined gas is inversely proportional to the volume. This means that the product of pressure and volume is constant:

$$PV = k \tag{30}$$

2. At constant volume, the pressure of a gas is directly proportional to the absolute temperature,

$$P = kT \tag{31}$$

3. At constant pressure, the volume of a gas is directly proportional to the absolute temperature, or

$$V = kT \tag{32}$$

It is sufficient to remember that an increase in temperature or decrease in pressure will tend to increase the volume of a gas; and if the volume is increased, the pressure or temperature (or both) will decrease.

QUESTIONS

1. Which pair of units measures the same quantity? (1) kilogram and kilocalorie (2) kilocalorie and degree (3) joule and kilocalorie (4) degree and joule

2. A temperature of 50°C is the same as a Kelvin temperature of (1) −223° (2) 223° (3) 273° (4) 323°

3. Which is *not* a unit of energy? (1) newton (2) calorie (3) joule (4) watt-second

4. The kcal is a unit of (1) energy (2) force (3) power (4) temperature

5. Temperature is a measure of an object's (1) average molecular kinetic energy (2) average molecular potential energy (3) total molecular kinetic energy (4) total molecular potential energy

6. At what temperature is the internal energy of a body at a minimum? (1) 0°C (2) −273°C (3) 272°C (4) 373°C

7. Which is not a unit of power? (1) joule/sec (2) nt/sec (3) watt (4) kcal/sec

8. Which graph best represents the relationship between the Celsius temperature of an ideal gas and the average kinetic energy of its molecules?

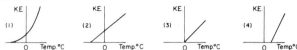

9. An increase in temperature of 54 Celsius degrees is equal to an increase in Kelvin degrees of (1) 54 (2) 219 (3) 327 (4) 454

10. When the internal energy of a body is at a minimum, its temperature is (1) $0°C$ (2) $-273°C$ (3) $-273°K$ (4) $100°K$

11. Which two temperatures are equivalent? (1) $0°C$ and $-273°K$ (2) $100°C$ and $273°K$ (3) $0°K$ and $273°C$ (4) $0°K$ and $-273°C$

12. Which represents a vector quantity? (1) force (2) temperature (3) mass (4) energy

13. The heat absorbed by an object can be measured in (1) degrees (2) newtons (3) watts (4) joules

14. What is the number of Kelvin degrees between the freezing point and boiling point of pure water at standard pressure? (1) 0 (2) 100 (3) 180 (4) 273

15. A pressure vs. temperature graph is drawn for a sample of an ideal gas in a closed container. The graph intercepts the temperature axis at (1) $0°C$ (2) $273°K$ (3) $-273°K$ (4) $-273°C$

16. As the Kelvin temperature of a body increases, the total internal energy of the body (1) decreases (2) increases (3) remains the same

17. As the kinetic energy of the molecules of an ideal gas increases, its absolute temperature (1) decreases (2) increases (3) remains the same

18. As the temperature of a substance approaches absolute zero, the random motion of the molecules (1) decreases (2) increases (3) remains the same

19. If only the potential energy of the molecules of a substance increases, the absolute temperature of the substance (1) decreases (2) increases (3) remains the same

20-23. Base your answers to Questions 20 through 23 on the Physics Reference Tables (page 162).

20. How many kcal of heat energy are required to raise the temperature of 0.2 kg of lead from $10°C$ to $20°C$? (1) 6 (2) 0.6 (3) 0.06 (4) 0.006

21. How many kcal of heat energy are required to melt 0.5 kg of iron at its melting point? (1) 0.055 (2) 3.95 (3) 8.00 (4) 39.5

22. How many kcal of heat energy are required to convert 0.8 kg of water at $100°C$ to steam at $100°C$? (1) 43.2 (2) 64 (3) 432 (4) 640

23. How many kg of ice at $0°C$ will have melted when 8000 kcal of heat energy have been absorbed by the ice? (1) 10 (2) 80 (3) 100 (4) 800

24-28. Base your answers to Questions 24 through 28 on the information below and on the Physics Reference Tables.

The temperature of 1 kg of mercury is changed from $-73°$ C to $727°$ C by the addition of heat energy at the rate of 1 kcal/min. (Assume atmospheric pressure and no heat loss to the surroundings.)

24. At which temperature can the mercury exist both as a liquid and as a gas? (1) $357°$ C (2) $396°$ C (3) $457°$ C (4) $1000°$ C

25. What is the total range of temperature in which mercury can exist as a liquid? (1) $39°$ C (2) $318°$ C (3) $357°$ C (4) $396°$ C

26. What amount of heat is necessary to melt completely the mercury at its melting point? (1) 2.8 kcal (2) 8.4 kcal (3) 39 kcal (4) 71 kcal

27. What amount of heat is necessary to raise the temperature of the mercury from $-1°$ C to $1°$ C? (1) 82 kcal (2) 2.0 kcal (3) 0.03 kcal (4) 0.06 kcal

28. How long will it take the mercury to change completely into a gas after it reaches its boiling point of $357°$ C? (1) 2.8 min (2) 39 min (3) 71 min (4) 357 min

29-33. Base your answers to Questions 29 through 33 on the following information.

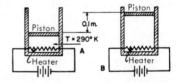

The accompanying diagram shows a frictionless piston which weighs 100 nt fitted into an insulated cylinder containing an ideal gas at $290°$ K. As 25 joules of heat energy are supplied by a heater, the piston rises 0.1 m.

29. What was the Celsius temperature of the gas before the heat energy was added? (1) $563°$ C (2) $290°$ C (3) $17°$ C (4) $0°$ C

30. How much work is done by the gas as it raises the piston 0.1 m? (1) 1.0 joules (2) 10 joules (3) 100 joules (4) 1000 joules

31. As the heat energy is supplied to the cylinder, the internal energy of the gas will (1) decrease (2) increase (3) remain the same

32. As the heat energy is supplied to the cylinder, the temperature of the gas will (1) decrease (2) increase (3) remain the same

33. Compared with diagram *A*, the pressure of the gas in diagram *B* is (1) greater (2) less (3) the same

34-38. Base your answers to Questions 34 through 38 on the following information.

Two kilograms of aluminum at a temperature of $300°$ C are placed on a block of ice whose temperature is $0°$ C. The ice melts until the system achieves equilibrium at $0°$ C.

34. What is the equilibrium temperature on the Kelvin scale? (1) $0°$ (2) $100°$ (3) $273°$ (4) $573°$

35. How many kcal are lost by the block of aluminum? (1) 63 (2) 126 (3) 154 (4) 600

36. Compared to the specific heat of ice, the specific heat of water (liquid) is (1) greater (2) less (3) the same

37. As the ice melts, the potential energy of its molecules (1) decreases (2) increases (3) remains the same

38. As the aluminum cools, the average kinetic energy of its molecules (1) decreases (2) increases (3) remains the same

39. Doubling the absolute temperature of an ideal gas will affect the molecules by doubling their average (1) kinetic energy (2) velocity (3) momentum (4) potential energy

40. Which graph shows the variation of pressure with absolute temperature for a fixed mass and volume of an ideal gas?

41-43. Base your answers to Questions 41 through 43 on the information below.

A 2.0 kg block of ice at 0°C is dropped into 4.0 kg of ethyl alcohol at 20°C. The final temperature of the mixture is 0°C.

41. What is the final temperature of this mixture in °K? (1) 0 (2) 273 (3) −273 (4) 373

42. What is the amount of heat in kcal given up by the alcohol? (1) 12 (2) 46 (3) 80 (4) 92

43. What is the amount of heat in kcal needed to melt the first 0.5 kg of ice? (1) 1 (2) 0.5 (3) 40 (4) 80

44-47. Base your answers to Questions 44 through 47 on the graph, which shows the temperature for 10 kg of an unknown substance as heat is added at a constant rate of 15 kcal/min. The substance is a solid at 0°C.

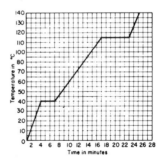

44. How much heat is added to the substance from the time that it stops melting to the time that it begins to boil? (1) 10 kcal (2) 15 kcal (3) 80 kcal (4) 150 kcal

45. What is the total heat necessary to change the substance at its melting point from a solid to a liquid? (1) 3 kcal (2) 40 kcal (3) 45 kcal (4) 90 kcal

46. From the 17th minute to the 23rd minute, the average kinetic energy of the molecules of the substance (1) decreases (2) increases (3) remains the same

47. As the temperature of the solid increases from 0°C to 40°C, its specific heat (1) decreases (2) increases (3) remains the same

WAVE PHENOMENA

1. INTRODUCTION TO WAVES

If a particle is moving back and forth about its average position, it is said to be *vibrating* or oscillating. If other particles nearby are set into vibration by the first one, the vibrations are said to be transferred or *propagated*. This propagation of vibration from one particle to the next is called *wave motion*.

Waves and Energy Transfer

Wave motion transfers *energy* from one place to another by means of repeated small motions (vibrations) of particles, or by repeated small changes in strength of a field. The first kind are called waves in a material medium; the second kind are called waves in space. Although the vibrating source itself moves back and forth, there is no actual transfer of mass from the source to the distant point. What does happen is that some faraway object is set into motion by the energy transferred. Sound waves are examples of waves in a material medium; light waves are instances of waves in an electrical field, which may be completely empty of matter.

Pulses and Waves

A non-repeating short disturbance is called a *pulse*. For example, the pulse produced on a stretched rope has a specific shape depending on how the rope was moved to make it. As the pulse moves *horizontally* along the rope, successive parts of the rope take this characteristic shape, moving *vertically* from their rest position. The pulse consists of this vertical motion transmitted horizontally.

The speed of the pulse is defined as the time it takes the pulse to move a unit distance through the medium. Pulse speed will be constant if the medium is of uniform material and in the same condition throughout. If the pulse reaches a new medium, a pulse of the same general shape but smaller size will be reflected back to the source, and a modified pulse, still of the same shape, will be transmitted through the new medium. If the original medium ends in a fixed unyielding body, then the pulse will be completely reflected, but will be inverted. Figure 8 illustrates this.

If the initial disturbance is regularly repeated without interruption, then the result is a continuous series of pulses, which is called a *wave train*. Although waves can have any number of shapes, even the most complex shapes can be resolved into combinations of single *sine* waves of different wavelengths (Figure 8).

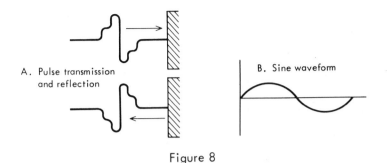

A. Pulse transmission and reflection

B. Sine waveform

Figure 8

Types of Wave Motion

Longitudinal Waves. A *longitudinal* wave is produced when the medium is disturbed in a direction *parallel* to the direction of wave travel. Sound waves and compression waves in springs are examples of such waves.

Transverse Waves. A *transverse* wave is produced by oscillations *perpendicular* to the direction of motion of the wave. For example, a transverse wave is produced in a rope by moving the end up and down or side to side. In the first case, the wave is in a vertical plane; in the second, it is in a horizontal plane. In both cases, the oscillation of the rope is perpendicular to the direction of wave travel.

Other Types of Waves. Longitudinal and transverse waves are basic types, but two other types of waves that are combinations of the basic types are important. Waves produced in a material medium by a combination of transverse and longitudinal motions are called *elliptical* waves. Large ocean waves and certain types of earthquake waves are elliptical. If a cylindrical rod is twisted at one end, the twist passes along the rod as a wave motion. This type of wave is called a *torsional* wave.

Polarization

When transverse waves are perpendicular to each other, they are said to be *polarized*. In the case of the vertical and horizontal waves in the rope, the first is polarized vertically, the second is polarized horizontally. Only transverse waves may be polarized, because longitudinal waves have only one possible direction of particle vibration: back and forth in the same direction as the direction of wave travel. Light and other forms of radiant energy are transmitted as transverse waves in electric fields. Ordinary light, however, is produced by many sources vibrating at different angles to one another. Some of the transverse waves produced are therefore polarized in a horizontal plane, others in a vertical plane, and still others in intermediate directions. Such light is said to be non-polarized, but by suitable means, such as polarizing filters, only those waves of a specific polarization may be selected from the light, producing *polarized light*.

2. COMMON CHARACTERISTICS OF WAVES

Frequency

The full series of changes at one point in a medium that constitute the passage of one full wave is called a *cycle*. The number of cycles each point undergoes in one second is called the *frequency* (*f*) of the wave. For example, if a point in a medium completes 10 cycles, representing the passage of 10 complete waves, in 1 sec, the frequency of the wave is 10/sec (or 10 cycles per sec). The unit 1/sec (sec^{-1} or "per second") is given the name *Hertz* (Hz) after Heinrich Hertz, who demonstrated the existence of radio waves (1888). A frequency of 10 cycles per sec is therefore written as 10 Hz.

Period

Another way of describing the rate of wave motion is to measure the time required for one full wave to pass a point of the medium. This is the time taken for a vibrating medium or wave to complete one cycle, and is called the *period* (*T*). Since a wave with a frequency of 10 Hz takes 1/10 sec to complete one cycle, its period is 1/10 sec. Since period is a unit of time, it is inversely proportional to frequency:

$$T = \frac{1}{f}, \text{ or } f = \frac{1}{T} \tag{33}$$

Amplitude

The maximum change in position (displacement) of a particle from its average position due to wave motion is called the *amplitude* of the wave. This term is also used for waves in a field, where it means the maximum change in a field from its normal strength due to a wave. For both transverse and longitudinal waves, the part of the wave where the maximum displacement occurs is called the *crest*, when the displacement is in the positive direction, and is called the *trough* when the displacement is in the negative direction.

The amplitude of a wave is proportional to the amount of energy being transmitted by the wave motion. The greater the amplitude of a sound wave, the louder the sound; the greater the amplitude of a light wave, the greater the intensity of the light.

Phase

The points on the successive waves in a wave train that are displaced by the same amount from their equilibrium (rest) positions and are changing in the same direction (increasing or decreasing with the progress of the wave) are said to be *in phase*. For example, in a wave train each wave crest is in phase with the other wave crests, and each trough is in phase with the other troughs. This is illustrated in Figure 9.

Since a wave can be represented by a sine graph, it is common practice to use the *x* axis of the sine graph, which is measured in

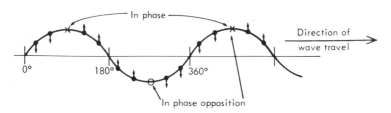

Figure 9. Sine waves and degree of phase.

angular degrees, to specify the difference in phase of two points on a wave. For example, points on the same wave that are an equal distance from their equilibrium positions and are moving in opposite directions with the same speed are said to be 180° out of phase, or in *phase opposition*. Figure 9 shows some points on a wave in phase and others in phase opposition. The points on a wave that move with maximum speed are those at the equilibrium position; the points that are momentarily at rest are at the crest and trough positions.

Wavelength

The distance between any two points in phase with one another in successive waves of a wave train is called the *wavelength* of the wave. Wavelength is usually given the symbol λ (Greek letter "lambda") and is measured in meters. Two points 180° out of phase on the same cycle of a waveform are therefore separated by ½ wavelength. For convenience, wavelengths are measured from successive crests or troughs, but any points in phase may be chosen. Wavelengths of waves that occur in nature vary from hundreds of meters to lengths smaller than the diameters of atomic particles.

Speed of Waves

The speed at which the successive waves in a wave train pass a given point depends on the properties of the medium. For a given medium, the speed of the wave is related to the wavelength and the frequency:

$$v = f\lambda \tag{34}$$

This relation between velocity of wave propagation, frequency, and wavelength holds true for all waves, longitudinal, transverse, material waves, and waves in fields.

Speed in Different Media

When a wave passes from one medium to another, the wave changes speed, becoming faster or slower depending on the nature of the second medium. However, the frequency, which is the number of waves produced per second by the source, does not change and because it remains constant, the change in speed will produce a change in wavelength (equation 34). If a wave of wavelength λ_1 travels with a speed v_1 in medium A, it will travel with wavelength λ_2 and speed v_2 in medium B. These quantities are related by the formula

$$\frac{\lambda_1}{\lambda_2} = \frac{v_1}{v_2} \qquad (35)$$

Dispersive Media. Most wave sources produce waves of different frequencies at the same time (polychromatic waves). In certain kinds of media, called *dispersive* media, waves of differing frequencies travel with different speeds. For example, light waves in glass travel at speeds that depend on the frequency of the light; the higher frequency waves travel slower than those of lower frequency. Glass is therefore a dispersive medium for light waves. With a correctly shaped glass block, it is possible to separate a polychromatic beam of light waves into its monochromatic components. Figure 10 illustrates Newton's earliest method of doing this.

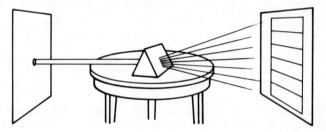

Figure 10. Effect of dispersive medium on poly-chromatic waves – Newton's prism.

Nondispersive Media. In other kinds of media, called *nondispersive* media, all the waves travel at the same speed. For example, polychromatic sound waves, such as those of the voice, all travel at the same speed in air. Air is therefore a non-dispersive medium for sound.

Doppler Effect

If the source and the observer of a series of waves are at rest relative to one another, the waves generated will always be observed to maintain the same frequency, although their wavelength may change, as when they enter a new medium. However, both frequency and wavelength will be observed to change, without change of medium, when source and observer are moving relative to one another. This change is called the *Doppler effect* for Christian Doppler, the physicist who first explained it (1842).

If the distance between source and observer is decreasing, the frequency appears to increase and the wavelength to decrease. The opposite occurs if the distance between them is increasing. For example, sound waves appear to rise in pitch, due to the decrease in wavelength and increase in frequency, when their source approaches the observer and to drop in pitch when the source recedes. Light waves are subject to the same effect, appearing to increase in frequency and decrease in wavelength as the light source approaches the observer, and to do the opposite as the light source recedes. Since higher frequencies (shorter wavelengths) are seen by the eye as blue light and the lower frequencies (longer wavelengths) are seen as red light, an approaching light source will appear slightly bluer and a receding one slightly redder. These color and wavelength relationships are summarized in Table 2.

Motion of Source	Frequency Change	Wavelength Change
None	None	None
Toward observer	Increase	Decrease
Away from observer	Decrease	Increase

If an object is a source of waves (sound or light) of known frequency, the Doppler effect can be used to measure the speed at which the object is moving toward or away from the observer.

Wave Propagation

Types of Wavefronts. When a pebble is dropped into a quiet pond, waves spread as a series of concentric circles from the source of the disturbance. These are known as *circular wavefronts*. Each point on a given circle is at the same phase, since such a circle represents the same part of a circular wavefront. For example, all points on the crest of a given wave circle are at the same phase. Successive wavefronts are separated from one another by one wavelength.

If the radius of a circular wavefront is extremely large, the wavefront approximates a straight line. Ocean waves often seem to consist of such wavefronts. Linear wavefronts can be generated in a ripple tank by using a straight bar as the wave source. In space, a point source can propagate wavefronts in all directions. In such cases, the wavefronts will form the surface of a sphere, the radii varying with the distance of the spherical wavefront from the source.

Huygens' Principle. In 1680, Christian Huygens, a Dutch physicist, discovered a principle which enabled him to construct the position of any succeeding wavefront from a given one. This principle assumes that every point on a given wavefront is a separate source of wavelets. These wavelets travel with the same speed as those issuing directly from the source. As these wavelets spread out from each point on the inner wavefront, they intersect one another, forming a circular pattern that constitutes the outer wavefront. This wavefront, in turn, becomes the inner wavefront that generates the next outer wavefront, and so on. The phenomenon of diffraction discussed in the following section is readily understood on the basis of Huygens' principle.

QUESTIONS

1. Which type of wave can be polarized? (1) sound (2) light (3) compression (4) torsional

2. A periodic wave that has a frequency of 5.0 Hz and a speed of 10 m/sec has a wavelength of (1) 50 m (2) 2.0 m (3) 0.50 m (4) 0.20 m

3. A point source vibrating up and down on the surface of a container of water produces a periodic surface wave. The wave fronts are (1) straight (2) vertical (3) spherical (4) circular

4. On the wave train at right, which point is in phase with point *A*? (1) *E* (2) *B* (3) *C* (4) *D*

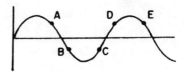

5. A wave has a frequency of 50 Hz. The period of the wave is (1) 0.02 sec (2) 0.2 sec (3) 2 sec (4) 20 sec

6. The speed of a wave in a nondispersive material medium is dependent upon (1) frequency (2) period (3) wavelength (4) characteristics of the medium

7. In the diagram at right, which two points are in phase? (1) *A* and *E* (2) *A* and *F* (3) *B* and *E* (4) *E* and *F*

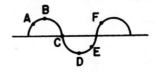

8. Which generally occurs when a pulse reaches a boundary between two different media? (1) The entire pulse will be reflected. (2) The entire pulse will be absorbed. (3) The entire pulse will be transmitted. (4) Part of the pulse will be transmitted and part reflected.

9. A periodic wave has a frequency of 10 Hz. The period of the wave is (1) 1 sec (2) 0.1 sec (3) 0.01 sec (4) 0.001 sec

10. A train of waves is moving along a string as shown at right. What is the number of meters in one wavelength? (1) 6 (2) 2 (3) 1.5 (4) 0.75

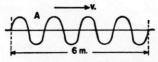

11. Longitudinal waves cannot be (1) reflected (2) refracted (3) diffracted (4) polarized

12. Two pulses approach each other in a spring, as shown. Which diagram best illustrates the appearance of the spring after the two pulses pass each other at point P?

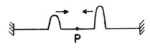

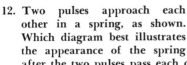

13. A pulse in a light spring approaches a heavier spring, as shown. Which pulse shape best represents the transmitted pulse in the heavy spring?

14. The maximum distance that the crest of a wave rises above its rest position is known as the wave's (1) amplitude (2) frequency (3) wavelength (4) velocity

15. What is the frequency of a water wave that has a speed of 0.4 m/sec and a wavelength of 0.02 m? (1) 10 Hz (2) 20 Hz (3) 0.008 Hz (4) 0.05 Hz

16. In the diagram at right, which point is in phase with point X? (1) A (2) B (3) C (4) D

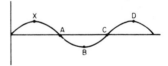

17. If the energy in a longitudinal wave travels from south to north, the particles of the medium move (1) from north to south, only (2) both north and south (3) from east to west, only (4) both east and west

18. A wave x meters long passes through a medium with a speed of y meters per second. The frequency of the wave could be expressed as (1) $\frac{y}{x}$ Hz (2) $\frac{x}{y}$ Hz (3) xy Hz (4) (x + y) Hz

19. If the frequency of a train of waves is 25 Hz, then the period of the waves is (1) 0.04 sec (2) 0.25 sec (3) 0.4 sec (4) 25 sec

20. A pulse in a spring transmits (1) energy only (2) mass only (3) both energy and mass (4) neither energy nor mass

21. In a certain medium, waves of different frequencies travel with different speeds. Such a medium is (1) opaque (2) coherent (3) periodic (4) dispersive

22. The water wave shown is moving toward the right. In which direction are the particles A and B moving? (1) Both A and B are moving upward. (2) Both A and B are moving downward. (3) A is moving upward and B is moving downward. (4) A is moving downward and B is moving upward.

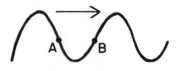

23. The frequency of a water wave is 6.0 Hz. If its wavelength is 2.0 m, then the speed of the wave is (1) 0.33 m/sec (2) 2.0 m/sec (3) 6.0 m/sec (4) 12 m/sec

24. As the frequency of a vibrating spring increases, its period of vibration (1) decreases (2) increases (3) remains the same

25. As the amplitude of a wave increases, the energy transported by the wave (1) decreases (2) increases (3) remains the same

26. As a wave travels into a medium in which its speed increases, its wavelength (1) decreases (2) increases (3) remains the same

27. As a pulse travels through a uniform medium, the speed of the pulse (1) decreases (2) increases (3) remains the same

28-32. Base your answers to Questions 28 through 32 on the diagram, which represents a wave travelling from left to right along a horizontal elastic medium. The horizontal distance from b to f is 0.08 m. The vertical distance from x to y is 0.06 m.

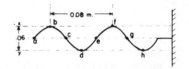

28. If the crest at b takes 2.0 sec to move from b to f, then what is the speed of the wave? (1) 0.03 m/sec (2) 0.04 m/sec (3) 0.05 m/sec (4) 0.06 m/sec

29. If the period of the wave is 2.0 sec, what is the frequency? (1) 0.5 Hz (2) 2.0 Hz (3) 5.0 Hz (4) 4.0 Hz

30. What is the amplitude of the wave? (1) 0.03 m (2) 0.04 m (3) 0.05 m (4) 0.06 m

31. As the wave moves to the right from its present position, in which direction will the medium at point e first move? (1) down (2) up (3) to the right (4) to the left

32. The frequency of the wave is now doubled. If the velocity remains constant, its wavelength is (1) quartered (2) halved (3) unchanged (4) doubled

33-37. Base your answers to Questions 33 through 37 on the following information.

The speed in air of the sound waves emitted by the tuning fork in the diagram is 340 m/sec.

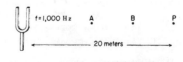

33. The time required for the waves to travel from the tuning fork to point P is (1) 0.020 sec (2) 0.059 sec (3) 0.59 sec (4) 2.9 sec

34. The wavelength of the sound waves produced by the tuning fork is (1) 0.29 m (2) 0.34 m (3) 0.43 m (4) 2.9 m

35. If the waves are in phase at points *A* and *B*, then the minimum distance between points *A* and *B* is (1) 1 wavelength (2) 2 wavelengths (3) ¼ wavelength (4) ½ wavelength

36. If the tuning fork, vibrating with a constant amplitude, is moved toward *P*, the amplitude of the waves reaching point *P* will (1) decrease (2) increase (3) remain the same

37. If the vibrating tuning fork is accelerated toward point *P*, the pitch observed at point *P* will (1) decrease (2) increase (3) remain the same

38-40. Base your answers to Questions 38 through 40 on the diagram, which shows four waves, all travelling in the same medium.

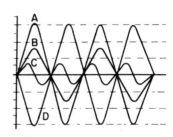

38. Which two waves will produce a resultant wave with the greatest amplitude? (1) *A* and *B* (2) *A* and *C* (3) *A* and *D* (4) *C* and *D*

39. Which pair of waves has the same amplitude? (1) *A* and *C* (2) *B* and *C* (3) *B* and *D* (4) *D* and *A*

40. Compared to the wavelength of wave *C*, the wavelength of wave *A* is (1) one-half as great (2) the same (3) twice as great (4) three times as great

3. PERIODIC WAVE PHENOMENA

The study of wave behavior requires the following definitions:
A straight line indicating the direction of wave travel is called a *ray*.

The surface where two media meet is called an *interface*.

A ray that originates in one medium and travels toward an interface is called an *incident* ray.

After an incident ray rebounds from the interface it is called a *reflected* ray.

A line perpendicular to an interface of the incident and reflected rays is called a *normal*.

The angle between the normal and the incident ray is called the *angle of incidence*, and the angle between the normal and the reflected ray is called the *angle of reflection*.

Reflection

The *Law of Reflection*, which may be stated in two parts, was discovered by Greek philosophers in ancient times through direct observation. They observed, first, that the angle of incidence is always equal to the angle of reflection. Second, all three lines, the incident ray, the reflected ray, and the normal, lie in one plane. Although originally observed in connection with light, the law of reflection is true for all wave phenomena. (See Figure 14)

Refraction

When a wave strikes an interface, it will be reflected, but it may also be transmitted in modified form through the second medium. Since the velocity of the wave in this new medium will, in general, be different from that in the original medium, waves incident at an angle other than 90° to the interface will be bent from their original direction. The ray is then said to have been *refracted*. Only if the incident ray lies along the normal will there be no refraction.

Snell's Law. The direction taken by the refracted ray depends upon the following mathematical law:

$$\frac{\sin \theta_1}{\sin \theta_2} = k \qquad (36)$$

Sin θ_1 is the sine of the angle of the ray with the normal in medium 1, and sin θ_2 is the sine of the angle of the ray with the normal in medium 2. This mathematical statement is known as *Snell's law*.

Speed and Refraction. When a ray enters a medium in which it is slowed, it will always be bent toward the normal extended into the second medium. Such is the case when light rays pass from air into water, as shown in *A*, Figure 11. When the ray enters a medium in which the speed is greater than the original speed in the first medium, then the refracted ray is bent away from the normal. *B*, Figure 11 illustrates this.

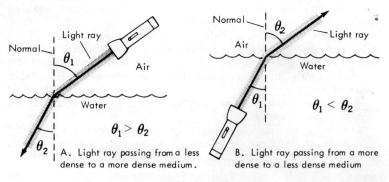

A. Light ray passing from a less dense to a more dense medium.

B. Light ray passing from a more dense to a less dense medium

Figure 11. Refraction.

The ratio of the velocities are the same as the ratio of the sines of the angles of incidence and refraction:

$$\frac{v_1}{v_2} = \frac{\sin \theta_1}{\sin \theta_2} \tag{37}$$

The frequencies f_1 and f_2 of the incident and refracted waves are the same. The wavelengths being proportional to the velocities, it follows therefore that

$$\frac{v_1}{v_2} = \frac{\lambda_1}{\lambda_2} \tag{38}$$

All of the above may be summarized as:

$$\frac{\sin \theta_1}{\sin \theta_2} = \frac{v_1}{v_2} = \frac{\lambda_1}{\lambda_2} \tag{39}$$

Diffraction

When an advancing wavefront in a ripple tank is partially blocked by an obstacle, the part of the wavefront that passes by the obstacle also bends around it. This bending of waves, whether of straight or circular wavefronts, into the region behind an obstruction is called *diffraction*. For example, a person speaking on one side of a solid fence can be heard on the other side, even though the speaker and the listener are not in line of sight.

The degree of diffraction of a wave depends upon the wavelength in relation to the width of the obstruction. The degree of diffraction increases as the ratio λ/d increases, where d is the width of the obstacle. At constant wavelength, the diffraction increases as the width of the obstacle decreases. For obstructions of constant width, the diffraction increases as the wavelength increases.

Diffraction may be explained in terms of Huygens' principle, in which each point on a wavefront is considered as a generator of small waves that combine to produce the next wavefront. The portion of the wavefront that passes nearest the end of a barrier acts as a source that generates the wavelets that combine behind the barrier to form the new wavefront. Figure 12 illustrates the spreading of such a wave behind the barrier in which a diffracted wavelet is generated at an aperture in the barrier.

Interference

The effect produced by two or more waves appearing simultaneously in the same region of a medium is called *interference*. At points where the two waves are in the same phase, as when two crests appear at the same point, there will be a net displacement of the medium equal to the *sum* of the two amplitudes. This is called constructive interference. When two waves meet at one point, crest to trough, there is *destructive interference*. There are variations in degree of interference between maximum and minimum net dis-

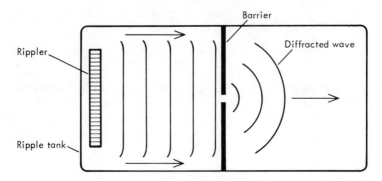

Figure 12. Diffraction in a ripple tank.

placements. The resultant displacement at any point may be found by the *algebraic sum* of the individual displacements due to each wave. The process of constructing the new waveform by finding this algebraic sum, point by point, for two or more waves is called *superposition*.

Amplitude of Combined Waves. If the amplitude of one wave is A and that of the other is B, both of the same wavelength, then the maximum displacement of the resultant wave is $(A + B)$, the minimum displacement is $(A - B)$. All other points will have displacements between these extremes. If both waves are of the same amplitude, A, then the maximum displacement of the resultant wave is $2A$ and the minimum is zero.

Standing Waves. When two waves of the same frequency and amplitude are present in the same medium at the same time, but travelling in opposite directions, the superposition of the waves produces a special waveform known as a *standing wave*. It is called by this name because the waveform seems not to move in any direction, although the particles of the medium are vibrating with different amplitudes. Those points where maximum constructive interference occurs, that is, where the medium oscillates at double amplitude, are called *antinodes*. Points one-half wavelength from these antinodes, where complete destructive interference (no oscillation) occurs, are called *nodes*. The pattern as a whole takes on the appearance of a set of waves where each half wave oscillates in phase opposition at double amplitude, but the pattern as a whole does not move through the medium. Standing waves most commonly occur where waves are reflected at a fixed boundary, because the incident and reflected waves have the same frequency, wavelength, and amplitude, but they move in opposite directions.

When two point sources in phase generate waves at opposite ends of a ripple tank, the pattern of nodes and antinodes spreads out on the water surface to form a set of mathematical curves called hyperbolas. The distance from any point on a nodal line to the two sources differs in path length by an *odd* number of half-wavelengths. In general, nodal lines form where the path difference is $(n - \frac{1}{2}\lambda)$, where n is the number of whole wavelengths. Antinodal lines form where the path lengths differ by an *even* number of half-wavelengths. This is illustrated in Figure 13. If a medium is limited so that reflection occurs at both ends of the wave pattern, and if the distance between the reflecting surfaces is $n\lambda/2$, a standing wave pattern will form.

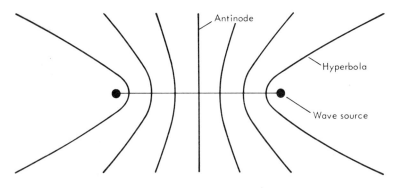

Figure 13. Standing waves.

QUESTIONS

1. The speed of light is changed when it is (1) polarized (2) refracted (3) reflected (4) diffracted
2. The spreading of a wave front into the region behind an obstruction is known as (1) reflection (2) refraction (3) diffraction (4) dispersion
3. Which phenomenon is evidence of the transverse nature of light? (1) polarization (2) reflection (3) diffraction (4) interference
4. The particles in a standing wave that do not move appreciably are located at the (1) crests (2) troughs (3) loops (4) nodes
5. As a periodic wave passes into a new medium where the wave speed is greater, the (1) frequency increases (2) frequency decreases (3) wavelength increases (4) wavelength decreases
6. Standing waves may be produced in the same medium if (1) the wavelength of one wave is half that of the other (2) two waves travel in the same direction (3) two waves travel in opposite directions and then back toward each other (4) the frequency of one wave is three times that of the other
7. What is the wavelength of the standing wave shown? (1) 1.0 m (2) 0.5 m (3) 3.0 m (4) 1.5 m

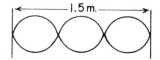

8. Two waves will produce a standing wave in a medium if they have (1) the same frequency, different amplitudes, and the same direction (2) the same frequency, the same amplitude, and the same direction ③ the same frequency, the same amplitude, and opposite directions (4) different frequencies, the same amplitude, and the same direction

9. The wave phenomenon that could not be demonstrated with a single wave pulse is ① a standing wave (2) diffraction (3) reflection (4) refraction

10. Refraction of a monochromatic light wave is caused by a change in the wave's (1) amplitude (2) frequency ③ wavelength (4) speed

11. Which phenomenon is associated only with transverse waves? (1) interference (2) dispersion (3) refraction ④ polarization

12. When two waves cross each other, maximum constructive interference will occur in places where the phase difference between the two waves is ① 0° (2) 45° (3) 90° (4) 180°

13. Sources that produce waves with a constant phase relation are said to be (1) polarized (2) diffused (3) refracted ④ coherent

14. The diagram shows light waves passing through slit S in barrier B. This is an example of (1) reflection (2) refraction (3) polarization ④ diffraction

15. A vibrator is used to produce standing waves in a stretched string. As the frequency of the vibrator increases, the number of nodes in the string (1) decreases ② increases (3) remains the same

16. As a periodic wave passes into a different medium in which the speed of the wave is decreased, the frequency of the wave ① decreases (2) increases (3) remains the same

17. The speed at which light passes through a material medium depends on the (1) frequency of the light only, ② nature of the medium, only (3) frequency of the light and the nature of the medium (4) angle of incidence to the medium

18. Which waves require a material medium for transmission? ① sound waves (2) radio waves (3) x rays (4) visible light

19. The change in direction which occurs when a wave passes obliquely from one medium into another is called (1) diffraction (2) interference ③ refraction (4) superposition

4. LIGHT

What we usually call light is an electromagnetic disturbance that gives rise to the sensation of sight. As mentioned earlier, the electromagnetic spectrum consists of a broad range of such disturbances, of which light is only a small portion.

Speed of Light

The speed of light is so great that accurate measurements of its magnitude could not be made until about 100 years ago. It is now known to travel at 300,000,000 (3.0×10^8) m/sec in vacuum and nearly at the same speed in air. In other media, its speed is always less than in vacuum. No other phenomenon in nature ever exhibits any greater speed. The theoretical importance of this velocity was pointed out by Albert Einstein in 1915 and is of great significance in modern physics. The transmission of light in vacuum can be viewed either as a spreading disturbance in the fields associated with electrical phenomena or as a movement of "particles" of energy (quanta). Today we know that light is only one portion of the electromagnetic radiation spectrum, and that all such radiations travel at the same velocity, c, in vacuum.

Reflection

The laws of reflection that describe the behavior of other wave phenomena also describe that of light waves. The angle of incidence equals the angle of reflection; the incident ray, the normal and the reflected ray all lie in one plane. However, when a beam of light strikes an irregular surface, such as the surface of running water, or of a sheet of paper, the reflected rays are scattered in all directions. Although each individual ray obeys the laws of reflection, the surface irregularities produce non-parallel normals, so that the reflected rays are not parallel. This prevents image formation. Such reflection is known as *diffuse* reflection.

When a light beam strikes a smooth plane surface, such as polished metal or smooth glass, the reflected rays will be parallel, enabling the eye to produce an image of the source. This regular reflection from the surface of plane mirrors is shown by geometrical construction of rays reflected from an object. *A,* Figure 14, shows two rays from the head of an object and two other rays from its base, each ray following paths described by the law of reflection. Each point on the object has a corresponding image point on the opposite side of the reflecting surface. Each image point seems the same distance behind the mirror as its corresponding object point is in front. Therefore, the image seems to be on the other side of the mirror, of the same size as the object itself. However, since the image cannot be cast on a screen and is not formed by the actual meeting of rays at a point in space, it is called a *virtual* image. Rays reflected from curved surfaces also follow the law of reflection, as shown in *B,* Figure 14.

Refraction

Light waves obey the laws of refraction as previously described, because their speeds differ in various media.

Index of Refraction. The amount of refraction is governed by Snell's law:

$$\frac{\sin \theta_1}{\sin \theta_2} = n \tag{40}$$

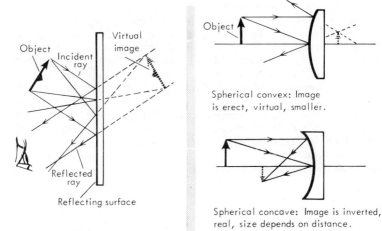

A. Plane mirror reflections

Spherical convex: Image is erect, virtual, smaller.

Spherical concave: Image is inverted, real, size depends on distance.

B. Curved mirror reflections

Figure 14. Reflection of light by mirrors.

The constant n is known as the *absolute index of refraction*, if medium 1, the medium in which the ray is travelling toward the interface, is a vacuum. It is a constant for any particular substance which acts as medium 2.

For any two media, Snell's law may be generalized in terms of the absolute index of refraction of each medium n_1 and n_2, in the following form:

$$n_1 \sin \theta_1 \ = \ n_2 \sin \theta_2 \tag{41}$$

In vacuum, $n = 1$.

The index of refraction of a medium may also be defined as the ratio of the speed of light in vacuum (c) to its speed in the medium (v):

$$n \ = \ \frac{c}{v} \tag{42}$$

The relation between the index of refraction and velocities of any two media is given by

$$\frac{n_1}{n_2} \ = \ \frac{v_2}{v_1} \tag{43}$$

The medium in which the speed of light is slower and n is greater is called the *optically dense* medium; the medium in which the speed of light is greater and n is smaller is called the *optically rare* medium.

In any ray diagram showing refraction, the relative angles of incidence and refraction will be the same when the source is interchanged with its final destination. If no clue is given as to which is the incident ray and which is the refracted ray, one could not tell merely by inspection of the ray traces. This phenomenon is known as the *principle of reversibility*. (See Figure 11.)

Critical Angle. Because the angle of refraction of light passing into a rarer medium will always be greater than the angle of incidence, the angle of incidence in the dense medium can be adjusted to give an angle of refraction equal to 90°, so that the refracted ray will graze the interface. The angle of incidence which produces a 90° angle of refraction is called the critical angle, θ_c. It is related to the index of refraction by the equation

$$n = \frac{1}{\sin \theta_c} \tag{44}$$

At angles of incidence in the denser medium greater than the critical angle no refraction into the rare medium can occur. All incident rays are reflected back into the dense medium. This type of reflection is known as *total internal reflection.*

Dispersion of Light. Light waves of different frequency are interpreted by the eye as being of different color. Since the different frequencies may have different speeds in dispersive media, they will each have a different index of refraction in the same medium and will be refracted at different angles. A mixture of light of different frequencies, such as sunlight, will then be separated by the different refractions into component frequencies and colors, as diagrammed in Figure 15.

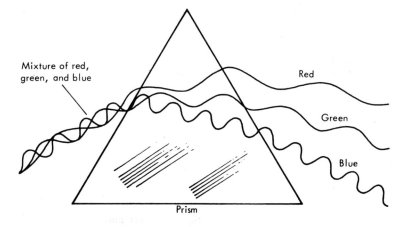

Figure 15.

The dispersion of polychromatic light by material media is used in the analysis of light waves. For example, yellow light produced by white light reflected from yellow-tinted glass may be dispersed into separate beams of red and green light. Yellow light from a sodium vapor lamp, however, is found to be only monochromatic; it cannot be dispersed.

Wave Nature of Light

Young's Experiment. The early Greek philosophers guessed that light consisted of a stream of minute particles, and explained the laws of reflection and refraction in terms of paths followed by these particles. This view persisted until the beginning of the nineteenth century, when Thomas Young demonstrated the interference of light and explained it in terms of waves. Based on this experiment, the wave nature of light was generally accepted. The polarization of light is evidence that it has the properties of transverse rather than longitudinal waves.

Interference of Light. Young used a double slit arrangement to provide two light sources from which the waves would always be in phase. Such light is said to be coherent, and is more readily produced today by means of the laser. When two such sources emit waves of the same frequency, amplitude, and phase, and these waves meet at the same point after travelling different paths, they will interfere with one another. If the paths from the two sources (or slits) to a point on a screen differ in length by one half-wavelength, then the two beams will produce a dark spot because the crest of one wave coincides with the trough of the other. Light must be assumed to have wave properties in order to explain this kind of complete interference. Conversely, physicists determined that radio, x rays, and gamma radiations had wave properties only after they demonstrated the ability of these radiations to show interference patterns.

(a) *Double Slit Interference.* If the paths from a point on a screen to the two sources differ in length by a multiple of a whole wavelength, the crests coincide at the point, producing a bright region on the screen. If they differ by a multiple of $\frac{1}{2}\lambda$, crests coincide with troughs, producing a dark region on the screen. Young's double slit experiment produced a series of dark and bright regions on the screen, demonstrating constructive and destructive interference, as shown in Figure 16. From the geometric arrangement of the experiment, the relationship between wavelength of the light, λ , the distance from source to screen, L, the separation between the slits, d, and the distance from the first bright line to the central bright line, x, was found to be

$$\lambda = \frac{dx}{L} \qquad\qquad (45)$$

The central bright line is always produced because the points on it are equidistant from each of the two slits. A series of slits very close together and equally spaced produces a similar pattern with

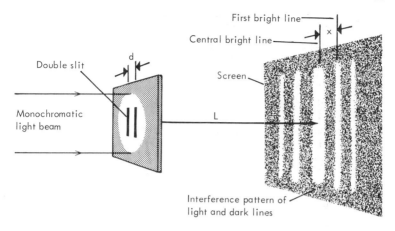

Figure 16. Young's double-slit interference pattern.

greatly enhanced effects, making it more useful in practical experimental work. This device is called a *diffraction grating*.

Since the d, x and L of equation 45 may readily be measured, the wavelength of the incident light may be calculated. Visible light was shown by this means to have wavelengths ranging approximately from 4×10^{-7} m (blue violet) to 8×10^{-7} m (deep red). The other colors of visible light have wavelengths between these extremes.

Note that according to equation 45, the distance between bright lines (or dark lines) is directly proportional to the wavelength and the distance from the screen, but inversely proportional to the distance between the slits.

(b) *Single Slit Interference—Optional Topic.* Light from a small single slit will also exhibit an interference pattern that is called a diffraction pattern, as shown in Figure 17. A broader bright central maximum spot is produced than in the double slit pattern. A double slit interference pattern is actually a combination of an interference pattern and diffraction patterns from the two slits.

(c) *Resolution—Optional Topic.* Because of diffraction and interference effects, light from two sources close together will have overlapping patterns. Such sources of light will appear to merge into one blurred mass. The ability of an optical instrument to distinguish between such closely spaced light sources is called its *power of resolution*. In general, the ability of a lens to *resolve* two closely spaced light sources, that is, to show them as separate, depends on the diameter of the lens used and the wavelength of the light. For a given wavelength, the larger the lens diameter, the greater its power of resolution.

(d) *Interference Fringes—Optional Topic.* Interference of light waves may also be observed when light is reflected from both the upper and lower surfaces of a thin layer of oil or soap films. In

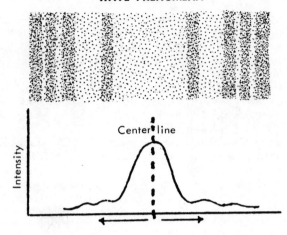

Figure 17. Single slit interference pattern.

such thin films, as in other instances, the difference in path lengths produces interference patterns. Waves with multiples of ½ λ path difference undergo destructive interference and waves with multiples of 1 λ path difference undergo constructive interference.

QUESTIONS

1. If the speed of light in a vacuum is *c*, then the speed of light in a medium with an index of refraction of 2 will be (1) $c/2$ (2) $2c$ (3) $c/4$ (4) $4c$

2. A ray of light travelling through water strikes the water-air interface with an angle of incidence equal to the critical angle. The angle of refraction will be (1) 180° (2) 90° (3) 45° (4) 30°

3. The frequency of infrared waves is generally greater than that of (1) visible light rays (2) radio waves (3) ultraviolet waves (4) x rays

4. If a ray of monochromatic yellow light ($λ = 5.9 \times 10^{-7}$ m) travelling through the air is incident to a refractive medium at an angle of 30°, the material that would produce the largest angle of refraction is (1) alcohol (2) water (3) glycerol (4) benzene (Refer to page 162.)

5. The speed of light through a medium is 3.0×10^8 m/sec. The index of refraction of the medium is (1) 1.0 (2) 1.45 (3) 3.0 (4) 2.5

6. The critical angle for light passing from a special glass into air is 41°. When the angle of incidence equals the critical angle, the angle of refraction will be (1) between 0° and 41° (2) 41° (3) between 41° and 90° (4) 90°

7. A beam of light travelling in air is incident upon a glass block. If the angle of refraction is 30°, the angle of incidence is (1) 0° (2) between 0° and 30° (3) between 30° and 90° (4) 90°

8. Which electromagnetic wave has the highest frequency? (1) radio (2) infrared (3) x ray (4) visible

9. The breaking up of white light into component colors as it passes through a triangular prism is an example of (1) dispersion (2) diffracion (3) diffusion (4) interference

10. Patterns obtained on a screen by passing light through a double slit can be explained in terms of (1) refraction and dispersion (2) diffraction and dispersion (3) diffraction and refraction (4) diffraction and interference

11. A beam of white light passes obliquely from air into glass. Which color experiences the greatest change in direction? (1) red (2) yellow (3) green (4) blue

12. One condition necessary for the formation of diffraction patterns from two light sources is that the two sources (1) have different frequencies (2) have different intensities (3) be coherent (4) be incoherent

13. The speed of light in a transparent medium is three-fourths that in a vacuum. The index of refraction of the medium is (1) $\dfrac{3}{4}$ (2) $\dfrac{4}{3}$ (3) $\dfrac{\sqrt{3}}{2}$ (4) $\dfrac{\sqrt{2}}{3}$

14. Maximum destructive interference occurs when the phase difference between two waves is (1) $0°$ (2) $90°$ (3) $180°$ (4) $270°$

15. The critical angle is that angle of incidence which produces an angle of refraction of (1) $0°$ (2) $45°$ (3) $60°$ (4) $90°$

16. What is the color of light with a wavelength of 7.9×10^{-7} m? (1) blue (2) green (3) yellow (4) red

17. At which point in the diagram will the object appear to the observer? (1) A (2) B (3) C (4) D

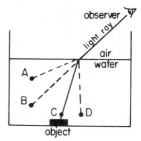

18. A light ray travelling through glass strikes a glass-air surface. The angle of incidence equals the critical angle of $42°$. The angle which the refracted ray makes with the normal is (1) $0°$ (2) $42°$ (3) $48°$ (4) $90°$

19. The diagram represents straight wave fronts passing through an opening in a barrier. The change in shape of the wave fronts is an example of (1) refraction (2) polarization (3) dispersion (4) diffraction

20. Light of a single frequency cannot be (1) dispersed (2) reflected (3) refracted (4) diffracted

21. Which instrument is usually used to analyze the color of light emitted by a star? (1) oscilioscope (2) spectroscope (3) electroscope (4) stroboscope

22. A wave passes obliquely from a medium having an index of refraction of 1.3 to a different medium. The wave will bend toward the normal if the index of refraction of the second medium is (1) 1.0 (2) 1.2 (3) 1.3 (4) 1.4

23. Double-slit interference experiments with light were important in establishing the (1) wave theory (2) corpuscular theory (3) quantum theory (4) electromagnetic theory

24. Which diagram shows the path that a monochromatic ray of light will travel as it passes through air, benzene, lucite, and back into air? (Refer to page 162.)

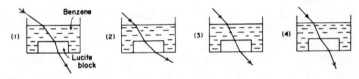

25. As the index of refraction of an alcohol and water mixture increases, the critical angle for the mixture (1) decreases (2) increases (3) remains the same

26. When the index of refraction of a medium increases, the apparent speed of light through the medium (1) decreases (2) increases (3) remains the same

27. A light ray travelling through glass strikes a glass-air surface. As the angle of incidence increases, the critical angle (1) decreases (2) increases (3) remains the same

28. As the absolute index of refraction of a substance increases, the speed of light in the substance (1) decreases (2) increases (3) remains the same

29. As a beam of light travels from a medium of low refractive index to one of high refractive index, the wavelength (1) decreases (2) increases (3) remains the same

30. As the width of a slit through which waves of constant frequency are passing decreases, the diffraction that takes place (1) decreases (2) increases (3) remains the same

31. A man standing on a straight railroad track hears the whistle of an approaching train. As the train approaches with a constant velocity, the frequency that the man observes (1) decreases (2) increases (3) remains the same

32. The speed of a ray of monochromatic blue light in glass, as compared with the speed of a ray of monochromatic red light in the same glass, is (1) greater (2) less (3) the same

33. A ray of monochromatic light passes from air into water. As the angle of incidence of the light ray increases, the index

of refraction of the water (1) decreases (2) increases (3) remains the same

34. As the angle of incidence of a light wave entering glass from air increases, the angle of refraction (1) decreases (2) increases (3) remains the same

35. Images produced by plane mirrors are (1) virtual, erect and the same size (2) virtual, inverted, and larger (3) real, inverted, and larger (4) real, erect, and smaller

36. A ray of light is reflected from a plane mirror. If the angle between the incident and reflected rays is 40°, the angle of incidence is (1) 20° (2) 35° (3) 50° (4) 70°

37. An arrow is drawn in front of the plane mirror *MM'*, as shown. The orientation of the image formed by the mirror is best represented by

38. The belief that light travels as a transverse wave is best supported by the fact that light can be (1) reflected (2) refracted (3) dispersed (4) polarized

39. Light rays emitted from point *P,* as seen by an observer at *B,* will seem to come from point (1) *A* (2) *B* (3) *C* (4) *D*

40. When a ray of light strikes a mirror perpendicular to its surface, the angle of reflection will be (1) 0° (2) 45° (3) 60° (4) 90°

41. A light beam from earth is reflected by an object in space. If the round trip takes 2.0 seconds, then the distance of the object from earth is (1) 6.7×10^7 m (2) 1.5×10^8 m (3) 3.0×10^8 m (4) 6.0×10^8 m

42-45. Base your answers to Questions 42 through 45 on the diagrams below, which show the paths of beams of monochromatic light as they reach the boundary between two media. *N* is the normal to the surface.

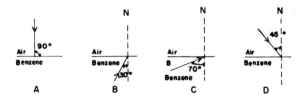

42. The direction of the beam of light will not change in diagram (1) *A* (2) *B* (3) *C* (4) *D*

43. The beam of light will undergo total internal reflection at the boundary in diagram (1) *A* (2) *B* (3) *C* (4) *D*

44. The angle of refraction of the beam of light will be greater than the angle of incidence in diagram (1) *A* (2) *B* (3) *C* (4) *D*

45. What is the sine of the angle of refraction for the beam of light in diagram *D*? (1) 1.00 (2) 0.707 (3) 0.47 (4) 0.30

46-50. Base your answers to Questions 46 through 50 on the diagram, which shows a glass prism surrounded by air. The dotted line *MN* is a normal.

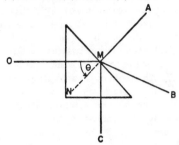

46. Which phenomenon would cause monochromatic light entering the prism along path *OM* to leave along path *MC*? (1) reflection (2) refraction (3) dispersion (4) diffraction

47. If the index of refraction of the prism is 1.5, then the speed of light in this prism is (1) 1.5×10^8 m/sec (2) 2.0×10^8 m/sec (3) 3.0×10^8 m/sec (4) 4.5×10^8 m/sec

48. A ray of light striking the prism along path *AM* will follow path (1) *MO* (2) *MN* (3) *MB* (4) *MC*

49. As compared with the index of refraction for blue light, the index of refraction of this glass prism for red light is (1) greater (2) less (3) the same

50. If all the light entering the prism along path *OM* emerges along path *MC*, then angle θ is (1) greater than the critical angle (2) less than the critical angle (3) equal to the critical angle

51-55. Base your answers to Questions 51 through 55 on the diagram, which represents three transparent media arranged one on top of the other. A light ray in air is incident on the upper surface of layer *A*.

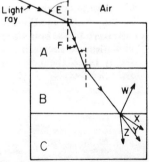

51. If layers *B* and *C* both have the same index of refraction, in which direction will the light ray travel after reaching the boundary between layers *B* and *C*? (1) *W* (2) *X* (3) *Y* (4) *Z*

52. If layer *A* were lucite, then layer *B* could be (1) water (2) diamond (3) benzene (4) flint glass (Refer to page 162.)

53. If angle E is 60° and layer A has an index of refraction of 1.61, the sine of angle F will be closest to (1) 1.00 (2) 0.866 (3) 0.538 (4) 0.400

54. If angle E were increased, then angle F would (1) decrease (2) increase (3) remain the same

55. Compared to the apparent speed of light in layer A, the apparent speed of light in layer B is (1) greater (2) the same (3) less

56-60. Base your answers to Questions 56 through 60 on the diagram, which shows a narrow beam of monochromatic yellow light passing from lucite into air. (Refer to page 162.)

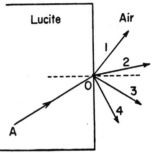

56. Which path will AO follow? (1) 1 (2) 2 (3) 3 (4) 4

57. The speed of the light beam in the lucite is (1) 1.0×10^8 m/sec (2) 2.0×10^8 m/sec (3) 3.0×10^8 m/sec (4) 4.5×10^8 m/sec

58. As the beam passes from lucite to air, its frequency (1) decreases (2) increases (3) remains the same

59. If the monochromatic yellow beam were replaced by a monochromatic violet beam, the speed of light in lucite would be (1) less (2) greater (3) the same

60. If the lucite were replaced by flint glass, the critical angle would be (1) smaller (2) larger (3) the same

61-64. Base your answers to Questions 61 through 64 on the diagram, which shows wave fronts passing from medium 1 into medium 2 at boundary BB'. The distance between the wave fronts in medium 1 is 0.04 m and in medium 2 is 0.02 m. The frequency of both waves is 10 Hz.

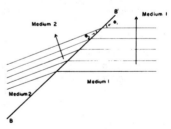

61. The change in the direction of the wave fronts is called (1) refraction (2) dispersion (3) diffraction (4) reflection

62. Compared to the speed of the waves in medium 2, the speed of the waves in medium 1 is (1) one half as great (2) the same (3) twice as great (4) four times as great

63. If angle θ_1 were increased, angle θ_2 would (1) decrease (2) increase (3) remain the same

64. The index of refraction of medium 2 relative to medium 1 is (1) less than 1 (2) equal to 1 (3) greater than 1

65-69. Base your answers to Questions 65 through 69 on the diagram, which shows a ray of monochromatic light as it passes through three transparent media. (Refer to page 162.)

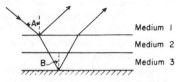

65. What happens to the light incident upon medium 2 from medium 1? (1) All of the light is refracted. (2) Part of the light is refracted and part is reflected. (3) Part of the light is refracted and part is dispersed. (4) Part of the light is diffracted and part is reflected.

66. If medium 2 is carbon tetrachloride, then medium 3 could be (1) crown glass (2) flint glass (3) lucite (4) fused quartz

67. As the light enters medium 2, its frequency (1) decreases (2) increases (3) remains the same

68. As angle A is increased, angle B will (1) decrease (2) increase (3) remain the same

69. If the frequency of the light is increased, its wavelength in medium 1 will (1) decrease (2) increase (3) remain the same

70-73. Base your answers to Questions 70 through 73 on the following information.

Two rays of monochromatic yellow light, A and B, originate in a tank of water as shown. Angle BON is the critical angle of water.

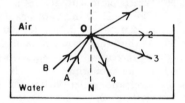

70. Ray A will travel along path (1) 1 (2) 2 (3) 3 (4) 4

71. The sine of the critical angle for water is equal to

(1) $\dfrac{1.33}{1}$ (2) $\dfrac{1}{1.33}$ (3) $\dfrac{3 \times 10^8}{1.33}$ (4) $3 \times 10^8 \times 1.33$

72. As a ray of light in the tank undergoes total internal reflection, its speed will (1) decrease (2) increase (3) remain the same

73. As a ray of light travelling along path NO enters the air, its speed will (1) decrease (2) increase (3) remain the same

74-78. Base your answers to Questions 73 through 78 on the diagram, which represents a lucite prism. HK is a narrow monochromatic yellow beam of light incident upon the prism at angle θ.

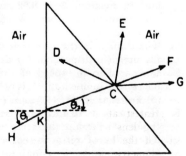

74. Which represents the path of *HK*? (1) *HKCD* (2) *HKCE* (3) *HKCF* (4) *HKCG*
75. The speed of the light beam through the lucite prism is (1) 1.0×10^8 m/sec (2) 2.0×10^8 m/sec (3) 3.0×10^8 m/sec (4) 4.0×10^8 m/sec
76. If angle θ_1 is 30°, the sine of angle θ_2 is

    (1) $\dfrac{0.50}{1.5}$ (2) $\dfrac{0.87}{1.5}$ (3) $\dfrac{1.5}{0.50}$ (4) $\dfrac{1.5}{0.87}$
77. If the monochromatic yellow beam is replaced by a monochromatic blue beam, angle θ_2 (1) decreases (2) increases (3) remains the same
78. As angle θ_1 increases from 20° to 30°, angle θ_2 (1) decreases (2) increases (3) remains the same

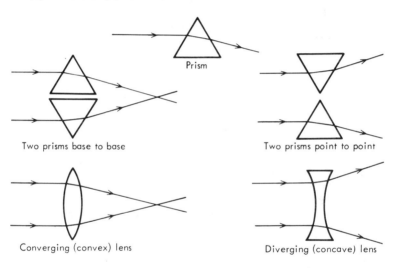

Figure 18. The relationship of converging and diverging lenses to prisms.

Lenses

Various transparent materials, especially glass, can be shaped so as to refract light rays in particular directions. These shapes are usually prisms or lenses. The paths of rays through lenses and prisms is shown in Figure 18.

Converging Lenses. A converging lens is one which refracts rays to a point. Its shape is convex, that is, its cross sectional thickness is greatest at its center. Parallel rays in air incident to a converging lens will be brought to a focus at a point on the opposite side of the lens. When these incident rays are parallel to the axis of symmetry of the lens (a line normal to the center of the lens surface), the refracted rays will converge at a point called the *focal point* of the lens. The distance of this point from the lens is called the *focal length* of the lens. The thickness of the lens is assumed to be negligible in comparison with the focal length.

Each converging lens has a specific focal length which is dependent upon the index of refraction of the optical material and the curvature of the two surfaces. The focal length, f, the distance of object from the lens, D_o, and the distance of the image from the lens, D_i, are related by the formula

$$\frac{1}{D_o} + \frac{1}{D_i} = \frac{1}{f} \tag{46}$$

The size of the image, S_i, is related to the size of the object, S_o, by the formula

$$\frac{S_o}{S_i} = \frac{D_o}{D_i} \tag{47}$$

EXAMPLE

An object is placed 0.5 m from a lens of focal length 0.1 m.
(a) The image is (1) real and inverted (2) real and upright (3) virtual and inverted (4) virtual and upright.
(b) Calculate the distance of the image from the lens (D_i*).*
(c) Calculate the size of the image if the object is 0.01 m high.

Solution:

(a) Choice (1)—real and inverted—because D_o is greater than f.

(b) $\dfrac{1}{D_o} + \dfrac{1}{D_i} = \dfrac{1}{f}$; $\dfrac{1}{0.5 \text{ m}} + \dfrac{1}{D_i} = \dfrac{1}{0.1 \text{ m}}$

$\dfrac{1}{D_i} = \dfrac{1}{0.1 \text{ m}} - \dfrac{1}{0.5 \text{ m}} = \dfrac{0.5 \text{ m} - 0.1 \text{ m}}{0.05 \text{ m}^2} = \dfrac{0.4}{0.05 \text{ m}}$

$D_i = \dfrac{0.05 \text{ m}}{0.4} = 0.13 \text{ m}$

(c) $\dfrac{S_o}{S_i} = \dfrac{D_o}{D_i}$

$S_i = \dfrac{S_o \times D_i}{D_o}$

$S_i = \dfrac{0.01 \text{ m} \times 0.13 \text{ m}}{0.5 \text{ m}} = 0.0026 \text{ m}$

When D_o is greater than f, an image will be formed on the other side of the lens. The image size increases as D_o increases toward the value of f, but the image formed is always inverted. At a point where $D_o = 2f$, the image size and the object size are equal. This fact is used by photographers in making a same-size copy of an original subject. When $D_o = f$, no image is formed (the image is said to be at infinity). A virtual, enlarged image on the same side of the lens as the object is formed when D_o is less than f. The relative size, location and position of the images produced with the converging lens may be obtained from scale drawings of the rays. Figure 19 illustrates this. In preparing such diagrams, the object, an

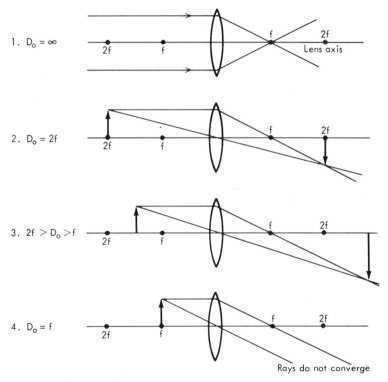

Figure 19. Converging lens ray diagram.

arrow, is usually placed to the left of the lens, with the foot of the arrow on the principal axis of the lens as shown. Two rays drawn from the top of the object to the lens are sufficient to determine the location of the image. One of these rays is drawn parallel to the principal axis and will be refracted through the focal point. This ray should be extended beyond this focal point.

The other ray is drawn through the lens center, is unrefracted, and is extended to meet the first ray. The point of intersection of the two rays determines the image point corresponding to the head of the object. A line perpendicular to the extended axis and terminating at the intersection gives the location of the image.

Images. There are two kinds of images, *real* and *virtual*. A *real* image can be projected on a screen because light rays from the object *converge* there. A *virtual* image is formed by the eye from light rays that *diverge* from a lens, and therefore appear to be coming from an object located at the point from which the rays diverge.

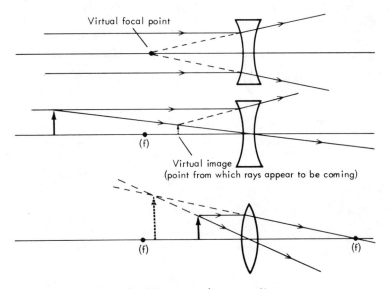

Figure 20. Diverging lens ray diagram.

Diverging lenses. A lens that is thicker at the edges than at the center is called a *concave* lens. Such a lens will always diverge a bundle of parallel light rays entering it, making them appear to be coming from a point called the *virtual focus*. Convex lenses also diverge light rays if they come from an object placed between the lens and its focal point. Ray diagrams for these lenses are given in Figure 20. Note that the concave lens always produces a virtual image that appears smaller than the object. The convex lens always forms a virtual image that appears larger than the object.

QUESTIONS

1. A real image can be produced by a (1) plane mirror (2) concave lens (3) convex lens (4) convex mirror

2. Which diagram correctly shows light rays passing through the lens?

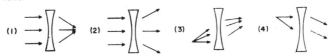

3. A spectrum is formed on a screen when white light is passing through a converging lens. This is an example of (1) interference (2) diffraction (3) reflection (4) dispersion

4-6. Base your answers to Questions 4 through 6 on the diagram, which represents a thin converging lens and its principal axis. *F* represents the principal focus.

4. If the light rays are parallel when they leave the lens, the light source must be placed (1) between *F* and the lens (2) at *F* (3) between *F* and *2F* (4) at *2F*

5. As an object is moved from point *A* toward point *B*, its image will (1) become erect (2) move toward the lens (3) change from real to virtual (4) become enlarged

6. If the image is located at *2F'* the object must be located (1) at *F* (2) between *F* and *2F* (3) at *2F* (4) beyond *2F*

7-11. Base your answers to Questions 7 through 11 on the diagram, which shows a lens whose focal length is 0.10 m.

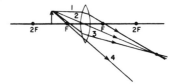

7. Which ray from the head of the arrow is not correctly drawn? (1) 1 (2) 2 (3) 3 (4) 4

8. If the object is 0.15 m from the lens, then the distance from the image to the lens is (1) 0.06 m (2) 0.10 m (3) 0.15 m (4) 0.30 m

9. If an object 0.24 m tall is placed at *2F*, then the height of the image is (1) 0.06 m (2) 0.12 m (3) 0.24 m (4) 0.48 m

10. As the object is moved from *2F* toward *F*, the size of the image (1) decreases (2) increases (3) remains the same

11. If the index of refraction of the lens increases, then the focal length of the lens (1) decreases (2) increases (3) remains the same

12-16. Base your answers to Questions 12 through 16 on the diagram, which represents a simple converging (convex) lens whose principal foci are at F and F'.

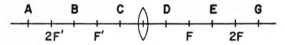

12. An object placed at $2F'$ will produce an image at (1) F (2) $2F$ (3) E (4) D
13. If an object is placed at point C, the resulting image is (1) real and smaller (2) real and larger (3) virtual and smaller (4) virtual and larger
14. An object placed 0.06 m to the left of the lens produces an image 0.03 m to the right of the lens. What is the focal length of the lens? (1) 0.015 m (2) 0.02 m (3) 0.2 m (4) 0.5 m
15. As an object is moved from A to B, the size of the image (1) decreases (2) increases (3) remains the same
16. As the size of an object placed a point A *increases,* the size of the image (1) decreases (2) increases (3) remains the same

17-21. Base your answers to Questions 17 through 21 on the diagram, which represents a thin convex lens and its optical axis. The principal foci are indicated at F and F'. The focal length of the lens is 0.20 m.

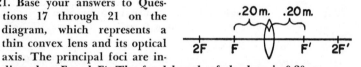

17. If the object is placed 0.30 m from the lens, then the distance from the lens to the image will be (1) 0.10 m (2) 0.12 m (3) 0.50 m (4) 0.60 m
18. A 0.12-m tall object is placed 0.40 m from the lens. The size of the image formed is (1) 0.06 m (2) 0.12 m (3) 0.24 m (4) 0.48 m
19. In order to form an image between F' and $2F'$, the object must be placed (1) at F (2) between F and $2F$ (3) at $2F$ (4) beyond $2F$
20. Which type of image cannot be formed by this lens? (1) a real image smaller than the object (2) a real image larger than the object (3) a virtual image smaller than the object (4) a virtual image larger than the object
21. For which color is the focal length of this lens greatest? (1) red (2) yellow (3) green (4) blue

22-25. Base your answers to Questions 22 through 25 on the following information.

A converging lens produces an image of a large, distant object. The object distance is 5000 m, and the image distance is 0.50 m.

22. What is the approximate focal length of the lens? (1) 1.0 m (2) 0.75 m (3) 0.50 m (4) 0.25 m
23. If the object size is 1000 m, what is the image size? (1) 0.050 m (2) 0.10 m (3) 0.15 m (4) 0.20 m

24. If the size of the object were increased, the size of the image would (1) decrease (2) increase (3) remain the same
25. If the index of refraction of the lens were increased, the focal length of the lens would be (1) smaller (2) the same (3) larger

Electromagnetic Radiation

From studies of the nature of electricity and magnetism, the British physicist James C. Maxwell in 1870 devised a set of equations, now called Maxwell's equations, which predicted the existence of transverse wave-like disturbances in electrical and magnetic fields. These *electromagnetic radiations*, generated by the acceleration of charged particles, have various wavelengths and are propagated at the speed of light. It was found that these waves exist and that visible light itself consists of such electromagnetic radiation of a particular range of wavelengths.

There are no sharp boundaries between the various wavelength ranges; they are classified for convenience according to the methods by which they are generated or received. The best known of the electromagnetic waves, light waves, originate in the motion of electrons within atoms. The frequency range of light waves is a narrow band compared to the total frequency range of the whole electromagnetic spectrum.

The Electromagnetic Spectrum. The band of frequencies of the electromagnetic waves is called a *spectrum*. Since all of these waves travel in vacuum at the same speed, c (3.0×10^8 m/sec), the wavelength, λ, is related to the frequency, f, by the equation

$$\lambda = \frac{c}{f} \qquad (48)$$

This equation is derived from equation 34 by substituting c as the velocity of wave propagation. Color ranges, frequency and wavelength data are given in Figure 21.

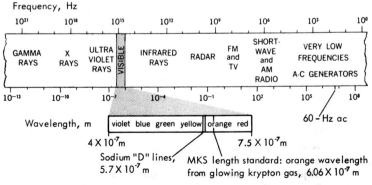

Figure 21.

Types of Spectra. Various sources produce different kinds of spectra. For example, glowing gases and vapors at low pressure, viewed in a spectroscope, show a *bright-line spectrum*, a series of distinct bright lines, each of which represents a distinct frequency. The different line series produced by different atoms are clues to the inner structure of the atom.

Incandescent solids and liquids, and incandescent gases under high pressure, produce *continuous spectra*, which show all the visible colors, each color merging into the next without gaps. Under certain conditions substances produce spectra consisting of regions of many closely spaced lines. These lines appear to merge, producing *band spectra*. Band spectra are closely related to the molecular structure of the substances and are a useful tool in chemical analysis.

QUESTIONS

1-5. Base your answers to Questions 1 through 5 on diagrams *A* through *D*, which represent four interference patterns. The dark bars indicate areas of *minimum* light intensity.

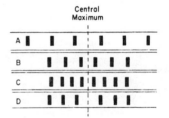

1. Which phenomenon was primarily responsible for producing all four interference patterns? (1) polarization (2) dispersion (3) refraction (4) diffraction

2. If the distance from the slits to the screen upon which pattern *B* is displayed is increased, then the most likely pattern to appear would be (1) *A* (2) *B* (3) *C* (4) *D*

3. In pattern *C*, the distance between the central maximum and the first bright line is 2.0×10^{-2} m. The separation of the double slit is 1.0×10^{-4} m and the distance from the slits to the screen is 4.0 m. The wavelength of the source is (1) 2.2×10^{-3} m (2) 8.0×10^2 m (3) 5.0×10^{-7} m (4) 1.5×10^{-6} m

4. Which pattern was produced by passing light through a single slit? (1) *A* (2) *B* (3) *C* (4) *D*

5. If pattern *B* is produced by using monochromatic green light and the source is changed to monochromatic red light, then the pattern produced would become like pattern (1) *A* (2) *B* (3) *C* (4) *D*

6-9. Base your answers to Questions 6 through 9 on the following information.

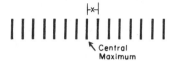

The dark bars in the diagram represent the bright areas in an interference pattern produced by a source of monochromatic light with a wavelength of 6.0×10^{-7} m. The light is incident upon two slits that are 2.0×10^{-5} m apart and 2.0 m from the screen.

6. The color of the incident light is (1) green (2) yellow (3) red (4) orange

7. Distance x is equal to (1) 1.7×10^{-2} m (2) 3.0×10^{-2} m (3) 6.0×10^{-2} m (4) 1.2×10^{-1} m

8. If the distance between the slits and the screen is increased, then distance x will (1) decrease (2) increase (3) remain the same

9. If the light source is made brighter, then distance x will (1) decrease (2) increase (3) remain the same

10-14. Base your answers to Questions 10 through 14 on diagrams A, B, C, D, and E, which represent a specific bright line from the helium spectrum. Diagram A was observed with a standard stationary source in a laboratory. Diagrams B, C, D, and E represent the same line observed from moving sources.

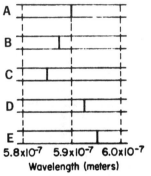

10. The frequency of the helium line in diagram A is (1) 2.0×10^{-14} Hz (2) 1.8×10^{1} Hz (3) 5.1×10^{14} Hz (4) 3.2×10^{11} Hz

11. Diagram B indicates an increase in the wave's observed (1) frequency (2) wavelength (3) speed (4) amplitude

12. Two sources travelling with constant but different velocities approach a stationary observer. The observer examining the spectral line of the source with the greater velocity would see the line shown in diagram (1) E (2) B (3) C (4) D

13. The above spectral line could have been emitted by (1) a luminous gas at low pressure (2) an incandescent liquid at low pressure (3) an incandescent liquid at high pressure (4) an incandescent solid at high pressure

14. The apparent shift of the radiation is a phenomenon whose explanation is credited to (1) Newton (2) Doppler (3) Huygens (4) Snell

15-19. Base your answers to Questions 15 through 19 on the diagram, which represents light from a monochromatic source, K, passing through narrow slits S_1 and S_2. A central bright band is observed at C and a first order bright band is observed at B. The two slits are 1.1×10^{-4} m apart, distance OC is 2 m, and distance CB is 1.0×10^{-2} m.

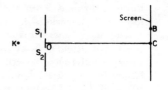

15. Light arrives at point B from slit S_2 because of (1) dispersion (2) refraction (3) diffraction (4) polarization

16. The bright band at B is caused by (1) interference (2) refraction (3) dispersion (4) polarization

17. What is the color of the light coming from source K? (1) orange (2) yellow (3) blue (4) green

18. If red light had been used, the distance BC would have been (1) larger (2) smaller (3) the same

19. If the two slits are moved closer together, the distance BC will be (1) larger (2) smaller (3) the same

20-24. Base your answers to Questions 20 through 24 on the following information.

Two parallel slits 2.0×10^{-6} m apart are illuminated by parallel rays of monochromatic light of wavelength 6.0×10^{-7} m, as shown. The interference pattern is formed on a screen 2.0 m from the slits.

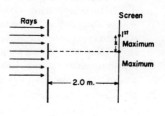

20. The distance X is (1) 6.0×10^{-1} m (2) 6.0×10^{-7} m (3) 3.0×10^{-1} m (4) 3.3 m

21. The difference in path length for the light from the two slits to the first maximum is (1) λ (2) 2λ (3) $\lambda/2$ (4) 0

22. If the wavelength of the light passing through the slits is doubled, the distance from the central maximum to the first maximum (1) decreases (2) increases (3) remains the same

23. If the screen is moved closer to the slits, the distance between the central maximum and the first maximum (1) decreases (2) increases (3) remains the same

24. If the distance between the slits decreases, the distance between the central maximum and the first maximum (1) decreases (2) increases (3) remains the same

25-29. Base your answers to Questions 25 through 29 on the following information.

Two speakers are arranged as shown so that initially they will emit tones which are in phase, equal in volume, and equal in frequency. A microphone is placed at position *A*, which is equidistant from both speakers, and then is moved along a line parallel to the line joining the speakers until it reaches a point (position *B*) at which it picks up no sound.

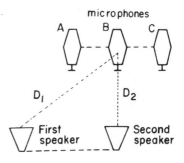

The microphone is then moved to position *C*, where it again picks up sound.

25. Which phenomenon caused the sound to be louder at position *C* than at position *B*? (1) reflection (2) dispersion (3) polarization (4) interference

26. Distance D_2 is shorter than distance D_1 by an amount equal to (1) the wavelength of the emitted sound (2) one half the wavelength of the emitted sound (3) twice the wavelength of the emitted sound (4) the distance between the two speakers

27. If the sound waves emitted by D_1 and D_2 have a frequency of 660 Hz and a speed of 330 m/sec, their wavelength is (1) 1.0 m (2) 2.0 m (3) 0.25 m (4) 0.50 m

28. As the first speaker is adjusted so that the sound which it emits is 180° out of phase with the sound emitted by the second speaker, the loudness of the sound received at *A* is (1) greater (2) less (3) the same

29. If speaker D_1 were removed and speaker D_2 were accelerated toward microphone *B*, the frequency of the waves detected at *B* would (1) decrease (2) increase (3) remain the same

30-34. Base your answers to Questions 30 through 34 on the diagram, which shows monochromatic yellow light ($\lambda = 5.9 \times 10^{-7}$ m) directed upon two narrow slits 1.0×10^{-3} m apart.

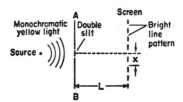

30. The first bright line is 5.9×10^{-3} m from the central axis of the pattern. The distance (*L*) between the screen and *AB* is (1) 1 m (2) 10 m (3) 100 m (4) 1000 m

31. If the screen is placed 1 m from *AB*, the separation of the central maximum and the first order bright line (*x*) is (1) 5.9×10^{-6} m (2) 1.18×10^{-5} m (3) 1.18×10^{-3} m (4) 5.9×10^{-4} m

32. This double slit pattern is a result of (1) polarization (2) refraction (3) diffraction (4) dispersion

33. As the separation between the slits increases, the space between the bright lines on the screen (1) decreases (2) increases (3) remains the same

34. As the wavelength of the light decreases, the separation of the bright lines on the screen (1) decreases (2) increases (3) remains the same

35-39. Base your answers to Questions 35 through 39 on the following information.

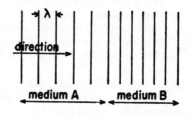

Waves with a frequency of 1.0×10^2 Hz and a wavelength $\lambda = 2.0 \times 10^{-1}$ m in medium A are travelling into medium B as shown. The wavelength in medium B is 1.0×10^{-1} m.

35. The speed of the wave travelling in medium A is (1) 3.0×10^8 m/sec (2) 2.0×10^3 m/sec (3) 2.0×10^1 m/sec (4) 2.0×10^{-3} m/sec

36. The wave frequency in medium B is (1) 5.0×10^1 Hz (2) 1.0×10^2 Hz (3) 2.0×10^2 Hz (4) 3.0×10^8 Hz

37. If the index of refraction of medium A is 1.0, then the index of refraction of medium B is (1) 1.0 (2) 2.0 (3) 3.0 (4) 0.50

38. The period T of the wave in medium A is (1) 1.0×10^2 sec (2) 5.0×10^2 sec (3) 1.0×10^{-2} sec (4) 3.0×10^{-7} sec

39. If the frequency in medium A is doubled, then the (1) speed in medium A is doubled (2) speed in medium A is halved (3) wavelength in medium A is doubled (4) wavelength in medium A is halved

40-44. Base your answers to Questions 40 through 44 on the diagram, in which the lines represent bright lines in the visible spectrum.

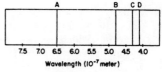

Wavelength (10^{-7} meter)

40. The color of line A is (1) red (2) orange (3) blue (4) violet

41. What is the frequency of line A in Hz? (1) 1.6×10^{14} (2) 4.6×10^{14} (3) 4.9×10^{-7} (4) 1.6×10^{15}

42. This spectrum could have been emitted by (1) an incandescent solid (2) an incandescent liquid (3) a cold solid (4) a luminous gas at low pressure

43. The speed of the light which produces line A, compared to that of the light which produces line B, is (1) less (2) greater (3) the same

44. A photograph of the spectrum of a distant star shows the

above lines displaced slightly to the left. This indicates that our distance from the star is (1) decreasing (2) increasing (3) not changing

45-47. Base your answers to Questions 45 through 47 on the following information.

When monochromatic light passes through a single narrow slit to a screen, a pattern is formed on the screen.

45. Compared to the bright regions on the sides of the pattern, the intensity of the central bright region is (1) greater (2) less (3) the same

46. As the intensity of the light source is increased, the width of the bright regions will (1) decrease (2) increase (3) remain the same

47. As the width of the slit is decreased, the width of the central maximum will (1) decrease (2) increase (3) remain the same

48. Which group of electromagnetic radiations is arranged in order of increasing frequency? (1) ultraviolet, visible, infrared, x ray (2) x ray, visible, infrared, radio (3) ultraviolet, visible, radio, infrared (4) radio, visible, x ray, gamma ray

49. Which electromagnetic wave has the highest frequency? (1) radio (2) infrared (3) x ray (4) visible

50. The frequency of ultraviolet radiation is less than that of (1) radio wave radiation (2) infrared radiation (3) violet radiation (4) gamma radiation

ELECTRICITY

1. STATIC ELECTRICITY

Electrically charged objects exert forces upon each other that depend on the quantity of charge, the distance between charges, and on whether or not the objects are at rest relative to each other. The study of these forces between charges *at rest* is the subject matter of static electricity. Note that the term "at rest" means that there is no net transfer of charge in any direction, although charged parts of a given object may be in motion relative to each other.

Microstructure of Matter

The following review of atomic structure is given to aid the study of electricity.

The matter in the universe is composed of various combinations of about one hundred different elements. Each element consists of one kind of atom, but all of these atoms consist of only three basic particles. Two of these particles are electrically charged and the other is neutral. The least massive particle, the *electron*, carries a negative (−) charge. The *proton*, which is 1836 times as massive as the electron, carries a positive (+) charge equal in magnitude to that of the negative electron charge. These *elementary units of charge* are the smallest that have ever been observed. The third particle is the *neutron*. It bears no charge, and is of approximately the same mass as the proton.

Protons and neutrons are found only in the central core, the *nucleus*, of the atom. The electrons are in motion outside the nucleus and possess specific levels of energy. Energy applied to atoms in the form of friction, heat, light, etc. may remove some of the electrons, but neither protons nor neutrons can be separated from atoms by ordinary means. This means that, in general, objects become charged only by gaining or losing electrons (units of negative charge).

Charged Objects

Atoms as a whole are electrically neutral because the number of protons in the nucleus is the same as the number of electrons outside it. When electrons are lost or gained by the neutral atom, the resulting particle is electrically charged and is called an *ion*. The charge of an ion depends on the nature and quantity of particles in excess. For example, an atom with 11 protons and 11 electrons is neutral, but if one electron (one unit of negative charge) is removed from this atom, leaving 11 protons and 10 electrons, the resulting ion will show a single unit of positive charge. Similarly, an ion with 16 protons and 18 electrons has a net negative charge of 2 units.

When two charged bodies of like sign are brought near one another, they are *repelled* by an electrical force acting on each in opposite directions. When the bodies each carry charge of opposite sign, they are *attracted* to one another by an electrical force acting on each, also in opposite directions. A charged electroscope shows the presence and nature of an electrical charge by the collapse or spread of its leaves or vanes. If, when a charged object is brought near the electroscope, the electroscope vanes spread further, the charge is the same as that of the electroscope; if the vanes move toward one another, the charge is of opposite sign.

Transfer of Charges

Conservation of Charge. In a system isolated so that electric charge cannot enter or leave, the total net charge in the system is constant. This means that whatever changes occur within the system, the algebraic sum of all positive and negative charges never changes. This observation is known as the *law of conservation of charge.* For example, the objects in a system in which the net charge is $+5$ units may exchange these charges back and forth, but the net charge will remain 5 units of positive elementary charge.

Charging by Contact. A system consisting of neutral objects will have a total net charge equal to zero. Objects within the system may exchange electrons, becoming charged relative to each other, but the system as a whole will remain neutral. This can occur if the objects are in contact, especially when they rub against each other. If one object loses electrons, becoming positively charged, the object in contact with it will acquire the electrons, becoming negatively charged. The sum of the charges of the two, however, will remain zero.

Conduction. In a system containing a charged object and a neutral one, both may become charged if they come into contact. This is called charging by *conduction.* Some of the charge of the charged object has been conducted to the neutral object, which has acquired the same polarity (sign) of charge as that of the original charged object. Of course, the sum of the charge of the two objects will remain constant during this process, according to the law of charge conservation.

Induction. When a charged object is brought near, but not touching, a neutral one, the charged object influences the uncharged one over the intervening space. The neutral object contains equal numbers of positive and negative charges within its atoms. In response to the charged object, the charges in the neutral object become redistributed, due to repulsion of like charges and attraction of unlike. In this condition of unbalanced charge, the neutral object is said to be *polarized*, exhibiting a positively charged end and a negatively charged end, although the object is still neutral overall. (See Figure 22.) This effect, a temporary one, is called *electrostatic induction.* If, during this unbalance, charge is removed from the neutral object by grounding, it will acquire a permanent charge of opposite sign to the charging body.

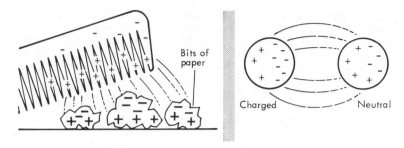

Figure 22. Effect of charged objects on neutral objects.

Elementary Charges

Although recent theories have predicted the existence of a smaller charge than that of the electron, there is no experimental evidence to confirm this prediction. The smallest charge observed to exist in nature is that of the electron (or of its equivalent, the proton). This charge, symbolized as $-e$ (or $+e$ for a positive charge) is extremely small compared to those dealt with in ordinary experience. The basic MKS unit of charge is the *coulomb* (coul, or sometimes C). It is equal to 6.25×10^{18} elementary charges. The charge on the electron is equal to -1.6×10^{-19} coul. That of the proton is $+1.6 \times 10^{-19}$ coul. The net charge on any larger object is always an integral multiple of $-e$ or $+e$. Thus, a body may have a charge of $2\,e$ ($= 3.2 \times 10^{-19}$ coul), $3\,e$ ($= 4.8 \times 10^{-19}$ coul), but can never have a charge of $2\frac{1}{2}\,e$ ($= 4.0 \times 10^{-19}$ coul).

Coulomb's Law

Experiment has shown that the magnitude of the force between charged objects at rest is directly proportional to the product of the charges carried by the objects. Thus, if all other conditions are unchanged, the force between an object carrying a charge of $+4\,e$ and one carrying a charge of $+3\,e$ is of the same magnitude as the force between two objects carrying charges of $+2\,e$ and $+6\,e$ respectively. Experiment also shows that the force between fixed charges varies inversely with the square of the distance separating them. Combining these two proportionalities yields the relationship called *Coulomb's Law*. This law is summarized in the equation

$$F = k\ \frac{q_1\,q_2}{r^2} \qquad (49)$$

The force F is given in newtons if q_1 and q_2 are expressed in coulombs and r in meters. The proportionality constant k has been found to be approximately equal to 9.0×10^9 newton-meter^2/coulomb^2. Note that, just as Newton's law of gravitational force is exact for "point" masses, Coulomb's law is exact only for "point" charges, that is, charged objects whose dimensions are insignificant compared to the

---

EXAMPLE

What is the force between two relatively small charged objects that carry charges of +0.1 coul and −0.1 coul respectively, if the distance between them is 1000 m?

Solution:

$$F = k \times \frac{q_1 q_2}{r^2} =$$

$$\frac{9 \times 10^9 \text{ nt-m}^2}{\text{coul}^2} \times \frac{(0.1 \text{ coul}) \times (-0.1 \text{ coul})}{(1000 \text{ m})^2} =$$

$$- \frac{9 \times 10^9 \times 10^{-2} \text{ nt}}{10^6} = -90 \text{ nt}$$

The negative sign indicates a force of attraction.

---

distance between them, and for charged spherical objects if r is the distance between their centers.

Electric Fields

The region in which electrical force acts between two electrically charged objects is called an *electric field*. By definition, the direction of the field at a given point is the direction in which force acts on a small *positively* charged object called a *test charge*. For example, if electric force acts on such a test charge in a northerly direction, then the electric field direction is north. At the same point in the field, a small negative charge would experience a force directed to the south. A *field line* is the line along which a test charge would move in an electric field. The strength of the field at any point is determined by the magnitude of the force exerted on the test charge. The equation for determining electric field strength, E, is

$$E = \frac{F}{q} \tag{50}$$

When the force F is given in newtons, and q, the magnitude of the test charge, in coulombs, the electric field strength E is measured in newtons/coulomb (nt/coul). For example, if an object carrying a charge of 2×10^{-6} coulomb is acted upon by an electric force of 0.06 nt, the electric field strength at that point is

$$E = \frac{6 \times 10^{-2} \text{ nt}}{2 \times 10^{-6} \text{ coul}} = 3 \times 10^4 \text{ nt/coul}$$

Electric field strength, E, must be designated both in magnitude and direction because it is a vector quantity. When two fields interact, the net field must be obtained by vector methods.

Field Around a "Point" (or Spherical) Charge. The origin of an electric field is a charged object. For any charged object on which charge can spread uniformly (a charged conductor), the electric field lines are normal to the surface. Depending upon the distribution of charges on the object, the intensity of its field will vary. Around a "point" charge, the electric field is directed radially, away from the charge if it is positive and toward it if negative. As indicated by equation 49, the intensity of the field around a point charge decreases inversely as the square of the distance from the charge. This is also true of the field around a charged conducting sphere. The field acts as if it were the result of a point charge located at the center of the sphere. Within a charged sphere itself, however, the field intensity is zero; that is, no force will be observed on a test charge inside a hollow charged sphere. The fields surrounding charged objects are shown in Figure 23.

Field Around a Charged Rod. The field around a charged rod is also directed radially from the long axis (the axis of symmetry) of the rod. The strength of the field also decreases with increasing distance

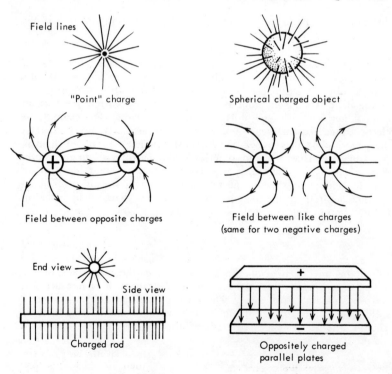

Figure 23. Fields surrounding charged objects.

from the rod, but, because the charged object is not spherical, the variation is not an inverse square relation. That is, the decrease of electric force with distance from a charged rod is inversely proportional to r rather than r^2. For example, if the distance from a charged sphere is doubled, the field strength is decreased by $\frac{1}{4}$. If the distance from a charged rod is doubled, the field strength is decreased only by $\frac{1}{2}$.

Field Between Parallel Charged Plates. The electric field that exists in the region between two oppositely charged parallel plates is uniform if the distance between the plates is small relative to their size. This means that the field strength is the same at each point between the plates. A test charge within this region of uniform field will experience the same force in the same direction wherever it is placed.

Electric Potential. Since work would be required to move a test charge against the force that acts on it in an electric field, the field can be described in terms of work (or energy). The work required to bring a positive unit charge from an infinite distance to a given point in an electric field is called the electric potential of that point in the field. The electric potential V may then be calculated from the equation

$$V = \frac{W}{q} \tag{51}$$

When W is measured in joules and q in coulombs, the unit of electric potential, V, is the joule/coulomb. This unit, the MKS unit of electric potential difference, is called the *volt* in honor of the Italian physicist Alessandro Volta, who invented the electric battery (1800). A field may thus be described by stating the field strength, E, in newtons per coulomb, or by stating the potential V, in joules per coulomb (volts). For example, in a field in which 12 joules of work is required to bring a charge of 3 coul from infinity to a given point, the electric field potential at that point is

$$V = \frac{12 \text{ joules}}{3 \text{ coul}} = 4 \text{ joules/coul} = 4 \text{ volts}$$

Potential Difference

Voltage and Potential Difference. Since the volt is a measure of the electric potential difference between points in an electric field, it can be used to calculate the energy required to transfer a given charge between these points. For example, to move 2 coul of charge across a potential difference of 3 volts, the work required is 3 volts $\times$ 2 coul = 6 joules. The potential difference between two points in an electric field is therefore the change in energy per unit charge as a charge is moved between the points.

If an electric charge is moved in the direction of lower potential from a point at higher potential in a field, then the field has performed work on the charge. For example, an electric toaster connected to two points at a potential difference of 120 volts will receive 120 joules of energy for each coulomb of charge that passes through the toaster. On the other hand, when a 12-volt battery is charged from some external energy source, for every coulomb of charge transferred from one terminal of the battery to the other, 12 joules of energy are expended by the outside source.

The basic equation for potential difference is therefore

$$\Delta V = \frac{W}{q} \qquad (52)$$

ΔV is the potential difference between two points in volts when W is given in joules and q in coulombs. If one of the points has a zero potential, then ΔV is the same as V and the equation may be written as $V = W/q$ (equation 51). Similarly, if the potential difference between two points is known, and the quantity of charge transported is known, then the total energy transferred between the two points is

$$W = Q\Delta V \quad or \quad W = qV \qquad (53)$$

Electron-Volts. If the charge transported is the elementary charge of the electron, e, and the potential difference is 1 volt, then the energy is 1 *electron-volt* (ev). The electron-volt is an *energy* unit. It is extremely small in comparison with the joule, but is the magnitude of the energy commonly involved in chemical reactions between atoms and ions. For example, the energy needed to ionize (remove the electron from) a hydrogen atom is 13.6 ev. An electron transferred from a point of 4-volt potential to one of 7-volt potential will undergo an energy change of 3 ev.

Relationship of Field Intensity to Field Potential—Optional Topic. The electric field intensity between two points can be expressed in terms of the potential difference between the points and the distance separating the two points. Thus the electric field intensity, E, may be defined in terms of potential difference, ΔV, existing between two points separated by a distance d.

$$E = \frac{\Delta V}{d} \qquad (54)$$

When ΔV is expressed in volts and d in meters, E is in units of volts/meter. This is identical with the unit newton/coulomb, since

$$\frac{\text{volt}}{\text{meter}} = \frac{\text{joule/coulomb}}{\text{meter}} = \frac{\text{joule}}{\text{coulomb-meter}} = \frac{\text{newton-meter}}{\text{coulomb-meter}} = \frac{\text{newton}}{\text{coulomb}}$$

Discovery of the Fundamental Unit of Charge

The existence of a smallest unit of charge, the charge on the electron, was discovered by the American physicist R. A. Millikan in 1909 in the "oil drop" experiment. In this experiment, Millikan measured the ratio between the gravitational force and the electrical force on charged oil droplets in the uniform electric field between parallel charged plates. His results showed that the electric charge on the tiny droplets was always a whole-number multiple of a small constant value, meaning that there is a smallest fundamental unit of charge.

QUESTIONS

1. A metal (conducting) sphere with $+11$ elementary charges touches an identical sphere with $+15$ elementary charges. After touching, the number of elementary charges on the first sphere is ① $+13$ (2) $+26$ (3) -4 (4) $+4$

2. What amount of work is needed to transfer 10 coul of charge between two points having a potential difference of 120 volts? (1) 1/12 joule (2) 12 joules (3) 600 joules ④ 1200 joules

3. As a positively charged rod is brought near to but not allowed to touch the knob of an uncharged electroscope, the leaves will diverge because (1) negative charges are transferred from the electroscope to the rod (2) negative charges are attracted to the knob of the electroscope ③ positive charges are repelled to the leaves of the electroscope (4) positive charges are transferred from the rod to the electroscope

4. An electron may be placed at positions *A*, *B*, or *C* between the two parallel charged metal plates shown.

   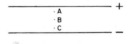

   The electric force on the electron will be (1) greater at *A* (2) greatest at *B* ③ greatest at *C* (4) the same at all three positions

5. Which graph best represents the electric force between two point charges as a function of the distance between the charges?

   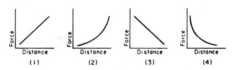

6. When a positively charged body touches a neutral body, the neutral body will (1) gain protons (2) lose protons (3) gain electrons ④ lose electrons

7. Two point charges 1 m apart repel each other with a force of 9 nt. What is the force of repulsion when these two charges are 3 m apart? ① 1 nt (2) 27 nt (3) 3 nt (4) 81 nt

8. An electron gains 2 ev·of energy as it is transferred from point *A* to point *B*. The potential difference between points *A* and *B* is (1) 3.2×10^{-19} volt ② 2 volts (3) 32 volts (4) 1.25×10^{19} volts

9. Two parallel metal plates have a potential difference of 50 volts. How much work is done in moving a charge of 4.0×10^{-5} coul from one plate to the other? (1) 8.0×10^{-7} joule (2) 1.6×10^{-3} joule ③ 2.0×10^{-3} joule (4) 1.3×10^{6} joules

10. One metallic sphere has a charge of $+16$ units and a second identical sphere has a charge of -4 units. After the two spheres are touched together, the charge on each sphere is (1) $+6$ units (2) $+12$ units (3) $+20$ units (4) -20 units

11. If object A becomes positively charged when rubbed with object B, then object B has (1) gained electrons (2) lost electrons (3) gained protons (4) lost protons

12. Which is the simplest device used to detect the presence of charge on an object? (1) spectroscope (2) stroboscope (3) oscilloscope (4) electroscope

13. If the distance between 2 protons is tripled, then the force they exert on each other, compared with the original force, will be (1) one-ninth as great (2) one-third as great (3) three times as great (4) nine times as great

14. Which will occur when a neutral hard rubber rod is rubbed with wool and the rod becomes negatively charged? (1) The rod will lose protons. (2) The rod will lose electrons. (3) The wool will lose protons. (4) The wool will lose electrons.

15. An energy of 2.0×10^4 ev is equal to (1) 1.6×10^{-19} joule (2) 3.2×10^{-19} joule (3) 3.2×10^{-15} joule (4) 5.0×10^{-5} joule

16. A and B are two identical uncharged metal spheres. Sphere A is given an electrical charge of $+q$, touched to sphere B, and then removed. The charge on sphere A after separation is (1) $+q$ (2) $-q$ (3) $+q/2$ (4) $-q/2$

17. Three electric charges are arranged as shown. Which vector best represents the resultant force which charges q_2 and q_3 exert on charge q_1?

(1) ←———   **(2)** ↘   **(3)** ←—   **(4)** ↑

18. The work required to transfer 1 coul of charge between two points whose potential difference is 2 volts is (1) ½ joule (2) 2 joules (3) 3 joules (4) 4 joules

19. An electron moves through a potential difference of 3.00 volts. The energy acquired by the charge is (1) 5.33×10^{-19} joule (2) 1.60×10^{-19} joule (3) 4.80×10^{-19} joule (4) 3.00 joules

20. A and B are two points in an electric field. If 6.0 joules of work are done in transferring 2.0 coul of electric charge from point A to point B, then the potential difference between points A and B is (1) 0.0 volts (2) 1.5 volts (3) 3.0 volts (4) 12 volts

21. How is a positive charge usually given to a neutral object? (1) Electrons are added to the object. (2) Electrons are re-

moved from the object. (3) Protons are added to the object. (4) Protons are removed from the object.

22. When two objects are rubbed together, which particle is most likely to be dislodged? (1) alpha particle (2) electron (3) proton (4) neutron

23. The electron-volt is a unit of (1) current (2) power (3) resistance (4) energy

24. The repulsive force between two positively charged spheres is *F* nt. If the charge on one of the spheres is doubled, the force will be (1) ¼*F* nt (2) ½*F* nt (3) 2*F* nt (4) 4*F* nt

25. The electric force between two charged spheres is 18 nt. If the distance between the centers of the spheres is tripled, the resulting electric force will be (1) 6 nt (2) 2 nt (3) 3 nt (4) 54 nt

26. The diagram represents a charged electroscope and the charging object. The electroscope was charged by (1) conduction (2) contact (3) induction (4) radiation

27. In general, solid materials become electrically charged because of transfer of (1) positrons (2) electrons (3) protons (4) neutrons

28. As an electron approaches a proton, electrostatic force acts on (1) the electron only (2) the proton only (3) both the electron and proton (4) neither the electron nor the proton

29. The energy of an electron is increased by 8×10^{-17} joule as a result of moving through a potential difference of (1) 0.002 volt (2) 200 volts (3) 500 volts (4) 5000 volts

30. If the distance between two point sources of equal charge is halved, the electrical force between them is (1) halved (2) quadrupled (3) doubled (4) unchanged

31. A charge of 8.0×10^{-5} coul is moved by a force of 2.0×10^{-2} nt between two points 0.10 m apart in a uniform electric field. The potential difference between the two points is (1) 25 volts (2) 40 volts (3) 75 volts (4) 160 volts

32. An electron is projected horizontally between two parallel charged plates from *D* toward *B* as shown. The electric force acting on the electron will be directed toward (1) *A* (2) *B* (3) *C* (4) *D*

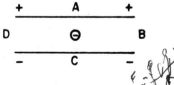

33. The relationship of the force between two point charges and the distance between them is best shown by graph

34. Four electric charges, A, B, C, and D, are arranged as shown. The electric force will be least between charges (1) A and B (2) A and C (3) A and D (4) B and D

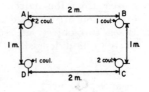

35. Which diagram best represents the electric field surrounding two positively charged spheres?

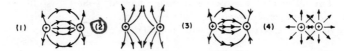

36. Which graph best illustrates the relationship of electrostatic force to distance between two point charges?

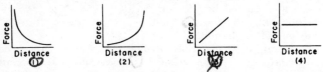

37. As the amount of charge held on an object increases, the voltage required to add additional charges to it (1) decreases (2) increases (3) remains the same

38. As a charged object is moved parallel to the central region of a long uniformly charged rod, the electrical force on the object (1) decreases (2) increases (3) remains the same

39. As the electric charge on the surface of a hollow metal sphere increases, the electric field intensity inside the sphere (1) decreases (2) increases (3) remains the same

40. As the kinetic energy of an electron increases, its momentum (1) decreases (2) increases (3) remains the same

41. As an electron approaches a proton, the electrical force between them (1) decreases (2) increases (3) remains the same

42. As body *A* charges body *B* by induction, the quantity of charge on body *A* (1) is decreased (2) is increased (3) remains the same

43. As a negatively charged rod moves toward the tip of a positively charged electroscope, the number of electrons in the tip of the electroscope (1) decreases (2) increases (3) remains the same

44. A battery of constant voltage is attached to two parallel plates. As the distance between the plates is increased, the field strength between the plates (1) decreases (2) increases (3) remains the same

45-49. Base your answers to Questions 45 through 49 on the following information.

Two particles, *A* and *B*, are placed between two parallel plates

6.0 $\times$ 10^{-2} m apart in a vacuum. The potential difference across the plates is 90 volts. The charge on A is $+1$ elementary charge and that on B is -1 elementary charge. The mass of A is 4 times the mass of B.

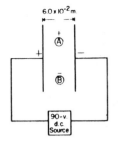

45. What is the increase in the kinetic energy of particle A as it moves from the positive to the negative plate? (1) 1.44 $\times$ 10^{-17} ev (2) 1.60 $\times$ 10^{-19} ev (3) 90 ev (4) 360 ev
46. What is the increase in the kinetic energy of particle B as it moves from the negative to the positive plate? (1) 1.44 $\times$ 10^{-17} joule (2) 1.60 $\times$ 10^{-19} joule (3) 22.5 joules (4) 90 joules
47. The ratio of the increase in the kinetic energy of particle A to the increase in the kinetic energy of particle B is *(1)* 1/1 (2) 2/1 (3) 1/2 (4) 4/1
48. What is the electric field intensity between the two plates, in newtons per coulomb? (1) 5.4 (2) 1.5 $\times 10^3$ (3) 6.7 $\times$ 10^{-2} (4) 2.4 $\times$ 10^{-16}
49. If the distance between the plates is decreased while other factors remain the same, there will be no change in the (1) charge on the plates (2) capacitance of the plates (3) electric field between the plates (4) potential difference across the plates

50-54. Base your answers to Questions 50 through 54 on the following information.

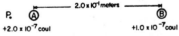

Two identical metal spheres, A and B, are given charges of $+2.0$ $\times$ 10^{-7} coul and $+1.0$ $\times$ 10^{-7} coul, respectively. The separation between their centers is 2 $\times$ 10^{-1} m.

50. The electric force exerted on B by A will be directed (1) to the left (2) to the right (3) upward (4) downward into the page
51. If the magnitude of the electric force on B is equal to F, the magnitude of the electric force on A will be equal to (1) F (2) $2F$ (3) $F/2$ (4) $4F$
52. The magnitude of the electric force exerted on B is equal (1) 9.0 $\times$ 10^3 nt (2) 9.0 $\times$ 10^{-4} nt (3) 4.5 $\times$ 10^4 nt (4) 4.5 $\times$ 10^{-3} nt
53. A positive charge of 1.0 $\times$ 10^{-10} coul at a point P near sphere A is acted upon by a force of 2.0 $\times$ 10^{-15} nt. What is the intensity of the electrical field at point P in newtons/coulomb? (1) 2.0 $\times$ 10^{-15} (2) 2.0 $\times$ 10^{-5} (3) 2.0 $\times$ 10^5 (4) 5.0 $\times$ 10^{-6}
54. If A and B are brought into contact, which will gain electrons? (1) A, only (2) B, only (3) both A and B (4) neither A nor B

55-59. Base your answers to Questions 55 through 59 on the following information.

A metal sphere, *A*, has a charge of −*q* coul. An identical metal sphere, *B*, has a charge

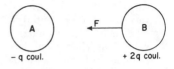

of +2*q* coul. The magnitude of the electric force on *B* due to *A* is *F* newtons.

55. The magnitude of the electric force on *A* due to *B* is (1) $\frac{1}{2}F$ (2) *F* (3) 2*F* (4) 4*F*

56. If the distance between the centers of the spheres is halved, the magnitude of the force on *B* due to *A* will be (1) $\frac{1}{2}F$ (2) *F* (3) 2*F* (4) 4*F*

57. If an electron were placed midway between *A* and *B*, the resultant electric force on the electron would be (1) toward *A* (2) toward *B* (3) up (4) down

58. If *A* and *B* are connected by a copper wire whose surface is negligible compared with that of the spheres, charge will flow through the connecting wire until the charge on **B** becomes (1) 0 coul (2) +*q*/2 coul (3) +*q* coul (4) −*q* coul

59. The current in the wire consists of a flow of (1) protons from *A* to *B* (2) protons from *B* to *A* (3) electrons from *B* to *A* (4) electrons from *A* to *B*

60-63. Base your answers to Questions 60 through 63 on the diagram, which represents two large parallel metal plates with a small charged sphere between them.

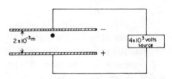

60. The energy gained by the charged sphere as it moves from the negative plate to the positive plate can be measured in (1) electron-volts (2) volt-meters (3) coulombs/volt (4) volts/meter

61. What is the intensity of the electric field between the two charged plates? (1) 5.0 × 10⁻¹⁷ meter/volt (2) 2.0 × 10⁶ volts/meter (3) 1.6 × 10⁻¹⁶ coulomb/meter (4) 8.0 volt-meters

62. If the distance between the plates were increased, the field intensity would (1) decrease (2) increase (3) remain the same

63. As the sphere moves from the negative plate to the positive plate, the force on the sphere (1) decreases (2) increases (3) remains the same

64-66. Base your answers to Questions 64 through 66 on the following information.

Charge +*q* is located a distance *r* from charge +*Q*. Each charge is 1 coul.

64. The electric field due to charge +*Q* at distance *r* is equal to (1) $\frac{kQ}{F}$ (2) $\frac{kQq}{r}$ (3) $\frac{Q}{r^2}$ (4) $\frac{kQ}{r^2}$

65. If 200 joules of work were required to move $+q$ through distance r to $+Q$, the potential difference between the two charges would be (1) 100 volts (2) 200 volts (3) 800 volts (4) 50 volts

66. If distance r is doubled, then the force that $+Q$ exerts on $+q$ is (1) quartered (2) halved (3) unchanged (4) doubled

67-71. Base your answers to Questions 67 through 71 on the following information.

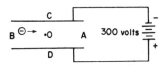

An electron is projected into the vacuum space between two charged parallel plates, as shown. The plates are 0.03 m apart. The potential difference between the plates is 300 volts.

67. The direction of the electric field at point O between the plates is toward (1) A (2) B (3) C (4) D

68. The magnitude of the electric field at point O between the plates, in newtons per coulomb, is (1) 1.00×10^4 (2) 1.50×10^{-3} (3) 9.00×10^{-3} (4) 6.67×10^{-11}

69. An electron moving from B toward A between the plates will be acted upon by an electric force that is always directed (1) toward the positive plate (2) toward the negative plate (3) parallel to the plate surfaces (4) at right angles to the instantaneous velocity of the electron

70. As the electron moves between the plates, its kinetic energy (1) decreases (2) increases (3) remains the same

71. If the distance between the plates is increased, the intensity of the electric field between them (1) decreases (2) increases (3) remains the same

72-76. Base your answers to Questions 72 through 76 on the following information.

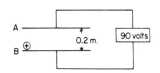

A proton (represented by $\oplus$) is placed between the two parallel plates, A and B, as shown. The plates are 0.2 m apart and connected to a 90-volt battery. The proton has a force exerted on it toward A.

72. The direction of the electric field between the two plates is from (1) positive plate A to negative plate B (2) negative plate A to positive plate B (3) positive plate B to negative plate A (4) negative plate B to positive plate A

73. The magnitude of the electric field intensity between the two plates is (1) 18 nt/coul (2) 45 nt/coul (3) 180 nt/coul (4) 450 nt/coul

74. The kinetic energy gained by the proton in moving from plate B to plate A is (1) 1.4×10^{-21} joule (2) 1.8×10^{-21} joule (3) 1.4×10^{-17} joule (4) 1.8×10^{-17} joule

75. If the proton is now moved back toward plate B, its potential energy will (1) decrease (2) increase (3) remain the same

76. As the separation between plates A and B is increased, the electric field intensity between the plates will (1) decrease (2) increase (3) remain the same

77-81. Base your answers to Questions 77 through 81 on the accompanying diagram, in which circular lines are drawn at 60 volts, 30 volts, and 20 volts about electric charge $+q$. Positions A through D on the equipotential lines are indicated.

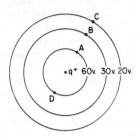

77. The total work done in moving 1 coul of charge from A to D is (1) 0 joules (2) 40 joules (3) 60 joules (4) 80 joules

78. The total work done in moving 2 coul of positive charge from position C to position A is (1) 0 joules (2) 40 joules (3) 60 joules (4) 80 joules

79. If 5 coul of charge moves from position A to position B, the energy expended will be (1) 5 joules (2) 6 joules (3) 30 joules (4) 150 joules

80. Compared with A, the magnitude of the electric field intensity at B is (1) greater (2) less (3) the same

81. If $+q$ is increased to $+2q$, the potential at B (1) decreases (2) increases (3) remains the same

82-86. Base your answers to Questions 82 through 86 on the following information.

Plates A and B are parallel, and a potential difference of 50 volts is maintained across them. A positive test charge ($\oplus$) is located as shown.

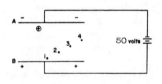

82. If the separation of the plates is 1.0×10^{-1} m, then the electric field intensity between them is (1) 8.0×10^{-16} volt/meter (2) 5.0×10^2 volts/meter (3) 5.0×10^{-1} volt/meter (4) 3.1×10^{18} volts/meter

83. How much work would be required to move a charge of $+2.0$ coul from plate A to plate B? (1) 5.0×10^1 joules (2) 2.0×10^1 joules (3) 1.0×10^2 joules (4) 6.25×10^{18} joules

84. The greatest amount of work would be required to move the positive test charge ($\oplus$) from its present position to point (1) 1 (2) 2 (3) 3 (4) 4

85. An electron moving freely from plate A to plate B would acquire a kinetic energy of (1) 4.5×10^{-31} ev (2) 2.5 ev (3) 5.0×10^1 ev (4) 1.0×10^2 ev

86. The electrical potential energy of the positive test charge is greatest if it is located at position (1) 1 (2) 2 (3) 3 (4) 4

87-91. Base your answers to Questions 87 through 91 on the following information.

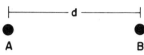

The diagram represents two equal negative point charges, *A* and *B*, that are a distance *d* apart.

87. Which diagram best represents the electrostatic lines of force between charge *A* and charge *B*?

88. Where would the electric field intensity of the two charges be minimum? (1) one quarter of the way between *A* and *B* (2) midway between *A* and *B* (3) on the surface of *B* (4) on the surface of *A*

89. Which graph expresses the relationship of the distance between the charges and the force between them?

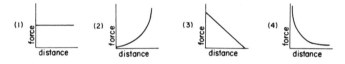

90. If charge *A* is doubled, the force between *A* and *B* will be (1) quartered (2) halved (3) doubled (4) quadrupled

91. If *A* has an excess of 2.5×10^{19} electrons, its charge in coulombs is (1) 1.6 (2) 2.5 (3) 6.5 (4) 4.0

2. ELECTRIC CURRENT

Unit of Current

A stream of electrically charged particles passing through a given area is called a *current*. A current of one coulomb of charge passing through a given surface each second is called one *ampere* (amp) of current. Therefore, 1 amp = 1 coul/sec.

Conductivity

Various materials differ in their ability to conduct charge. The metals, especially silver and copper, are good conductors and are extensively used in electrical circuits. Nonmetals, such as glass, wax, and plastics, are extremely poor conductors and are often used as insulating materials. The conductivity of solids depends in general upon the presence of electrons that are not bound to any particular atom within the material. In pure metals, the electron is the only type of charge carrier; all currents in metals are due to the transport of electrons. Some materials, called *semiconductors* because they are somewhat poorer conductors than metals, have a crystal structure in which passage of electrons in one direction produces a movement of virtual positive charge (electron "holes") in the opposite direction. Some solids, such as table salt, although composed entirely of ionized atoms, are nonconductors in the solid state because these ions are not free to move through the solid. When melted, such ionic substances become excellent conductors because the ions become able to move.

Water solutions of ionic substances and of substances that react chemically with water to produce ions are also good conductors. However, pure substances that are liquids at room temperature, such as pure water, are usually poor conductors. Similarly, substances that are gases at room temperature are composed of neutral molecules and therefore do not conduct electricity. All substances, however, can be ionized by intense electric fields so as to produce both positive and negative ions that will carry currents. In cases where current is due to movement of both positive and negative charges, as in conductive solutions or fluorescent tubes, the total current is the sum of the positive and negative currents. By definition, the direction of current is that of the direction of *positive* charge movement. When electron (negative) current is being discussed, it must be clearly indicated. See Figure 24 for illustrations of charge movement and current.

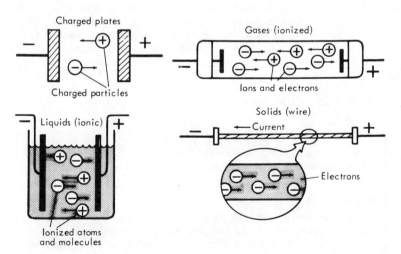

Figure 24. Currents and charge movements; conduction in solids, liquids, and gases.

Electric Circuits

The closed path along which electric charge moves is called an *electric circuit*. In order to maintain this movement, a difference in potential must exist between two points in the circuit. From the definition of the terms positive and negative, electrons in a circuit will move from points of lower potential to points of higher potential, whereas positive charge will move from points of higher to points of lower potential.

Ohm's Law. The size of the current that can be produced in a given material by a given potential difference is determined by a property called the *resistance* of the material. If the ratio of potential difference in volts to the current in amperes is 1:1, then the resistance is said to be one *ohm*. The formula for this relationship is

$$R = \frac{V}{I} \tag{55}$$

where R represents the resistance in ohms, V the potential difference in volts and I the current in amperes. Alternatively this may also be written as

$$V = IR \tag{56}$$

The Greek capital letter omega, Ω, is the symbol for resistance in ohms. This relation between current, voltage and resistance is known as Ohm's law; it holds true for entire circuits and for any portion of a circuit.

For a particular sample of material, the resistance will be constant if the temperature does not change. The resistance of metals is directly related to temperature. As the temperature of a metal conductor increases, its resistance also increases. The resistance of non-metals, however, generally decreases with increase in temperature.

EXAMPLE

A current of 0.1 amp was found to flow through a lamp in a 12-volt circuit. What was the resistance of the lamp?

Solution: $V = 12$ volts; $I = 0.1$ amp

$$\frac{V}{I} = R; \quad R = \frac{12 \text{ volts}}{0.1 \text{ amp}} = 120 \text{ ohms}$$

Resistivity. If a conductor, such as a wire, is of uniform cross-sectional area and uniform composition, its resistance varies directly as its length and inversely as its cross-sectional area. For example, if two wires have the same composition and length, but one is double the thickness of the other, the thicker wire will have ¼ the resistance of the thinner one. If the length of either wire were doubled, its resistance would be doubled. This relationship is expressed by the formula

$$R = \frac{kL}{A} \tag{57}$$

where R is measured in ohms, L in meters and A in square meters. The proportionality constant k is called *resistivity*. Its units are ohm-meters and its magnitude depends on the particular material of which the conductor is made.

Types of Electric Circuits

The simplest type of electric circuit consists of a *source* of electrical energy and a *circuit element*, or component, which is a device that converts the electric energy to some other form. The source may be a battery; the circuit element may be a resistor, a device that converts electric energy to heat energy. The current in the circuit depends on the potential difference, V, established by the battery at the ends of the resistor, and the resistance, R, of the resistor, according to Ohm's law (equation 56). For example, the current across a 2-ohm resistor in a 12-volt circuit is shown in Figure 25.

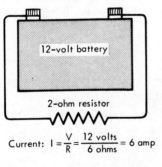

Current: $I = \frac{V}{R} = \frac{12 \text{ volts}}{6 \text{ ohms}} = 6 \text{ amp}$

Figure 25. Resistance in a
simple circuit.

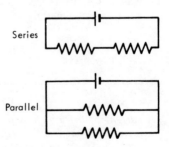

Figure 26. Resistances in
series and
parallel circuits.

Series Circuits. When more than one resistor is present in the circuit, there are two basic methods of connecting them. The first is called the *series* circuit, shown in Figure 26, in which the same current exists in each resistor, since there is only one path for the charged particles to follow. Therefore, for resistors in series, if I_1 is the current in R_1, I_2 is the current in R_2, I_3 is the current in R_3, etc., then

$$I_1 = I_2 = I_3, \text{etc.} \tag{58}$$

The resistance of the series circuit as a whole, R_t, is the sum of the individual resistances:

$$R_t = R_1 + R_2 + R_3, \text{etc.} \tag{59}$$

The difference in potential across each resistor, V_1 and V_2, is proportional to the resistances:

$$\frac{V_1}{V_2} = \frac{R_1}{R_2} \tag{60}$$

The voltage, V, at the terminals of the battery is equal to the sum of the potential differences across the resistors:

$$V_t = V_1 + V_2 + V_3, \text{etc.} \tag{61}$$

Parallel Circuits. The second method of connecting two resistors to form an electric circuit is known as the *parallel* circuit. In this circuit, current is divided among the branches of the circuit, as shown in Figure 26. The currents present in the branches are inversely proportional to the resistances of the branches:

$$\frac{I_1}{I_2} = \frac{R_2}{R_1} \tag{62}$$

The sum of the currents in each branch, however, is equal to the current from the source:

$$I_t = I_1 + I_2 + I_3, \text{etc.} \tag{63}$$

The potential differences across each branch are equal, and in the example shown in Figure 26, they are the same as that of the battery:

$$V_t = V_1 = V_2 = V_3, \text{etc.} \tag{64}$$

The resistance of the entire circuit, R_t, however, is always less than the resistance of the smallest resistor. It is found from the equation

$$\frac{1}{R_t} = \frac{1}{R_1} + \frac{1}{R_2} + \frac{1}{R_3}, \text{etc.} \tag{65}$$

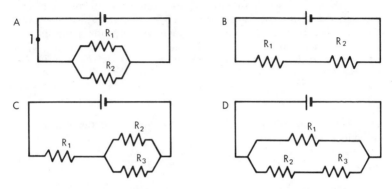

Figure 27. Some combinations of simple circuits.

Conservation of Charge and Energy in Electric Circuits; Kirchoff's Laws

All circuits consist of series and parallel circuits, either alone or in combination. Figure 27 shows some possible combinations. However, no matter how complex the circuit, both charge and energy of currents are conserved throughout the circuit. This means, in general, that the total energy and the total charge entering any portion of a circuit are equal to the total energy and the total charge leaving that portion of the circuit. For example, as shown in *A*, Figure 27, if a current of 10 amp (10 coul/sec) is measured at point 1 and 4 amp in resistor R_1, then a 6-amp current must exist in R_2, because charge cannot be created or destroyed in a circuit. This rule is called *Kirchoff's first law*. Its formal statement is: The algebraic sum of the currents entering any circuit junction is equal to zero.

In the same circuit diagram, according to the law of conservation of energy, it is clear that the voltage loss (potential difference) across each resistor, and therefore the energy per coulomb of charge consumed by the resistors, must be equal to the energy per coulomb (the voltage) supplied by the source. This rule is called *Kirchoff's second law*. The formal statement is: The algebraic sum of all the potential drops and applied voltages around a complete circuit is equal to zero.

Electric Power

In electricity, as in mechanics, the time rate of consumption of energy is called *power* and is measured in terms of the watt (joule per second) :

$$P = \frac{W}{t} \tag{66}$$

P is expressed in watts, W in joules, and t in seconds. In electric circuits, the product of current, I, and potential difference, V, is also equal to the power consumed, P:

$$P = IV \qquad (67)$$

P is in watts, I in amperes and V in volts. This is true because current is charge per unit time (coul/sec) and potential difference (voltage) is energy per unit charge (joule/coul). Therefore

$$\frac{joule}{coul} \times \frac{coul}{sec} = \frac{joule}{sec}$$

Since $V = IR$, from Ohm's law (equation 56), it also follows that

$$P = I^2R \qquad (68)$$

The total electric energy consumed (that is, converted to other forms) in a circuit may be obtained by multiplying the power consumption, P, of the circuit by the time of charge flow, t. Thus the energy, W, consumed is

$$W = Pt = I^2Rt = VIt \qquad (69)$$

The energy in joules may be computed from either equation 68 or 69. Note that, when a circuit element, such as a resistor, converts electric energy to heat, the amount of heat in kcal can be calculated from the mechanical equivalent of heat, $J = 4.19 \times 10^3$ joules/kcal. This value is supplied in the Physics Reference Tables. (See page 162)

EXAMPLE

The current measured in a 10-ohm resistor is 4 amp.
(a) How much energy is used by the resistor in 10 sec?
(b) If all this energy were converted to heat, how many kcal would be produced?

Solution:

(a) $W = I^2Rt =$

$$(4 \text{ amp})^2 \times (10 \text{ ohms}) \times (10 \text{ sec}) = 1600 \text{ joules}$$

(b) $1600 \text{ joules} \times \dfrac{1 \text{ kcal}}{4.19 \times 10^3 \text{ joules}} = 0.382 \text{ kcal}$

QUESTIONS

1. If three resistors of 3 ohms, 6 ohms, and 9 ohms are connected in parallel, the combined resistance will be (1) greater than 9 ohms (2) between 6 ohms and 9 ohms (3) between 3 ohms and 6 ohms (4) less than 3 ohms

2. How much electric energy is dissipated when a 120-volt appliance operates at 2 amp for 1 sec? (1) 60 joules (2) 240 joules (3) 480 joules (4) 28,880 joules

3. Which is a unit of electric power? (1) watt (2) volt (3) ampere (4) kilowatt-hour

4. To reduce the resistance of a metal conductor one should (1) cool the conductor to a low temperature (2) heat the conductor to a high temperature (3) coat the conductor with an insulator (4) wire the conductor in series with another resistor

5. Two copper wires have the same length, but the cross-sectional area of wire *A* is twice that of wire *B*. Compared to the resistance of wire *B*, the resistance of wire *A* is (1) one-quarter as great (2) one-half as great (3) twice as great (4) four times as great

6. A 6.0-ohm resistor is connected in series with a 12-ohm resistor in an operating circuit. If the current in the 12-ohm resistor is 3.0 amp, then the voltage drop across the 6.0-ohm resistor is (1) 1.5 volts (2) 18 volts (3) 3.0 volts (4) 36 volts

7. A resistor carries a current of 0.10 amp when the potential difference across it is 5.0 volts. The resistance of the resistor is (1) 0.020 ohms (2) 0.50 ohms (3) 5.0 ohms (4) 50 ohms

8. An electric motor lifts a 10-kg mass 100 m in 10 sec. The power developed by the motor is (1) 9.8 watts (2) 98 watts (3) 980 watts (4) 9800 watts

9. Compared to the current in the 10-ohm resistor, the current in the 5-ohm resistor, in the circuit shown, will be (1) one-third as great (2) one-half as great (3) the same (4) twice as great

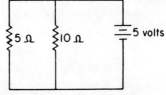

10. If energy is used in an electric circuit at a rate of 20 joules/sec, then the power of this circuit is (1) 5 watts (2) 20 watts (3) 25 watts (4) 100 watts

11. One ampere is equivalent to one (1) coulomb per second (2) joule per coulomb (3) electron-volt (4) newton per coulomb

12. Energy is being consumed at the greatest rate in an appliance drawing (1) 5 amp at 110 volts (2) 5 amp at 220 volts (3) 10 amp at 110 volts (4) 10 amp at 220 volts

13. If three resistors have a value of R ohms, the total resistance of the three resistors connected in parallel is (1) $R/3$ ohms (2) $2R$ ohms (3) $3R$ ohms (4) R ohms

14. A 5-ohm resistor and a 10-ohm resistor are connected in series. If the current in the 5-ohm resistor is 2 amp, then the current in the 10-ohm resistor is (1) 1 amp (2) 2 amp (3) ½ amp (4) 4 amp

15. If the voltage across a 4-ohm resistor is 2 volts, the current through the resistor is (1) 1 amp (2) 2 amp (3) ½ amp (4) 8 amp

16. Three ammeters (current-measuring devices) are located near junction P in a direct current electric circuit as shown. If A_1 reads 8 amp and A_2 reads 2 amp, then the reading of ammeter A_3 could be (1) 16 amp (2) 6 amp (3) 5 amp (4) 4 amp

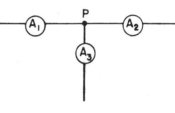

17. Which voltage would cause a current of 0.5 amp in a circuit that has a resistance of 24 ohms? (1) 6.0 volts (2) 12 volts (3) 24 volts (4) 48 volts

18. What is the current in a circuit if 15 coul of electric charge move past a given point in 3 sec? (1) 5 amp (2) 12 amp (3) 18 amp (4) 45 amp

19. A series circuit contains a 4-ohm and a 2-ohm resistor connected to a 110-volt source. Compared to the energy dissipated in the 2-ohm resistor, the energy dissipated in the 4-ohm resistor during the time is, (1) one half as great (2) the same (3) twice as great (4) four times as great

20. Assuming total conversion of electrical energy to heat energy, how many joules of heat energy are produced by a 20-watt heating unit in 5 sec? (1) 100 (2) 25 (3) 24 (4) 4

21. A circuit carries a current of 4.0 amp for 8.0 sec. The electric charge passing any point in the circuit in 8.0 sec is (1) 32 coul (2) 2.0 coul (3) 8.0 coul (4) 4.0 coul

22. The ratio of the potential difference across a conductor to the current in it is (1) electromotive force (2) energy (3) power (4) resistance

23. An operating lamp has a current of 2.0 amp at 6.0 volts. The resistance of the lamp is (1) 1.5 ohms (2) 6.0 ohms (3) 3.0 ohms (4) 12 ohms

24. Electric charge Q_1 is transferred through a conductor in time t. The quantity Q_1/t measures average (1) current (2) potential (3) power (4) resistance

25. In the diagram, ammeter *A* reads 5 amp and ammeter *B* reads 2 amp, as shown. The reading of ammeter *C* is (1) 1.4 amp (2) 5 amp (3) 3 amp (4) 7 amp

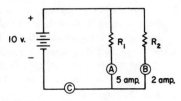

26. What is the current in ammeter *A*? (1) 200 amp (2) 100 amp (3) 25 amp (4) 4 amp

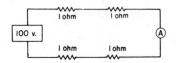

27. A resistor of 20 ohms carries a current of 2 amp. The electrical energy used in 1 sec is (1) 5 watts (2) 40 watts (3) 40 joules (4) 80 joules

28. In the diagram, the current through ammeter *A* is 1 amp. Resistor *B* has a resistance of (1) 9 ohms (2) 6 ohms (3) 3 ohms (4) 1/3 ohm

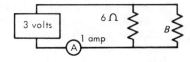

29. In a series circuit where the resistance remains constant, the graph that best represents the relationship between current and voltage in that circuit is

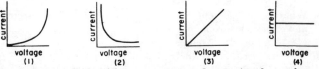

30. A circuit is supplied with a constant voltage. As the resistance of the circuit decreases, the power dissipated by the circuit (1) decreases (2) increases (3) remains the same

31. If the length and the cross-sectional area of a wire are both halved, the resistance of the wire will (1) decrease (2) increase (3) remain the same

32. As additional resistors are connected in parallel to a source of constant voltage, the current in the circuit (1) decreases (2) increases (3) remains the same

33. Two lamps of different resistances are connected in series to a battery. As electrons flow from the lamp of higher resistance through the lamp of lower resistance, the rate of electron flow (1) decreases (2) increases (3) remains the same

34. A light bulb is in series with a rheostat (variable resistor) and a fixed voltage is applied across the total circuit. As the resistance of the rheostat decreases, the brightness of the bulb (1) decreases (2) increases (3) remains the same

35. As the temperature of a metal increases, its electrical resistance usually (1) decreases (2) increases (3) remains the same

36. As resistors are added in parallel to a circuit, the current in the circuit (1) decreases (2) increases (3) remains the same

37. A 6-volt battery is connected to a 3-ohm resistor. As additional resistors are connected in series, the potential difference across each resistor (1) decreases (2) increases (3) remains the same

38. A constant potential difference is applied to a variable resistor. As the value of the resistance increases, the current through it (1) decreases (2) increases (3) remains the same

39-43. Base your answers to Questions 39 through 43 on the diagram, which shows a 3-ohm metal wire resistor connected to a 6-volt battery. (Neglect the resistance of the source and connecting wires.)

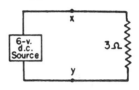

39. How many coulombs of charge pass point X in 1 sec? (1) 6 (2) 2 (3) 12 (4) 18

40. The amount of energy which a coulomb of charge loses in moving from X to Y through the resistor is (1) 6 joules (2) 2 joules (3) 12 joules (4) 18 joules

41. In this circuit, electrical energy is converted to heat at the rate of (1) 6 volts (2) 2 amp (3) 12 watts (4) 18 joules

42. If one coulomb of charge passes point X during a given time interval, the amount of charge that passes point Y in the same time interval is (1) less than one coulomb (2) one coulomb (3) more than one coulomb

43. As the temperature of the resistor increases, the current in the circuit (1) increases (2) decreases (3) remains the same

44-47. Base your answers to Questions 44 through 47 on the diagram below.

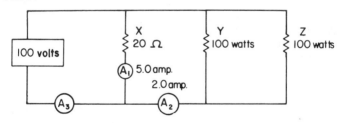

44. The reading of ammeter A_3 is (1) 1 amp (2) 5 amp (3) 7 amp (4) 15 amp

45. The current in resistor Y is (1) 1.0 amp (2) 2.0 amp (3) 0.5 amp (4) 5.0 amp

46. The power dissipated by resistor X is (1) 100 watts (2) 200 watts (3) 220 watts (4) 500 watts

47. The energy used by resistor Y in 10 min is (1) 10 joules (2) 100 joules (3) 1000 joules (4) 60,000 joules

48-52. Base your answers to Questions 48 through 52 on the information given in the diagram.

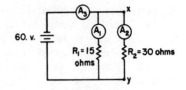

48. The equivalent resistance of R_1 and R_2 is (1) 10 ohms (2) 20 ohms (3) 25 ohms (4) 45 ohms

49. Ammeter A_1 reads (1) 1 amp (2) 2 amp (3) 8 amp (4) 4 amp

50. If ammeter A_3 reads 6.0 amp, at what rate does the battery supply energy to the circuit? (1) 360 watts (2) 66 watts (3) 54 watts (4) 10 watts

51. The potential difference in joules per coulomb between points X and Y is (1) 60 (2) 40 (3) 30 (4) 15

52. If ammeter A_3 reads 6.0 amp, the number of coulombs passing through it in 8.0 sec is (1) 75 (2) 2.0 (3) 14 (4) 48

53-57. Base your answers to Questions 53 through 57 on the diagram, which shows a 0.5-ohm resistor, R, and a light bulb, which are connected in series to a 6.0-volt battery. The current in resistor R is 4.0 amp.

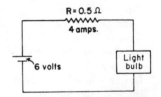

53. The potential difference between the two ends of the resistor is (1) 0.13 volts (2) 2.0 volts (3) 6.0 volts (4) 8.0 volts

54. The electric current through the light bulb is (1) 0.67 amp (2) 2.0 amp (3) 6.0 amp (4) 4.0 amp

55. How much chemical energy will the battery convert to electrical energy in 10 sec? (1) 24 joules (2) 240 joules (3) 360 joules (4) 600 joules

56. The resistance of the light bulb is (1) 1.0 ohm (2) 0.5 ohm (3) 0.17 ohm (4) 23.5 ohms

57. What is the rate at which heat energy is being dissipated in resistor R? (1) 8 joules/sec (2) joules/sec (3) 3 joules/sec (4) 24 joules/sec

58-62. Base your answers to Questions 58 through 62 on the diagram, which shows a resistor R and an ammeter A connected to a 24-volt battery. Ammeter A reads 0.5 amp. (Neglect the resistance of the source, meter, and connecting wires.)

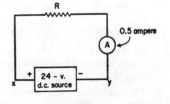

58. What is the resistance of resistor R? (1) 0.02 ohm (2) 12 ohms (3) 48 ohms (4) 100 ohms

59. How many coulombs of charge move past point X in 10 sec?
(1) 0.50 (2) 5.0 (3) 12 (4) 48

60. Energy is being dissipated in resistor R at a rate of (1) 6 joules/sec (2) 12 joules/sec (3) 24 joules/sec (4) 48 joules/sec

61. Another resistor with the same value as resistor R is placed in series with resistor R. The total resistance of the circuit will be (1) halved (2) unchanged (3) doubled (4) quadrupled

62. Compared with the original circuit, the power dissipated by the circuit in Question 61 is (1) quartered (2) halved (3) doubled (4) quadrupled

63-67. Base your answers to Questions 63 through 67 on the diagram, which represents a direct-current motor connected in series with a 12-volt battery, a resistance R, and an ammeter A. Mass M is suspended from a pulley that is attached to the shaft of the motor.

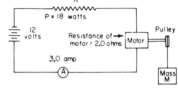

63. What is the resistance of resistor R? (1) 8.0 ohms (2) 2.0 ohms (3) 3.0 ohms (4) 6.0 ohms

64. What is the potential difference across resistor R? (1) 0 volts (2) 12 volts (3) 6.0 volts (4) 4.0 volts

65. What is the rate at which the motor uses electrical energy? (1) 0 watts (2) 18 watts (3) 36 watts (4) 4.0 watts

66. What is the total charge that will pass through the motor in 5.0 sec? (1) 0.60 coul (2) 15 coul (3) 3.0 coul (4) 4.0 coul

67. If the motor were 100% efficient, how much would the gravitational potential energy of mass M change in 10 sec? (1) 9.8 joules (2) 12 joules (3) 18 joules (4) 180 joules

68-71. Base your answers to Questions 68 through 71 on the diagram at right.

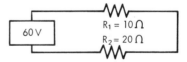

68. What is the total resistance of the circuit? (1) 6.6 ohms (2) 10 ohms (3) 20 ohms (4) 30 ohms

69. If the potential difference across R_1 is V volts, the potential difference in volts across R_2 would equal (1) V (2) $\frac{1}{2}(60 - V)$ (3) $(60 - V)$ (4) $(60 + V)$

70. If the potential difference of the source were decreased, the total heat developed in the circuit would (1) decrease (2) increase (3) remain the same

71. Compared to the current in R_1, the current in R_2 is (1) less (2) greater (3) the same

3. MAGNETISM

It is common experience that magnets exert forces on each other, that they have areas called *poles* where the magnetic force is concentrated, and that like poles repel each other, whereas opposite poles attract. The needle of a compass, for example, is magnetized so that opposite poles are at opposite ends of the needle. The compass needle therefore points toward the magnetic poles of the earth.

Magnetic Force

When current is switched on in a conductor, a nearby compass needle will move. The magnetic force acting on the needle is assumed to be the result of movement of charge in the conductor, because the needle will return to its original position when the current is switched off. This observation, supported by all experimental evidence, has led to the conclusion that all magnetic force is due to the motion of charged objects relative to each other. The magnetism of a magnet is due to the nonsymmetrical motion of electrons in the atoms of the magnetic material. Even magnets at rest relative to each other will therefore exert magnetic forces because the electrons within them are in motion.

Magnetic Field

Just as a gravitational field surrounds a mass, and an electric field surrounds a charged object, a magnetic field surrounds a charged object *in motion*. The moving charged object may be a proton or other ion, an electron moving within an atom, or an electron current in a conducting material. In each case, a magnetic field exists in the vicinity of the charged particle in motion.

The existence of a field is shown by the action of a force on an appropriate test object. For example, the presence of a gravitational field is shown by the force on a test *mass*, an electric field by the force on a test *charge*, and a magnetic field by the force on a test charge *in motion*. The standard test object for a magnetic field, called a *current element*, consists of a wire of length l carrying a current, I. The unit current element is defined as a wire 1 m long carrying a current of 1 amp. In a magnetic field, a current element will be acted upon by a force that is perpendicular to both the magnetic field and to the direction of the current. The direction of the magnetic field is defined as the direction in which the N pole of a compass would point in the field. A convention known as a *hand rule* is used to show the correct directions of force, current, and magnetic field relative to each other, as shown in Figure 28.

Magnetic Field Intensity and Flux. The force acting on a current element in a magnetic field is proportional to the intensity of the field. To indicate this intensity, a number of lines proportional to the magnitude of the force are drawn in the direction of the magnetic field. These lines are called *lines of magnetic flux* (from a Latin word meaning "flow"). Such lines are of course imaginary, but they

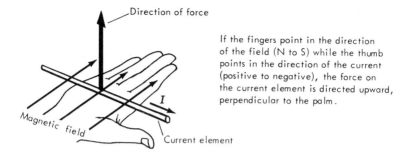

Direction of force

If the fingers point in the direction of the field (N to S) while the thumb points in the direction of the current (positive to negative), the force on the current element is directed upward, perpendicular to the palm.

I

Magnetic field

Current element

Figure 28. Right-hand rule.

serve as a convenient method of visualizing the intensity and direction of a magnetic field. Their pattern resembles that made by sprinkling iron filings on a card held in the field. These lines always form closed paths, and never cross.

Flux Density. The concept of magnetic field lines is used to represent field intensity. The total intensity of the field is measured in terms of the *weber*. The number of lines per unit area (in a plane perpendicular to the lines) is called the *flux density* and is measured in webers per square meter (weber/m^2).

The relationship of flux density to field intensity is shown by the force acting on a current element in the field. If the maximum force on a unit current element (1 amp in a conductor 1 m long) in the field is 1 nt, then the field intensity is 1 newton/ampere-meter (nt/amp-m). In such a field, the flux density is 1 weber/m^2, making the two field units identical in magnitude. This unit, the weber/m^2 (or nt/amp-m), has been given the official name *tesla* (T), in honor of the inventor who developed the use of alternating current. Both field units are given the symbol *B*, analogous to *E* for an electric field and *g* for a gravitational field.

The magnetic field intensity, *B*, like the electric field strength *E* and the gravitational field strength *g*, is a vector quantity. It must be specified both in direction and in magnitude.

Field Around a Straight Conductor. When a current is present in a conductor, the field surrounding the conductor is represented as a series of concentric circles in a plane perpendicular to the conductor. The strength of the field decreases with increasing distance from the conductor, but increases with increase in current. The direction of the field at any point is tangent to the line of flux at the point, as indicated by the hand rule in *A*, Figure 29.

Field Around a Loop. When current is present in a conductor that is shaped into a loop or circle, the magnetic field surrounding the loop is shaped like that of a small magnet with poles perpendicular to the plane of the loop. The location of south and north directions

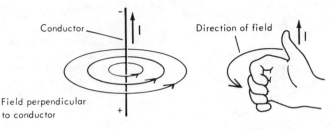

A. Hand rule for field direction around a
   straight conductor (positive current)

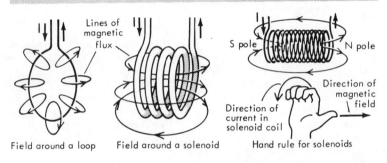

B. Field around a solenoid

Figure 29. Hand rules for determining magnetic
field direction in conductors.

of the magnetic field through the center of the loop is found by
the hand rule given in *B*, Figure 29.

Field Around a Solenoid. If a wire is wound as a solenoid (a coil
with many parallel turns of the same diameter), its magnetic field
resembles that of a bar magnet. The lines of magnetic flux emerge
from the N-pole at one end of the solenoid and curve around to
reenter the S-pole at the other end. Inside the solenoid, near the
center, the lines of flux are practically parallel to one another and
to the coil axis. They emerge almost perpendicular to the face of
the coil, where the flux density is a maximum. The intensity of the
field increases as the number of turns is increased, and as the current
in the coil is increased.

Permeability. Materials placed in a magnetic field have the property
of changing the number of lines of force present, compared to the
number that would exist in a field free of matter. This property is
called *permeability*. For example, if an iron rod is inserted in the
solenoid parallel to the coil axis, the flux density will be increased
greatly because iron has high permeability. The permeability of

vacuum is assigned a value of 1; that of air is slightly greater than 1. Cast iron has a permeability of 5000. Solenoids with iron alloys inserted in the core are called *electromagnets*.

Force on a Current Element in a Magnetic Field

As explained previously, in a uniform magnetic field, the magnetic force acting on a current element is *perpendicular* to both the direction of the field and the direction of the current in the element (Figure 28). By contrast, the force on a mass in a gravitational field, or on a positive charge in an electric field, acts in the *same* direction as the field. The force is a maximum when the current element is perpendicular to the field, but zero when the element is parallel to the field. The magnitude of the force is given by

$$F = BIl \tag{70}$$

where F is in newtons, B in newtons/ampere-meter, and (Il) is the product of current and length of the current element, expressed in ampere-meters. Solving this equation for magnetic field intensity, B, gives the equation

$$B = \frac{F}{Il} \tag{71}$$

B is again given in nt/amp-m, which is equivalent to webers/m^2.

Force Between Straight Parallel Conductors; Definition of the Ampere

If two parallel straight conductors carry current in the same direction, each will be attracted toward the other. The two magnetic fields interact, producing a magnetic force of attraction if the currents are in the same direction and a repulsion if the currents are in opposite directions. The force on each conductor is directly proportional to the product of the currents, but inversely proportional to the distance separating them. This interaction is used to define officially the basic unit of current, the ampere, as follows: If two conductors, both very long compared to the distance between them ("infinite length"), are placed parallel to each other one meter apart, the current in each that produces a force between them of exactly 2.0×10^{-7} newtons per meter of conductor length is one ampere. From this definition of the ampere, the coulomb is defined as the quantity of charge that is transported in one second by a current of one ampere.

Magnetic Effects on Moving Charges

Force on a Moving Charged Particle. The force acting upon a charged particle moving in a magnetic field depends on the strength of the field, B, the charge q on the particle, and the speed v of the particle. The force is equal to the product of the three factors:

$$F = qvB \tag{72}$$

F is measured in newtons, v in m/sec and B in nt/amp-m or webers/m². The direction of the force on the particle, as in the case of a current element, is perpendicular to both the magnetic field and the direction in which the charge moves (the direction of the "current"), and obeys the same hand rule (Figure 28). No magnetic force acts on the charge when it moves along a line of magnetic flux, that is, parallel to the direction of the field. The magnitude of the force on the charge is a maximum when the charge moves perpendicular to the field. When the charge moves at an angle between 0° and 90° to the field, that is, between parallel and perpendicular, the force varies between zero and maximum, depending on the magnitude of the velocity component perpendicular to the field.

Force on a Current-Carrying Loop or Solenoid. When a loop of wire or a solenoid carries current and is inserted in a magnetic field, the interaction of the solenoid field with the external field produces a resultant force, called a torque, that tends to turn the loop or coil until the resultant force is a minimum. This principle is used in making motors, galvanometers, loudspeakers, and other devices where magnetic force is used to produce motion.

Magnets

Modern theory indicates that permanent magnetic materials owe their properties to the circulation of electrons within atoms. Atoms of all elements have magnetic properties. In *diamagnetic* substances, these properties combine to *reduce* the flux density of an applied magnetic field. In *paramagnetic* substances, the flux density of an applied field is *increased*. In *ferromagnetic* substances, such as iron, nickel, and cobalt, the electron currents tend to align the atoms in clusters called *domains*. Within a domain the magnetic fields of the aligned atoms add to produce a relatively strong field, but, normally, the axes of the domains are randomly arranged so that the fields cancel. In a magnet, however, some domains are enlarged relative to others, producing a net field. When a permanent magnet is in the shape of a bar with poles at the ends, the overall effect of the atomic current elements is the same as that of a current-carrying solenoid wound around the bar. Concentrated lines of flux emerge from one end of the bar, called the N-pole, and enter the other end, the S-pole, after curving around outside the bar to produce the external field.

Electromagnetic Induction

In a constant magnetic field, no magnetic force will act on the electrons in a conductor, such as a wire, if it carries no current. However, if the magnetic field *changes* in magnitude or in direction, then magnetic force will act on the free electrons in the conductor because moving the field relative to the charge has the same effect as moving the charge relative to the field. Since these electrons are able to move through the wire, they will do so, causing an excess at one end of the wire and a shortage at the other end. This produces excess negative and positive charges at the ends, creating a difference of potential between these points and therefore an electric field inside the wire. The potential difference, measured in volts, depends upon the rate of change of the magnetic field that is inducing the voltage. The potential difference produced in this manner is sometimes called *emf* (derived from an incorrect term, electromotive force). The production of voltage by changing magnetic fields is called *electromagnetic induction*. Moving the source of the field, moving the conductor in a uniform field, or varying the intensity of the field all constitute the motion of the lines of flux relative to the conductor that is necessary to induce voltage.

Magnitude of Induced Voltage. If the conductor is made part of a complete electric circuit, the potential difference induced in the section that cuts the lines of magnetic flux will produce a current in the circuit. In accord with Ohm's law, the magnitude of the current depends on both the magnitude of the induced voltage and the resistance of the circuit. The direction of the induced current is found from a rule called *Lenz's law*, an application of the law of conservation of energy. Whenever a current is induced in a conductor, a magnetic field is produced by the current. According to Lenz's law, the direction of this induced magnetic field surrounding the conductor is always such that it opposes the original applied magnetic field. Since the direction of the *applied* field is known, and the direction of the *induced* field is always in the opposite direction, the direction of the current in the conductor can be found by using the familiar hand rule (Figure 28). From this, the positive and negative terminals of the induced voltage can be determined.

The magnitude of the induced voltage, that is, the actual voltage at the terminals of the conductor, depends on three factors: the length of conductor in the applied field, the field intensity (flux density) of the applied field, and the time rate of change of the field with respect to the conductor, which is represented by velocity, as if the conductor alone were moving. Increase of each of these factors will increase the induced voltage. For a conductor of length l moving with speed v perpendicular to a field of intensity B, the induced voltage is

$$E = Blv \qquad (73)$$

E is in volts when the field intensity B is given in newtons/ampere-meter (or weber/meter^2), l in meters, and v in meters/second.

Generator Principle. The production of voltage and current by electromagnetic induction is the basis of all mechanical generators of electricity. In commercial generators, the conductor, a tightly wound coil of wire with many turns, is rotated in a magnetic field at high speed, producing large currents. The mechanical energy of rotation is converted into electrical energy.

Maximum voltage and current are produced during the instant the plane of the coils (loops) is parallel to the magnetic field; minimum voltage is produced when the plane is perpendicular to the field. Since the loops or coils are rotating in the field, the direction of the voltage and current reverses with each half-turn. Such a current is called alternating current (ac) in contrast to the direct current (dc) produced by chemical action in batteries. The magnetic fields produced around conductors carrying alternating currents are also alternating in intensity and are therefore useful in the construction of many practical electrical devices, such as transformers, that depend chiefly on such alternating magnetic fields.

5. ELECTROMAGNETIC RADIATION

The alternating voltage and current produced in rotating loops by electromagnetic induction are the result of the motion of electrons back and forth in the conductor. This motion, or oscillation, means that the charges are accelerating alternately in opposite directions at twice the frequency of rotation of the loop. As explained previously, such oscillating charges produce changing electric and magnetic fields that radiate outward into the surrounding space in the form of waves. This combined electric and magnetic wave, called an *electromagnetic wave*, is propagated by interchange of energy between the electric and magnetic fields, which are always perpendicular to one another in free space. These waves are part of the electromagnetic spectrum, discussed earlier, and in a vacuum they travel at *c*, the speed of light.

6. ELECTRON BEAMS—OPTIONAL TOPIC

Thermionic Emission

When metallic filaments or wires are heated strongly they emit electrons. This phenomenon is called *thermionic emission*. Inside a closed evacuated tube (an electron or vacuum tube), the emitted electrons surround the filament, forming a negative charge in the space around it. This negative space charge prevents the further emission of electrons. As the wire is made to glow brighter, the electron emission increases, but at any specific temperature an equilibrium exists between the number of electrons emitted and those falling back onto the filament. The rate of electron emission can therefore be controlled by control of the filament temperature.

Electron Beams in an Electric Field

Thermionic emission is used in vacuum tubes in electronic circuits to produce electron beams and currents by application of an electric field between the electron emitter and a metal plate inside the tube. When the plate is at a higher potential than the emitter, the electric field accelerates the electrons toward the plate as soon as they are emitted. The electron emitter is called a *cathode* and the positive plate is called an *anode*. Because the electron current is always in one direction, toward the anode, and because it can be controlled both by temperature and electric field strength, this basic device is widely used. It is called a *diode* and was the first practical electron tube. All radio and television tubes are based on this tube and are modifications of it.

Control of Electron Beams

Electrons produced by thermionic emission can be shaped by electric and magnetic fields into narrow beams that can be controlled and pointed in given directions by changing the directions and intensities of the applied fields. If the beam enters the uniform electric field in the region between two parallel oppositely charged plates, it will be deflected toward the positive plate. Its path will be a parabola if the electrons have a velocity perpendicular to the electric field. The beam can be aimed by changing the electric field strength and direction.

A magnetic field can also deflect the electron beam. If the magnetic field is perpendicular to the beam, the electrons will be deflected into a circular path. The radius of this path is controlled by changing the magnetic field intensity. For example, the ordinary TV picture tube uses two magnetic fields at right angles to one another to move the beam in a scanning motion so that it covers the entire face of the tube in producing the TV image.

QUESTIONS

1-4. Base your answers to Questions 1 through 4 on the following information.

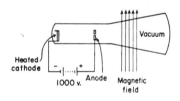

The diagram represents an electron vacuum tube with a heated cathode and an anode connected to a 1000-volt d-c source. A uniform magnetic field is applied as shown. Some of the electrons emitted by the cathode pass through the hole in the anode and move through the magnetic field.

1. What is the kinetic energy gained by each electron as it moves from the cathode to the anode? (1) 1.0×10^3 ev (2) 1.6×10^{-19} ev (3) 9.1×10^{-31} ev (4) 6.6×10^{-34} ev

2. If the speed of the electron leaving the anode is 1.9×10^7 m/sec and the flux density (B) is 2.0×10^{-4} nt/amp-m, the magnetic force on each electron is (1) 4.3×10^{-12} nt (2) 6.1×10^{-16} nt (3) 8.2×10^{-14} nt (4) 9.4×10^{-16} nt

3. If the voltage on the anode increases, the kinetic energy of the electrons reaching it (1) decreases (2) increases (3) remains the same

4. If the direction of the magnetic field is reversed, the magnitude of the magnetic force on the electrons (1) decreases (2) increases (3) remains the same

Charge to Mass Ratio of the Electron

One of the first uses of electric and magnetic fields resulted in the discovery of a basic property of the electron, the ratio of its charge to its mass. In 1897, J. J. Thomson, an English physicist, projected a beam of electrons through a dual field consisting of oppositely acting electric and magnetic fields. These fields were adjusted to produce a zero net force on the electrons. Under such conditions, theory showed that the ratio of electron charge to electron mass, e/m, depended on the readily measured values of B and E of the applied fields. The numerical value of this ratio was calculated and was used later by R. A. Millikan to determine the charge of the electron in the "oil drop" experiment (see page 92).

QUESTIONS

1. In the diagram, the direction of the magnetic field at point P is toward point (1) A (2) B (3) C (4) D

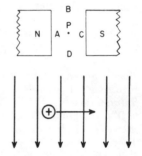

2-5. Base your answers to Questions 2 through 5 on the diagram, which shows a unit positive charge moving in a vacuum at a constant speed perpendicular to the direction of a magnetic field.

2. If the unit positive charge on the particle were replaced by a unit negative charge, the magnitude of the force exerted on the particle would be (1) quartered (2) halved (3) doubled (4) unaffected

3. If the magnetic field strength were doubled, the force exerted on the particle would be (1) halved (2) unaffected (3) doubled (4) quadrupled

4. If the charge on the particle were doubled, the force exerted on the particle would be (1) halved (2) unaffected (3) doubled (4) quadrupled

5. If the speed of the particle were doubled, the force exerted on the particle would be (1) halved (2) unaffected (3) doubled (4) quadrupled

6-9. Base your answers to Questions 6 through 9 on the following information.

Two conducting spheres, A and B, are separated by a distance of 2 m between centers. Sphere A has a charge of $+2 \times 10^{-4}$ coul, and sphere B has a charge of $+6 \times 10^{-4}$ coul.

6. Which diagram best represents the electric lines of force around sphere *A* and sphere *B*?

7. The force that these two spheres exert upon each other is (1) 3.0×10^{-8} nt (2) $+5.4 \times 10^2$ nt (3) 9.0×10^9 nt (4) 2.7×10^2 nt

8. As the distance between the two positively charged spheres increases, the force of repulsion between them (1) decreases (2) increases (3) remains the same

9. The spheres are brought together until they touch and are then separated. As compared to the original total charge on the spheres, the net charge after separation is (1) less (2) greater (3) the same

10-12. Base your answers to Questions 10 through 12 on the diagram, which shows conductor *xy* moving through a uniform magnetic field toward point *A*, as indicated by the arrow. The length of the wire is 0.20 m and the magnetic field strength is 0.50 nt/amp-m. The wire moves at a uniform velocity of 1.0 m/sec.

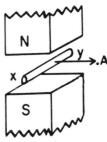

10. Which vector correctly represents the direction of the magnetic field between the north and south poles of the magnet?

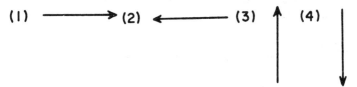

11. What is the magnitude of the induced voltage in conductor *xy*? (1) 0.0 volts (2) 0.10 volt (3) 2.5 volts (4) 10 volts

12. If the conductor were moving from its position directly toward the N-pole, then the magnitude of the induced voltage in the conductor would be (1) 0.0 volts (2) 0.1 volt (3) 2.5 volts (4) 10.0 volts

13. Two fixed parallel wires, each carrying a current of 1.0 amp, attract each other with a force of 1.2×10^{-6} nt. If the current in one of the wires is doubled, the force of attraction between them will become (1) 1.2×10^{-6} nt (2) 2.4×10^{-6} nt (3) 4.8×10^{-6} nt (4) 6.0×10^{-6} nt

14. An electric potential difference will be induced between the ends of the conductor shown in the diagram when the conductor moves in direction (1) *A* (2) *B* (3) *C* (4) *D*

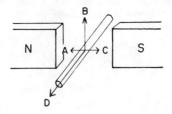

15. The diagram represents magnetic flux intersecting a plane at right angles. If the magnitude of the flux is 16 webers, the average flux density intersecting the plane is (1) 64 webers/m² (2) 16 webers/m² (3) 8 webers/m² (4) 4 webers/m²

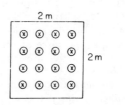

16. An electron moving parallel to a magnetic field as shown in the diagram will experience (1) no magnetic force (2) a magnetic downward force (3) a magnetic force out of the page (4) a magnetic force into the page

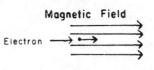

17. If the electrons in the wire shown are flowing eastward, in which direction will the needle of a compass held above the wire point? (1) north (2) south (3) east (4) west

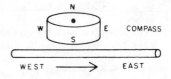

18. The north pole of the solenoid shown would be located at point (1) *A* (2) *B* (3) *C* (4) *D*

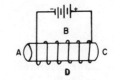

19. A beam of electrons is moving from north to south as shown. The direction of the magnetic field above the beam is toward the (1) north (2) south (3) east (4) west

20. The direction of the electron flow in a conductor is from east to west as shown.

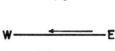

What is the direction of the magnetic field at point *P*? (1) north (2) south (3) into the page (4) out of the page

21. Which magnetic field configuration is not possible?

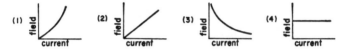

22. Which graph best represents the strength of a magnetic field at a point near a current-carrying straight wire?

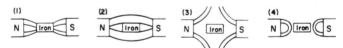

23. What information must be known to calculate the magnetic force on a charge as it moves perpendicularly through a magnetic field? (1) the speed of the charge, only (2) the speed and the magnetic field intensity, only (3) the magnetic field intensity and the magnitude of the charge, only (4) the speed, the magnetic field intensity, and the magnitude of the charge

24. A small, soft iron bar is placed between a north and a south pole. Which diagram represents the resulting magnetic field between these two poles?

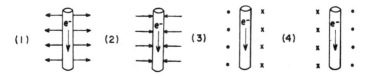

25. Which diagram best represents the magnetic field around a wire conductor in which electrons are moving as shown? (The **x** indicates that the field is into the page; the • indicates that the field is out of the page.)

26. Magnetic flux density may be measured in (1) nt/m^2 (2) webers/m^2 (3) oersteds/m^2 (4) gauss/m^2

27. An electron, *e*, is projected into the page through a magnetic field, as shown. The magnetic force acting on the electron is toward (1) *A* (2) *B* (3) *C* (4) *D*

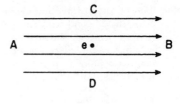

28. At point *X* above the current-carrying wire, the direction of the magnetic lines of force is (1) into the page (2) out of the page (3) to the left (4) to the right·

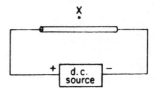

29. In the diagram, the end pole of a permanent magnet is thrust into end *A* of the air core coil. Which law best explains why the direction of electron flow in the external resistance is from right to left? (1) Coulomb's law (2) Ohm's law (3) law of conservation of energy (4) Snell's law

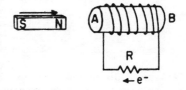

30. As materials of increasing permeability are placed at position *X* in the diagram, the flux density at position *X* (1) decreases (2) increases (3) remains the same

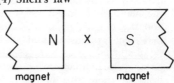

31. As the difference in potential across the terminals of a solenoid increases, its magnetic flux density (1) decreases (2) increases (3) remains the same

32. A loop of wire rotating in a magnetic field is part of a closed circuit. As the current in this circuit increases, the force required to rotate the loop at constant speed (1) decreases (2) increases (3) remains the same

33. As the current in a pair of parallel wires increases, the force between them (1) decreases (2) increases (3) remains the same

34. When the current in a coil is halved and the number of turns is doubled, the magnetic field strength of the coil (1) decreases (2) increases (3) remains the same

35. If the permeability of the core of a solenoid increases, its magnetic field strength (1) decreases (2) increases (3) remains the same

36. A wire conductor is perpendicular to the direction of a uniform magnetic field. As the current in the wire increases, the force exerted upon the wire by the magnetic field (1) decreases (2) increases (3) remains the same

37. Given the diagram at right, at the moment when switch S_1 is closed, the force of the magnet on the soft iron core (1) decreases (2) increases (3) remains the same

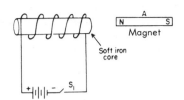

38. As the current in a circular loop of wire increases, the magnetic field strength at the center of the loop (1) decreases (2) increases (3) remains the same

39. As the current in a conductor is increased, the intensity of the magnetic field at a point near the wire (1) decreases (2) increases (3) remains the same

40. An electron is moving perpendicular to the lines of force of a uniform magnetic field. As the speed of the electron increases, the magnetic force on the electron (1) decreases (2) increases (3) remains the same

41. As the number of ampere-turns on an electromagnet is increased, the pole strength of the electromagnet (1) decreases (2) increases (3) remains the same

42. As the charge on a particle travelling perpendicular to a magnetic field is increased, the deflecting force on the particle (1) decreases (2) increases (3) remains the same

43-47. Base your answers to Questions 43 through 47 on the following information.

The current in the electromagnet shown is 5.0 amp. The magnitude of the flux density, B, of the magnet is 1.0×10^{-2} nt/amp-m. A beam of electrons passes from right to left be-

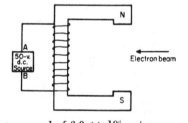

tween the poles of the magnet at a speed of 3.0×10^6 m/sec.

43. The resistance of the magnet coil is (1) 5.0 ohms (2) 10 ohms (3) 15 ohms (4) 250 ohms

44. At which point in the circuit is there a positive electrical potential? (1) A (2) B (3) S (4) N

45. The number of joules of electrical energy used per second by the magnet is (1) 0.01 (2) 0.05 (3) 10 (4) 250

46. As the electron beam passes between the poles of the electromagnet, it will be deflected (1) toward pole N (2) toward pole S (3) into the page (4) out of the page

47. The magnitude of the force exerted on each electron by the magnetic field is (1) 4.8×10^{-15} nt (2) 4.0×10^{-2} nt (3) 3.0×10^4 nt (4) 1.5×10^5 nt

48-52. Base your answers to Questions 48 through 52 on the diagram, which shows a conducting loop in a uniform magnetic field of 5.6 × 10⁻² weber/m².

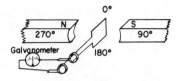

48. As the loop is rotated clockwise through 360°, the galvanometer needle will (1) deflect only to the left (2) deflect only to the right (3) deflect first in one direction and then in the other (4) not deflect in either direction

49. As the loop rotates, the induced voltage will be a maximum at (1) 0° and 90° (2) 0° and 180° (3) 90° and 270° (4) 180° and 270°

50. As the loop is made smaller, the maximum induced voltage will (1) decrease (2) increase (3) remain the same

51. As the speed of rotation of the coil increases, the flux density of the field due to the magnets (1) decreases (2) increases (3) remains the same

52. As the north and south poles are moved farther apart, the induced voltage (1) decreases (2) increases (3) remains the same

53-57. Base your answers to Questions 53 through 57 on the diagram, which shows a beam of electrons moving perpendicular to a uniform magnetic field.

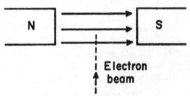

53. In which direction is the electron beam deflected by the magnetic field? (1) to the right (2) to the left (3) out of the page (4) into the page

54. Which will occur if only the direction of the magnetic field is reversed? (1) The magnitude of the force exerted on the beam of electrons will decrease. (2) The magnitude of the force exerted on the beam of electrons will increase. (3) The direction of the force exerted on the beam of electrons will change. (4) The speed of the electron beam will increase.

55. If the magnetic flux density is 1.0 weber/m² and the electron speed is 2 × 10⁷ m/sec, what is the force exerted by the magnetic field on one electron? (1) 3.0 × 10¹¹ nt (2) 3.2 × 10⁻¹² nt (3) 4.0 × 10⁻⁶ nt (4) 6.4 × 10⁻⁵ nt

56. If the speed of the electrons in the beam is decreased, then the force exerted by the magnetic field on the beam of electrons will (1) decrease (2) increase (3) remain the same

57. If the beam of electrons were replaced by a beam of protons travelling at the same speed, the force exerted by the magnetic field would (1) decrease (2) increase (3) remain the same

58-61. Base your answers to Questions 58 through 61 on the diagram shown, which represents the end view of a closed rectangular loop of wire rotating at a constant speed in a uniform magnetic field.

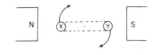

58. If the flux density between the two poles increases, the magnitude of the maximum induced electromotive force will (1) decrease (2) increase (3) remain the same

59. During one revolution of the loop, the direction of the current in the X side of the loop would be (1) out of the page, only (2) into the page, only (3) both out of and into the page

60. If the speed of rotation decreases, the magnitude of the maximum induced electromotive force will (1) decrease (2) increase (3) remain the same

61. As the loop rotates through an angle of 90° from the position shown, the magnitude of the maximum induced voltage will (1) decrease (2) increase (3) remain the same

62-66. Base your answers to Questions 62 through 66 on the diagram, which represents a straight conductor perpendicular to the page, rotating at constant speed in a uniform magnetic field. Points A, B, C, and D represent different positions of the wire as it rotates.

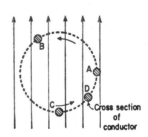

Cross section of conductor

62. The largest voltage will be induced in the conductor as it moves through position (1) A (2) B (3) C (4) D

63. When the conductor is moving through position B, the direction of the force on the electrons in the conductor will be (1) into the page (2) out of the page (3) toward the top of the page (4) toward the bottom of the page

64. If the strength of the magnetic field is increased, then the maximum induced voltage will (1) decrease (2) increase (3) remain the same

65. If the speed of the rotation of the conductor is decreased and the magnetic field strength is kept constant, then the maximum induced voltage will (1) decrease (2) increase (3) remain the same

66. If the ends of the conductor are now connected to a light bulb, then the force needed to rotate the conductor at the same speed will (1) decrease (2) increase (3) remain the same

67-71. Base your answers to Questions 67 through 71 on the following information.

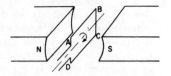

The diagram represents a rectangular wire loop, *ABCD*, rotating between two magnetic poles. Sides *AB* and *CD* move at a constant speed of 1.0 m/sec. The strength of the uniform magnetic field between the magnetic poles is 5.0 webers/m². Side *AB* is 0.30 m long.

67. The maximum voltage induced in side *AB* is approximately (1) 1.5 volts (2) 2.0 volts (3) 3.0 volts (4) 6.0 volts

68. The induced voltage will be a maximum when the angle between the plane of the loop and the direction of the magnetic field is (1) 0° (2) 30° (3) 45° (4) 90°

69. If the number of loops in the coils is increased, the maximum voltage induced in the coil will (1) decrease (2) increase (3) remain the same

70. If the strength of the magnetic field is decreased and the rate at which the coil rotates remains constant, the maximum induced voltage will (1) decrease (2) increase (3) remain the same

71. If the speed at which the loop is rotating is increased, the maximum induced voltage will (1) decrease (2) increase (3) remain the same

ATOMIC AND NUCLEAR PHYSICS

The modern understanding of atomic structure and the fundamental nature of matter resulted from studies of the nature of light, of the interaction of light with matter, and of radioactivity. These lines of study are presented in this section to help the student trace the development of modern atomic and nuclear theory.

1. DUAL NATURE OF LIGHT

Wave Phenomena

Until the 18th century, most scientists thought of light as being made up of tiny particles of some unknown composition. In the 19th century, the wave character of light was revealed by demonstrations of diffraction, interference, Doppler effect, and polarization of light. Maxwell's equations showed that light and other electromagnetic radiations could be considered as waves that are propagated by an interchange of energy between electric and magnetic fields.

Particle Phenomena—The Photoelectric Effect

Other observations, however, contradicted the wave theory of light. Near the beginning of the 20th century, a phenomenon known as the *photoelectric effect* was observed. It was found that substances emitted electrons when struck by light above a certain frequency limit, and that this lower limit, called the *threshold frequency*, was different for different substances. For a given substance, light frequencies below the threshold frequency, no matter how intense, would not cause electrons to be emitted. This contradicted wave theory, which predicted that light of any frequency should cause the emission of at least some electrons. It was also found that, for a given substance, if the frequency of the incident light is constant, and above the threshold frequency, then increasing the brightness of the light produces an increase in the number of electrons emitted, but the maximum kinetic energy, E_{max}, of the emitted electrons remains unchanged. This result also contradicted wave theory, which predicted that E_{max} should be directly proportional to light intensity.

2. QUANTUM THEORY

Quantized Radiation

The explanation of the photoelectric effect, given in 1905 by Albert Einstein, depended on the *quantum theory*, which was proposed in 1900 by Max Planck, a German physicist. The quantum theory was developed to explain the distribution of intensity (energy) observed in the spectra of radiations emitted by heated objects. To explain these observations (which the wave theory of light had failed to predict), Planck had to assume that atoms could not emit electromagnetic radiation in a continuous stream, but only in short bursts or packets (*quanta*) of energy. He predicted that the amount of energy, E, of each quantum would be directly proportional to the frequency, f, of the radiation. For example, a quantum of blue light (higher frequency) would contain more energy than a quantum of red light (lower frequency). This proportionality is written

$$E = hf \qquad (74)$$

where h is a constant of proportionality called *Planck's constant*. If E is given in joules and f in Hz (that is, $\sec^{-1}$), the units of h are joule-sec. Note that, since $f = c/\lambda$ (from equation 48), this proportionality can also be written

$$E = \frac{hc}{\lambda} \qquad (75)$$

where c is the constant velocity of light, 3×10^8 m/sec, and λ is wavelength.

Planck's Constant

Since the energy in joules of a single quantum is small, and since frequencies are large numbers, h must necessarily be an extremely small factor. Indirect measurements indicate that $h = 6.6 \times 10^{-34}$ joule-sec. A quantum of visible light ($f =$ nearly 10^{15} Hz) would therefore have an energy on the order of 10^{-19} joule, which is on the order of 1 electron-volt (1 ev $= 1.6 \times 10^{-19}$ joule).

Explanation of the Photoelectric Effect

Photons. Quanta of electromagnetic energy are called *photons*. In explaining the photoelectric effect, Einstein assumed that electromagnetic radiations are not only *emitted* as photons, they are also *received* as separate photons. That is, each photon interacts individually with an atom of the receiving substance. In the interaction, part of the photon energy is used in releasing an electron from the material; the remainder is converted to kinetic energy of the released electron.

Photoelectric Equation. By applying the law of conservation of energy to this interaction, Einstein developed an equation, called the *photoelectric equation*, that relates the maximum kinetic energy, E_{max}, of the photoelectrons to the energy, hf, of the incoming photons. The equation is

$$E_{max} = hf - w \qquad (76)$$

The term w, called the work function, is constant for a given material. It is the energy required to release an electron from the surface of the material. Thus if the energy, hf, of an incident photon is 5 ev, and the work function, w, of the given material is 2 ev, then the maximum kinetic energy of the photoelectron is 5 ev − 2 ev = 3 ev. If the photon energy were greater, 7 ev for example, then the maximum kinetic energy of the photoelectrons would be 7 ev − 2 ev = 5 ev. Illuminated by light of a given frequency, materials with lower work functions produce photoelectrons with higher maximum kinetic energies. For example, if metal A has a work function w_A = 2 ev and metal B has a work function w_B = 3 ev, then a photon of energy hf = 6 ev would release photoelectrons having a maximum energy E_{max} = 6 ev − 2 ev = 4 ev from metal A, and E_{max} = 6 ev − 3 ev = 3 ev from metal B.

The graph of equation 76 is a straight line of slope h, with frequency as the x axis and energy as the y axis, as shown in Figure 30.

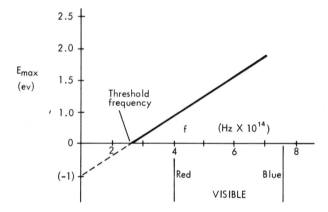

Figure 30. Theoretical photoelectric emission curve for a material whose work function is w = -1.0 ev.

The point where the line intersects the x axis is the threshold frequency, f_0, for the given material, showing the dependence of threshold frequency on the work function of the material. If the frequency of the incoming photon is less than the threshold frequency, then the value of E_{max}, given by $hf − w$, would be less than 0. In other words, no electrons could be emitted. For the production of photoelectrons, the frequency of the light must therefore be greater than f_0 and therefore greater than w/h.

The photon theory also explained the effect of intensity on photoelectron emission. An increase in intensity of light means an increase in the number of incoming photons per unit time, resulting in an increase in the number of photoelectrons emitted from a substance per unit time.

Photon-Particle Collisions—The Compton Effect

Photons having much larger energy than those of visible light, such as x-ray photons, were found to behave like particles in interactions with electrons. It was found that a photon-electron collision obeyed the laws of conservation of energy and momentum. This kind of interaction is called the *Compton effect* after its discoverer. The momentum of a photon was found to be given by the equation

$$p \doteq \frac{E}{c} \tag{77}$$

If E is given in joules, and c is the speed of light, 3.0×10^8 m/sec, p is measured in kilogram-meters/second. Since $c = f \lambda$, equation 77 can be written as

$$p = \frac{E}{c} = \frac{hf}{f\lambda} = \frac{h}{\lambda} \tag{78}$$

The momentum of photons therefore depends only on the frequency, or wavelength, of the photon because photons always move with the speed of light, c, and do not exist at rest.

QUESTIONS

1. In the photoelectric effect, photoelectrons may be removed from a metallic surface by means of (1) an electron beam (2) electromagnetic radiation (3) alpha particles (4) high temperature

2. During collisions between x-ray photons and electrons, there is a conservation of (1) momentum but not energy (2) energy but not momentum (3) neither momentum nor energy (4) both momentum and energy

3. Charged particles can be accelerated by (1) a gravitational field only (2) an electric field only (3) a magnetic field only (4) both an electric field and a magnetic field

4. Which color of visible light has the greatest quantum energy? (1) blue (2) green (3) yellow (4) orange

5. Only the particle theory of light can explain (1) interference (2) polarization (3) diffraction (4) the photoelectric effect

6. The maximum kinetic energy of electrons emitted from a photosensitive surface can be increased by increasing the (1) frequency of the incident light (2) intensity of the incident light (3) area of the surface (4) work function of the photosensitive material

7. The photon model of light is more appropriate than the wave model in explaining (1) interference (2) refraction (3) polarization (4) photoelectric emission

8. What is the energy in joules of a photon with a frequency of 3.00×10^{13} Hz? (1) 2.21×10^{-48} (2) 2.21×10^{-46} (3) 6.63×10^{-34} (4) 1.99×10^{-20}

9. Light falls on a photoelectric material and no electrons are emitted. Electrons may be emitted if the (1) intensity of the

light is decreased (2) intensity of the light is increased (3) frequency of the light is decreased (4) frequency of the light is increased

10. What is the frequency of a photon with 6.63×10^{-19} joule of energy? (1) 3.00×10^{15} Hz (2) 1.00×10^{15} Hz (3) 3.00×10^{-7} Hz (4) 1.00×10^{-5} Hz

11. The energy of a photon that has a frequency of 3.3×10^{14} Hz is approximately (1) 2.0×10^{-48} joule (2) 2.0×10^{-19} joule (3) 5.0×10^{-19} joule (4) 5.0×10^{48} joules

12. When photons with an energy of 3.0 ev strike a photoelectric surface, the maximum kinetic energy of the emitted photoelectrons is 2.0 ev. What is the work function of the surface? (1) 1.0 ev (2) 0.67 ev (3) 1.5 ev (4) 5.0 ev

13. Interference experiments demonstrate the (1) particle nature of light (2) polarization of light (3) intensity of light (4) wave nature of light

14. Which property of incident radiation striking a surface determines the rate at which the surface emits photoelectrons? (1) frequency (2) intensity (3) velocity (4) wavelength

15. Which property of a particle has the greatest influence on its wave nature? (1) mass (2) shape (3) volume (4) specific heat

16. Which graph best represents the energy of a photon as a function of its frequency?

17. Which determines the number of electrons emitted by a photoelectric material? (1) intensity (2) color (3) frequency (4) wavelength

18. Which graph best represents the relationship between the wavelength and the momentum of a photon?

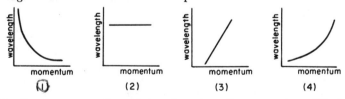

19. As the frequency of a photon increases, its momentum (1) decreases (2) increases (3) remains the same

20. As the intensity of monochromatic light on a photosensitive surface increases, the maximum velocity of the ejected electrons (1) decreases (2) increases (3) remains the same

21. As the frequency of electromagnetic radiation increases, the energy of the corresponding quanta (1) decreases (2) increases (3) remains the same

22. As the momentum of photons in a vacuum increases, the speed of the photons (1) decreases (2) increases (3) remains the same

23. As the frequency of radiation used to eject photoelectrons from a surface increases, the voltage needed to stop these electrons (1) decreases (2) increases (3) remains the same

24. As the momentum of a particle exhibiting wave properties increases, the wavelength of the particle (1) decreases (2) increases (3) remains the same

25-26. Base your answers to Questions 25 and 26 on the following information.

Monochromatic light strikes a metal surface that has a work function of 6.7×10^{-19} joule. Each photon has an energy of 8.0×10^{-19} joule.

25. What is the maximum kinetic energy of the photoelectrons emitted by the metal? (1) 1.3×10^{-19} joule (2) 2.6×10^{-19} joule (3) 6.7×10^{-19} joule (4) 8.0×10^{-19} joule

26. What is the energy of each photon expressed in electron-volts? (1) 5.4×10^{-37} ev (2) 1.6×10^{-19} ev (3) 8.0×10^{-19} ev (4) 5.0 ev

27-30. Base your answers to Questions 27 through 30 on the graph, which represents the relationship between the maximum photoelectron energy (E_{max}) and the frequency of the incident radiation (f) for four target metals: a, b, c, and d.

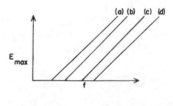

27. Which metal has the highest threshold frequency? (1) a (2) b (3) c (4) d

28. The energy of photons producing photoelectric emission from metal b is 4.2 ev. If the maximum energy of the photoelectrons is 2.5 ev, then the work function of the metal is (1) 1.7 ev (2) 3.5 ev (3) 4.2 ev (4) 6.7 ev

29. The energy of a photon with a frequency of 6×10^{14} Hz is approximately (1) 7×10^{-34} joule (2) 1×10^{-24} joule (3) 4×10^{-19} joule (4) 4×10^{48} joules

30. When light shines on a photoelectric surface, the maximum energy of the emitted photoelectrons depends upon the light's (1) intensity (2) frequency (3) speed (4) amplitude

31-35. Base your answers to Questions 31 through 35 on the following information.

Four different sources of electromagnetic radiation, A, B, C, and D, are used successively to illuminate a photoemissive metal. These sources produce photoelectrons of maximum kinetic energy 1, 2, 3, and 4 ev, respectively.

31. In this experiment, the source that produces the radiation with the longest wavelength is (1) A (2) B (3) C (4) D

32. Each photon from source *B* has an energy of 3 ev. The work function of the metal is (1) 1 ev (2) 2 ev (3) 3 ev (4) 4 ev

33. When source *C* is used, the maximum kinetic energy of the emitted photoelectrons is (1) 1.6×10^{-19} joule (2) 3.0×10^{-19} joule (3) 4.8×10^{-19} joule (4) 5.3×10^{-20} joule

34. As the intensity of source *A* increases, the maximum kinetic energy of the photoelectrons (1) decreases (2) increases (3) remains the same

35. If a metal with a lower work function is used in the experiment, the maximum kinetic energy of the photoelectrons produced by each source will (1) decrease (2) increase (3) remain the same

36-40. Base your answers to Questions 36 through 40 on the following information.

In the diagram, a photon beam is incident on photoemissive surface *A*. *B* represents the particle emitted as a photon strikes the surface.

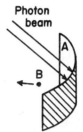

Photon beam

36. The particle emitted as a result of the photoelectric effect is (1) a proton (2) a photon (3) a neutron (4) an electron

37. If the wavelength of the incident photons is 6.0×10^{-7} m, the color of the beam is (1) blue (2) green (3) yellow (4) orange

38. The frequency of the incident photon is 5.0×10^{14} Hz. The energy of the photon in joules is (1) 3.3×10^{-19} (2) 6.0×10^{-7} (3) 8.0×10^{47} (4) 3.0×10^{48}

39. As the frequency of incident photons is increased, the energy of emitted particles (1) decreases (2) increases (3) remains the same

40. As the intensity of incident photons is increased, the rate of emission of particles (1) decreases (2) increases (3) remains the same

41. At constant photon energies, as the work function of the surface increases, the maximum kinetic energy of emitted photoelectrons (1) decreases (2) increases (3) remains the same

3. EARLY MODELS OF THE ATOM

Rutherford Model of the Atom

At the same time that Planck and Einstein were studying the nature of energy, other scientists were developing new theories about the nature of matter. In 1898 it was discovered that electrons are relatively light-weight, negatively charged particles present in atoms. This meant that part of the atom must also possess a positive charge equal to that of the electrons because atoms are normally electrically neutral. How this positive charge was arranged in the atom was discovered in 1911 by E. Rutherford in England from results of alpha particle scattering experiments.

Alpha Particles. Shortly after the discovery of radioactivity by Becquerel in 1895, Rutherford was able to show that radioactive emissions are of three kinds, which he named alpha, beta, and gamma. Alpha particles were later found to be helium atoms with their electrons removed. Upon emission from such radioactive elements as radium, these relatively massive, positively charged particles travel at approximately 1/10 the speed of light, and range in kinetic energy from 4.5 to 9.0 Mev (million electron-volts).

Alpha Particle Scattering. Rutherford directed a beam of alpha particles at extremely thin gold foil. It was expected that nearly all the alphas would be deflected through small angles by interaction with the atoms' positive charges. However, most of the alphas passed through the foil without being deflected at all. Only relatively few alphas were scattered, but many of these were scattered at large angles, even back toward the source at angles of nearly 180°. From the angles at which the alphas were deflected, Rutherford decided that the backward scattering of such massive and energetic particles must be due to collision with other even more massive particles with high positive charge. Assuming that atoms are symmetrical, he had to conclude that this concentration of mass and positive charge, which he called the *nucleus*, is located at the center of the atom. From the number of alphas deflected, he calculated that the nucleus is only 1/10,000 the diameter of the normal atom.

The "Rutherford Atom". Based on the results of his "gold foil" experiments, Rutherford was able to describe atoms as consisting of a tiny nucleus (less than 10^{-14} m in diameter) that contains all the positive charge of the atom and virtually all its mass, surrounded by a number of electrons, sufficient to balance the nuclear charge, moving in fixed orbits centered on the nucleus. Since atoms are normally on the order of 10^{-10} m in diameter, the Rutherford atom resembles the solar system, which also consists mostly of empty space, with the nucleus as the "sun" and the electrons as "planets", held by the Coulomb force of attraction between opposite charges rather than by gravity. This is essentially the modern view of atomic structure, except that the idea of electrons as particles in orbits has been replaced by a more complex mathematical description that accounts for the quantum theory of light and observations of atomic spectra.

Trajectories of Alpha Particles. Since the atom is mostly empty space, incoming alpha particles rarely meet the nucleus head-on. The distance between the actual path of the alpha and the path it would take for a head-on collision is called the impact parameter, P. As P gets smaller, θ, the angle of deflection from the alpha's original path, gets larger. At $P = 0$, which means a head-on collision, $\theta = 180°$, which means a deflection directly backward. Although a head-on collision between an alpha particle and a nucleus is possible, it is extremely rare. The average kinetic energy of the positively charged alpha particles is insufficient to allow them to overcome the Coulomb force of repulsion to reach the positively charged nucleus. The trajectory of the scattered alpha is therefore actually a hyperbola, strongly curved near the nucleus. The force of repulsion is given by equation 49, $F = k \times q_{alpha} \times q_{nucleus}/r^2$, where r is the distance between the centers of the gold nucleus and the alpha. For an atomic nucleus, $q = Ze$, where e is the elementary unit of charge, 1.6×10^{-19} coul, and Z is the atomic number, the number of positive charges in the nucleus.

Scattering and Atomic Number—Optional Topic. In Rutherford's experiment, the number of alphas scattered at large angles depended on the particular metallic element used as target material. It was found that, for alphas of a given energy, the number of alphas scattered at angles larger than a given angle is directly proportional to Z. Further experiment by Rutherford and his coworkers led him to conclude that the chemical and other properties of an element are determined by the number of positive charges (protons) in the nuclei of its atoms. All atoms of a given element have the same value of Z. Thus an alpha particle is the nucleus of a helium atom, atomic number 2, consisting of 2 protons and, as proved by later work, 2 neutrons.

Bohr Model of the Atom

Rutherford's atom model, as deduced from scattering experiments, contradicted the observation that accelerated charges radiate electromagnetic energy, losing kinetic energy in the process. In the "solar system" atom, the orbiting electrons, accelerated toward the nucleus by a Coulomb force of attraction, would have to lose orbital (angular) momentum very rapidly, emitting a prolonged burst of electromagnetic energy that increases in frequency as they spiral into the nucleus. Since atoms do not collapse but are stable for billions of years, Rutherford's model was incomplete in describing the manner of electron arrangement in the atom.

Bohr's Assumptions. In 1913, Niels Bohr, a Danish physicist, proposed a model of atomic structure which attempted to explain the atom's stability. He used Rutherford's model, agreeing with him about the features of nuclear structure, but in order to explain electron arrangement in the atom, he added an important assumption that was based on the quantum theory of light.

1. Bohr assumed that atoms could emit or absorb radiant energy when an electron changed from one orbit to another of different radius.

2. It was next necessary to assume that, since atoms do not collapse, the amount of energy they can emit, and therefore the radii of electron orbits, must be limited to certain set values.

3. The most important assumption of the Bohr model is that the angular momentum of the electrons, that is, the momentum due to their motion in orbit, is limited to certain set values, matching the values of the radii. This condition is called *quantized angular momentum*. The values are derived in the following way. For an ob-

ject of mass m travelling at velocity v in an orbit of radius r, the angular momentum is mvr. Bohr assumed that the angular momentum of an electron in orbit could only be a whole number multiple of the quantity $h/2\pi$, where h is Planck's constant. In formula form

$$mvr_n = n \left(\frac{h}{2\pi} \right) \tag{79}$$

where n is a whole number (not zero). This means not only that the number of orbits is limited, but also that there is a lower limit, a smallest orbit for which $n = 1$, below which the electron cannot go. This assumption explains the stability of the nuclear atom.

4. The electron in a given orbit is said to be in a *stationary state*. Different stationary states are possible, depending on the radius of the orbit. Different stationary states represent different quantities of energy, and electrons in different stationary states are said to be at different *energy levels*. The electron orbit of the smallest radius ($n = 1$) is called the *ground state* and is the lowest energy level. No loss of energy occurs as long as the atom is in a stationary state, in spite of the fact that the electron is accelerating during its motion within the particular orbit.

5. When an electron changes from a lower state to a higher state, a quantum of energy is *absorbed*. If it goes from a higher state to a lower one, a quantum of energy is *emitted*. The quantum of energy E_{photon}, is equal to the difference between the energies, E_2 and E_1, of the two states. By substituting in equation 74, this equation becomes

$$E_{\text{photon}} = E_2 - E_1 = hf \tag{80}$$

The frequency of the photon released or absorbed can therefore be calculated from the difference in energy between the two levels involved.

Energy Levels. The existence of energy states in atoms was demonstrated in 1914 by J. Franck and G. Hertz in an experiment with mercury vapor. They projected a beam of electrons into mercury vapor and found that atoms of mercury could only absorb certain values of energy. For example, incoming electrons with a kinetic energy of 4 ev were scattered elastically, but when their kinetic energy was raised to 5 ev, the electrons were found to have lost all but 0.1 ev. At the same time, the mercury atoms began to radiate a single frequency of ultraviolet light equal to 4.9 ev per photon. The absorption of kinetic energy from electrons raised the mercury atoms to an *excited state,* which is an energy level above the ground state. This process is called *excitation*. The atoms then radiated this energy as photons of ultraviolet light.

Different elements have different excitation energies. Atoms rapidly emit the energy of the various excited states in the form of photons of equivalent frequencies, accounting for the specific light frequencies observed in the spectra of different atoms.

Ionization Potential. The energy needed to remove an electron completely from (ionize) an atom is called the *ionization potential*. For example, the ionization potential of a hydrogen atom is 13.6 ev, which means that this much energy will remove an electron completely from a hydrogen atom in its ground state. For atoms in an excited state, a correspondingly smaller amount of energy is required to ionize the atom. Figure 31 shows some of the first few energy levels of the hydrogen atom, and the magnitude of the energy above ground level.

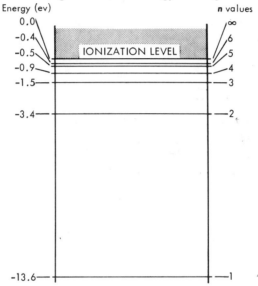

Figure 31. Energy levels of the hydrogen atom.

4. ATOMIC SPECTRA

A *spectrum* consists of the specific frequencies of light produced by elements excited by heat or other means. Each element produces a spectrum that distinguishes it from all other elements.

Emission (Bright Line) Spectra

The energy levels of the "Bohr atom" provided an explanation for spectra. Since there are many different energy levels associated with electrons in an atom, a large number of energy differences is possible. Each energy difference between two energy levels corresponds to a photon of specific frequency. Thus a set of frequencies characteristic of each atom is produced when the electrons of an atom in an excited state fall back to lower states or to the ground state. Since the atoms of different elements have electrons in different energy levels, no two elements produce identical spectra. As viewed in a spectroscope, an emission spectrum appears as a series of bright lines on a dark background, and is therefore called a *bright line* spectrum.

Absorption Spectra—Optional Topic

Atoms can also absorb photons whose energies are equal to the energies of the photons they can emit. Consequently, under certain conditions, if light of all frequencies (white light) is supplied to an element, the atoms will selectively absorb the same frequencies that they can emit when excited. These absorbed frequencies appear as dark lines in the white light spectrum. Such a spectrum is therefore called an *absorption spectrum*. Note that an atom will absorb a photon only if the photon energy is *exactly* the amount needed to raise the atom to one of its possible energy levels. Photons having energies other than these values will not excite the atom, except for photons whose energy is enough to ionize the atom.

In both the release of photons to make up the emission spectrum, and the absorption of photons to make up the dark line absorption spectrum, equation 80 gives the frequency of the photon emitted or absorbed.

Hydrogen Spectrum

In the visible part of the emission spectrum of hydrogen gas, there is a series of variously spaced bright lines called the *Balmer series* in honor of J. Balmer, who in 1885 devised an empirical formula relating their wavelengths. Calculations based on the Bohr atom model were also able to give the correct frequencies of these lines, which confirmed Bohr's theory, and in addition predicted the existence of other series of lines in the infrared and ultraviolet regions. Within a short time the predicted frequencies were discovered, further confirming Bohr's theory. The Balmer series was shown to be due to photons emitted by the transitions of electrons from higher energy states to the $n = 2$ level, which is one level above the ground state, as shown in Figure 32. The other predicted lines are produced when the excited atoms return to either the ground state, producing the Lyman series in the ultraviolet, or to the third, fourth, or fifth energy levels, producing three series of infrared lines.

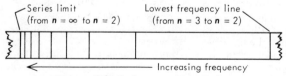

Figure 32. Balmer series of the
hydrogen spectrum.

5. WAVE-MECHANICAL MODEL OF THE ATOM

Despite its success in predicting the spectrum of hydrogen and of certain other elements, the theory failed to predict the spectra of all elements. In 1924, Louis de Broglie of France introduced a concept that led to the modern *wave-mechanical* model of the atom, a model that not only accounts for all atomic spectra, but also accounts for other phenomena that involve electrons, such as chemical bonding.

Matter Waves

De Broglie reasoned that, since the mathematics of particle motion could be applied to light, the mathematics of wave motion might usefully be applied to particles. He proposed that electrons in motion have wave properties, and that their "wavelength" in atoms depends on the length of their orbits. The length (circumference) of a circular orbit of radius r is $2\pi r$. By rearranging terms in equation 79, the formula for the circumference becomes

$$2\pi r = n \left(\frac{h}{mv}\right) \qquad (81)$$

De Broglie assumed that electrons could only occupy orbits whose length was a whole-number multiple of the electron "wavelength", because, in other orbits, destructive interference would occur. Thus the circumference must equal a whole number, n, times the electron wavelength λ :

$$2\pi r = n\lambda \qquad (82)$$

Substituting this term in equation 81 shows that the electron wavelength is inversely proportional to its momentum, mv:

$$\lambda = \frac{h}{mv} \qquad (83)$$

The predicted wave properties of electrons were demonstrated in 1927 by Davisson and Germer, who produced interference patterns with beams of electrons. The measured wavelengths agreed with de Broglie's predictions. Since then, the wave properties of other subatomic particles (protons, neutrons, etc.) have also been observed.

Note that, because the numerator in equation 83 is on the order of 10^{-34}, the wavelengths associated with relatively massive objects are too small to be observed. For particles of atomic size, however, such wave phenomena as diffraction and interference can be observed. This concept of the *matter wave* is the counterpart of the concept of the particle of radiation.

The Wave-Mechanical Atom—Optional Topic

In 1926, E. Schroedinger, an Austrian physicist, presented a strict mathematical interpretation of de Broglie's wave concept. Schroedinger's wave equations provide a model of the atom in which the electron waves occupy the entire space within the atom, and have shapes that depend on the kinetic energy of the electron. In this wave-mechanical model, as in the Bohr quantum-orbit model, the electron energy is quantized because the electrons can occupy only those energy states in which destructive interference of the wave patterns does not occur. Note that electrons themselves are not described by the wave equations. Instead, the equations give the *probability* of finding an electron of given energy within a given region of space inside the atom. These probability distributions are often represented pictorially as clouds of various shapes and densities surrounding the atomic nucleus.

The wave-mechanical model is mathematically complex, but it correctly predicts the spectra of all elements and is the model of the atom in current use. The Rutherford-Bohr model, however, can still be usefully applied to simple computations involving the energy levels and spectrum of the hydrogen atom.

QUESTIONS

1. The probability of a head-on collision between an alpha particle and a nucleus is (1) extremely small (2) very high (3) about 50% (4) zero

2. If a hydrogen atom changes from an energy level of $n = 4$ to the ground state in two steps, it can emit a photon whose energy is (1) 2.55 ev (2) 10.0 ev (3) 12.75 ev (4) 13.6 ev

3. The fact that most of the alpha particles directed at a thin metal foil pass through without being deflected indicates that the atom consists mostly of (1) electrons (2) neutrons (3) empty space (4) protons

4. If a hydrogen atom is in the $n = 5$ energy level, what is the minimum energy needed to ionize the atom? (1) 0.54 ev (2) 13.1 ev (3) 13.6 ev (4) 14.1 ev

5. What is the energy emitted by a hydrogen atom when the atom changes directly from the $n = 5$ state to the $n = 2$ state? (1) 13.6 ev (2) 3.4 ev (3) 2.86 ev (4) 0.54 ev

6. An element will emit its characteristic spectrum as its (1) atoms become ionized (2) nuclei are broken into protons and neutrons (3) atoms in high energy levels go to lower energy levels (4) atoms in low energy levels go to higher energy levels

7. The ionization potential of the hydrogen atom is (1) 10.2 ev (2) 12.1 ev (3) 13.1 ev (4) 13.6 ev

8. Rutherford based his model of the atom on evidence obtained from (1) the photoelectric effect (2) black body radiation (3) alpha particle scattering (4) absorption and emission spectra

9. Which property of a particle has the greatest influence on its wave nature? (1) mass (2) shape (3) volume (4) specific heat

10. As the momentum of a particle exhibiting wave properties increases, the wavelength of the particle (1) decreases (2) increases (3) remains the same

11-13. Base your answers to Questions 11 through 13 on the diagram, which represents three visible lines in the hydrogen spectrum. Either the energy or the frequency for each of these lines is given below the diagram.

11. What is the energy of the photons that produced line *B*? (1) 3.23 × 10^{-19} joule (2) 4.07 × 10^{-19} joule (3) 9.28 × 10^{-19} joule (4) 9.85 × 10^{-19} joule

12. Which energy level transition produced line *A*? (1) $n = 2$ to $n = 1$ (2) $n = 3$ to $n = 2$ (3) $n = 4$ to $n = 3$ (4) $n = 5$ to $n = 2$

13. If the diagram represented an absorption (dark line) spectrum, which energy level transition would have produced line *A*? (1) $n = 2$ to $n = 3$ (2) $n = 2$ to $n = 2$ (3) $n = 3$ to $n = 2$ (4) $n = 4$ to $n = 2$

14-18. Base your answers to Questions 14 through 18 on the information below and the Physics Reference Tables.

A photon with 14.6 ev of energy collides with a hydrogen atom in its ground state.

14. What is the energy of the incident photon? (1) 1.5 × 10^{-18} joule (2) 2.3 × 10^{-18} joule (3) 6.3 × 10^{-18} joule (4) 9.1 × 10^{-18} joule

15. What is the maximum potential energy that the hydrogen atom can gain in the collision without ionizing? (1) 0 ev (2) 1.0 ev (3) 13.6 ev (4) 14.6 ev

16. What will be the energy of the photon emitted by a hydrogen atom as the hydrogen atom moves from $n = 3$ to $n = 2$? (1) 1.0 ev (2) 1.5 ev (3) 1.9 ev (4) 12.1 ev

17. How many electron-volts of energy would be required to ionize a hydrogen atom in the $n = 3$ state? (1) 1.5 (2) 1.02 (3) 1.21 (4) 1.36

18. Which transition results in the emission of a photon with the highest frequency? (1) $n = 5$ to $n = 4$ (2) $n = 5$ to $n = 3$ (3) $n = 3$ to $n = 2$ (4) $n = 2$ to $n = 1$

19. How much energy is required to ionize a hydrogen atom in the ground state? (1) 0.03 ev (2) 1.5 ev (3) 3.4 ev (4) 13.6 ev

20. Of the following, the most energetic photon in the Balmer series is emitted when the hydrogen atom changes energy directly from (1) $n = 5$ to $n = 2$ (2) $n = 4$ to $n = 2$ (3) $n = 2$ to $n = 4$ (4) $n = 2$ to $n = 5$

21. Which diagram best represents the path of a positively charged particle as it passes near the nucleus of an atom?

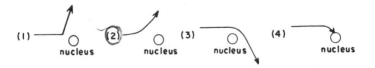

22. When a hydrogen atom changes from one energy level (E_1) to a lower energy level (E_2), the expression for the frequency of the emitted photon is

(1) $\dfrac{\lambda}{E}$ (2) $\dfrac{h}{E_1 - E_2}$ (3) $\dfrac{E_1 - E_2}{h}$ (4) $(E_1 - E_2)\dfrac{\lambda}{2}$

23. Alpha particle scattering may best be explained if one assumes that the interacting force is (1) nuclear (2) electrostatic (3) magnetic (4) gravitational

24. When alpha particles are directed against a thin metal foil, their deflection paths are (1) circular (2) elliptical (3) parabolic (4) hyperbolic

25. Which energy level transition in a hydrogen atom will emit a photon of the highest frequency? (1) $n = 2$ to $n = 1$ (2) $n = 3$ to $n = 2$ (3) $n = 3$ to $n = 1$ (4) $n = 4$ to $n = 2$

26. A hydrogen atom can be raised from the $n = 2$ state to the $n = 3$ state by a photon with an energy of (1) 1.9 ev (2) 10.2 ev (3) 12.1 ev (4) 22.3 ev

27. When an atom moves from a higher energy state to a lower energy state, it emits (1) electrons (2) protons (3) neutrons (4) photons

28. A hydrogen atom in the ground state can be ionized by a photon with an energy of (1) 1.9 ev (2) 3.4 ev (3) 10.2 ev (4) 13.6 ev

29. In the Rutherford experiment, a beam of alpha particles was directed at thin gold foil. The deflection pattern of the alpha particles showed that (1) the electrons of gold atoms have waves (2) the nuclear volume is a small part of the atomic volume (3) the energy levels of a gold atom are quantized (4) gold atoms can emit photons under bombardment

30. As an atom goes from the ground state to an excited state, its energy (1) decreases (2) increases (3) remains the same

31. In the Bohr model, as an electron in an atom moves in a circular path of constant radius around the nucleus, the total energy of the atom (1) decreases (2) increases (3) remains the same

32-36. Base your answers to Questions 32 through 36 on the Physics Reference Tables and the following information.

A hydrogen atom changes energy levels from $n = 1$ to $n = 2$.

32. This energy level change will occur if the atom (1) emits a 3.4-ev photon (2) emits a 10.2-ev photon (3) absorbs a 10.2-ev photon (4) absorbs a 3.4-ev photon

33. As a result of this transition, there is an increase in the (1) electric charge on the atom (2) electric force on the electron (3) speed of the electron along the path (4) total energy of the atom

34. The minimum energy required to ionize a hydrogen atom from the ground state is (1) 3.4 ev (2) 10.2 ev (3) 5.8 ev (4) 13.6 ev

35. The photon of greatest frequency would be emitted as a result of a transition from energy level (1) $n = 5$ to $n = 3$ (2) $n = 4$ to $n = 3$ (3) $n = 3$ to $n = 2$ (4) $n = 2$ to $n = 1$

36. The lines in the Balmer series are produced by transitions from higher energy levels to (1) $n = 1$ (2) $n = 2$ (3) $n = 3$ (4) $n = 4$

37-41. Base your answers to Questions 37 through 41 on the Physics Reference Tables and your knowledge of physics.

37. What is the minimum energy needed to ionize a hydrogen atom in the $n = 2$ state? (1) 1.9 ev (2) 3.4 ev (3) 10.2 ev (4) 13.6 ev

38. What is the minimum energy a photon must possess in order to excite a hydrogen atom in the ground state? (1) 13.05 ev (2) 12.08 ev (3) 10.20 ev (4) 3.40 ev

39. How many different energy photons could be emitted by hydrogen atoms as they drop from energy level $n = 4$ to energy level $n = 1$? (1) 1 (2) 6 (3) 3 (4) 7

40. As the frequency of a photon increases, its energy (1) decreases (2) increases (3) remains the same

41. As a hydrogen atom changes from energy level $n = 1$ to energy level $n = 3$, its total energy (1) decreases (2) increases (3) remains the same

42-46. Base your answers to Questions 42 through 46 on the diagram, which shows the path of a beam of alpha particles directed at a thin metal foil B. Screen $CDEF$ is used to detect the alpha particles that pass through the foil

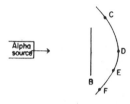

42. Most of the alpha particles that pass through the foil would be detected on the screen in the region of (1) E (2) F (3) C (4) D

43. Which is the maximum angle through which an alpha particle may be deflected? (1) 30° (2) 60° (3) 90° (4) 180°

44. Observed changes in the path of an alpha particle as it approaches a nucleus in the foil can be best explained in terms of (1) the Doppler effect (2) Ohm's law (3) Coulomb's law (4) the Bohr theory

45. If the energies of all the alpha particles in the beam are the same, the number of particles detected between C and D on the screen will be directly proportional to the (1) charge on an alpha particle (2) square of the charge on an alpha particle (3) charge on a foil nucleus (4) square of the charge on a foil nucleus

46. What kind of path have the alpha particles detected in the region of C followed? (1) linear (2) helical (3) hyperbolic (4) elliptical

47-51. Base your answers to Questions 47 through 51 on the following information.

The Balmer series of the hydrogen bright-line spectrum includes the following lines: (Refer to Table of Energy Levels for Hydrogen in the Physics Reference Tables.)

H_a—which results from an energy level change from $n = 3$ to $n = 2$
H_b—which results from an energy level change from $n = 4$ to $n = 2$
H_c—which results from an energy level change from $n = 5$ to $n = 2$

47. The H_a photon has an energy of (1) 12.08 ev (2) 10.2 ev (3) 2.55 ev (4) 1.88 ev

48. The H_b photon has an energy of (1) 1.6×10^{-19} joule (2) 2.55×10^{-19} joule (3) 4.1×10^{-19} joule (4) 4.6×10^{-19} joule

49. The H_a photon has an energy of 3.0×10^{-19} joule. The frequency of this photon is (1) 3.5×10^{14} Hz (2) 4.6×10^{14} Hz (3) 6.2×10^{14} Hz (4) 6.9×10^{14} Hz

50. The H$_c$ photon has an energy of 4.6×10^{-19} joule. What is the color of the H$_c$ line? (1) violet (2) blue (3) green (4) red

51. All the lines of the Lyman series result from changes to the energy level $n = 1$. In which part of the spectrum do these lines belong? (1) radio (2) ultraviolet (3) visible (4) infrared

52. Rutherford's experiment with the scattering of alpha particles by a metal foil led him to believe that the positive charge in an atom is (1) concentrated at its center (2) spread uniformly throughout its volume (3) in the form of positive electrons at some distance from its center (4) readily deflected by an incident alpha particle

53. According to the Bohr model of the hydrogen atom, an electron can revolve around a hydrogen nucleus indefinitely if its orbit (1) is a perfect circle (2) is sufficiently far from the nucleus (3) is less than its De Broglie wavelength in circumference (4) has a radius that makes the electron angular momentum a whole number multiple of $nh/2\pi$.

54. As an atom absorbs a photon of energy, one of its electrons will (1) exchange energy levels with another of its electrons (2) undergo a transition to a higher energy level (3) undergo a transition to a lower energy level (4) decrease its angular momentum

55. The Bohr model of the hydrogen atom contradicts classical physics by assuming that (1) a body can be in orbit without an unbalanced force acting upon it (2) an electron can be accelerated without radiating energy (3) the electron is in orbit around the nucleus (4) the total energy of the electron can change

56. Which graph best represents the change of photon momentum (p) with wavelength λ ?

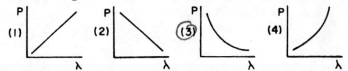

57. The wave characteristics of a batted ball cannot be observed because (1) its matter waves are too long (2) its speed is too small (3) its mass is too large (4) the ball is matter rather than energy

6. THE ATOMIC NUCLEUS

Observational Tools

Since subatomic particles are much too small to be directly visible, evidence for their presence must come from indirect observations. The presence of such particles is detected primarily by their electric charge or by the charges on atoms ionized by interaction with the particles. The simplest means of detecting charge is with an *electroscope*. If a known charge is placed on an electroscope, the rise or fall of its vanes indicates the presence and sign (+ or −) of charged particles.

In a *Geiger counter,* the passage of charged particles or high-energy photons produces ions in a small sample of gas, permitting a flow of current that indicates their presence. In the *scintillation counter,* atoms energized by the passage of a charged particle release the energy as a small flash of visible light. Such particles also leave tracks on a *photographic plate,* which are revealed when it is developed. By careful measurement of the length, thickness, and curvature of these tracks in magnetic or electric fields, the particles that made them can be identified. Other instruments that reveal the tracks made by particles are the *cloud chamber,* which makes particle tracks visible as a trail of droplets condensed from supercooled vapor, and the *bubble chamber,* in which particle tracks are made visible as a trail of bubbles in liquid hydrogen at its boiling point. In recent years this device has aided in the detection of many new particles. With the aid of these instruments, the modern physicist can observe clearly the interaction of fundamental particles.

Accelerators

The need to study interactions of subatomic particles under controlled conditions has led to the construction of devices called *accelerators.* These devices use electric and magnetic fields to accelerate electrons, protons, or other particles to high speeds at which they have enormous kinetic energies (on the order of 10^{11} ev). Such energetic particles are used to penetrate and smash atomic nuclei, so that the fragments can be studied. These fragments often consist of unusual high-energy, short-lived particles that do not normally exist. Studies of their modes of decay have greatly increased understanding of the fundamental nature of matter.

The *Van de Graaff generator,* the earliest type of particle accelerator, builds up very high potential differences between two points. Charged particles injected into the electric field are then accelerated to velocities proportional to the field intensity. However, because the effectiveness of this device is limited, more efficient methods of accelerating particles have been developed. In the *cyclotron,* and its later version the *synchrotron,* charged particles travel in circular orbits in a magnetic field and are accelerated by brief, intense pulses of an electric field. After many orbits and accelerating pulses, the particles have achieved the required high velocity and kinetic energy and are released as projectiles. The synchrotron is more efficient than the cyclotron because it times the accelerating pulses to match the increase in relativistic mass of the particles as they speed up, and thus is able to give them still greater energies. There is also a group of devices called *linear accelerators,* which give the particles a series of energizing pulses as they move in a straight path.

Nucleons

Scientists at first assumed that the nucleus contained both electrons and protons. According to modern theory, however, only protons and neutrons are present in the nucleus. The neutron was discovered in

1932 by J. Chadwick in England. The particles in the nucleus are called *nucleons*. The total number of nucleons in the nucleus is called the mass number *(A)*. The number of protons in the nucleus is called the *atomic number (Z)*.

Nuclear Force

The force binding the nucleons together within the nucleus is the strongest force known, but it is effective only at extremely short distances, less than 10^{-15} m. The short range of the nuclear binding force is in contrast to gravitational and electrical forces, which can act across astronomical distances.

Nuclear Mass and Binding Energy

The individual masses of protons and neutrons have been measured with high accuracy. The masses of many atomic nuclei are also known to the same degree of accuracy. It has been discovered, however, that the mass of a nucleus is always less than the sum of the masses of its component nucleons. This difference between calculated and actual mass of a nucleus is called the *mass defect*. Measurements also show that the energy released in the formation of nuclei from separate nucleons is equivalent to the missing mass, in accord with the mass-energy equivalence formula Einstein derived in his theory of relativity:

$$E = mc^2 \qquad (84)$$

where E is the energy in joules, m is the mass in kilograms, and c is the velocity of light, 3.0×10^8 m/sec. Energy equivalent to the binding energy must be supplied to the nucleus in order to separate it into individual protons and neutrons.

Isotopes

The chemical properties of different atoms depend only on the atomic number, the number of protons in the nucleus. Atoms of the same atomic number belong to the same element, but if they differ in the number of neutrons in the nucleus they differ in mass, and are called *isotopes*. Since isotopes of an element have the same atomic number, they have the same chemical properties. For example, the element oxygen, atomic number 8, has three common isotopes, oxygen-16, -17 and -18, having 8, 9, and 10 neutrons respectively. Each isotope will combine with hydrogen to form water, but the mass of each water molecule will be different.

7. NUCLEAR REACTIONS—OPTIONAL TOPIC

Natural Radioactivity

A nucleus that changes spontaneously, without any external influence, to a nucleus of different atomic number or mass number, or both, is said to be *naturally radioactive*. This process of radioactive decay is accompanied by the emission of one or more particles and extremely high-energy photons. Such decay processes can neither be speeded up nor slowed down by heat or chemical action. All of the isotopes of the elements above the atomic number 83 are radioactive, but every element has at least one radioactive isotope. Even hydrogen, for example, has the isotope hydrogen-3, called *tritium*, which is naturally radioactive.

Mass and Charge Conservation in Nuclear Changes. In all nuclear reactions, the sum of the *mass numbers* of the particles entering the reaction is equal to the sum of the mass numbers of the product particles. The same is true of the *charges* of the reactant and product particles: the sum of the charges of all particles entering the reaction must equal the sum of charges of the products. The descriptions of radioactive decay given in the following sections will provide examples of these rules.

Nuclear Equation Symbols. In writing equations for nuclear reactions, abbreviated forms are used. The chemical symbol of an element is used in place of its name, and its mass and charge are given as superscript and subscript, respectively. The general form for the symbol of a nucleus is $_Z^A\text{Sy}$ where Sy is the symbol of the element, A is the mass number, and Z is the atomic number. For example, the isotope hydrogen-3 is shown as $_1^3\text{H}$. The electron is $_{-1}^0e$ (because its mass number is counted as 0), the neutron is $_0^1n$, and the proton, which is in fact a hydrogen-1 nucleus, is $_1^1\text{H}$.

Alpha Decay. As mentioned previously, the decay of radium is accompanied by the emission of alpha particles. Further study revealed that the alpha particle is a helium-4 nucleus, which consists of 2 protons and 2 neutrons. Loss of such a particle therefore reduces the mass number of a nucleus by 4 and its atomic number by 2. In the case of alpha decay of radium, $_{88}^{226}\text{Ra}$, the reaction is written

$$\text{radium-226} \rightarrow \text{radon-222} + \text{alpha particle}$$
$$_{88}^{226}\text{Ra} \rightarrow {}_{86}^{222}\text{Rn} + {}_2^4\text{He}$$

Note that the total mass number on the left of the equation, 226, is equal to the sum of mass numbers on the right, $222 + 4$, and that, for the charge, $88 = 86 + 2$.

Beta Decay. The emission of a beta particle from a radioactive nucleus is called *beta decay*. Loss of a beta particle, which is actually an electron, results in no change of mass number, but increases the atomic number of the product nucleus by 1. For example, when the isotope lead-210, atomic number 82, emits a beta particle (electron), it becomes bismuth-210, atomic number 83. The equation for this reaction is

$$_{82}^{210}\text{Pb} \rightarrow {}_{83}^{210}\text{Bi} + {}_{-1}^0e$$

Again, note the conservation of charge and mass number in this reaction.

Gamma Radiation. The high-energy, high-frequency electromagnetic radiations emitted as a result of radioactivity are called *gamma rays*.

These are high-energy photons produced by a decrease in the internal energy of the nucleus itself. Loss of energy in the form of photons, which have no mass and no charge, results in no change of either mass number or atomic number. In this reaction, the nucleus resembles an excited atom emitting a photon as it drops from a higher to a lower energy level.

Half-Life

The time required for the decay of one half of the number of nuclei of a radioactive isotope is called the half-life of the isotope. For example, if the initial mass of a sample of $^{32}_{15}P$ (phosphorus-32) is 6 grams, after 14 days tests will show only half of the sample, 3 grams, is still phosphorus-32. The remainder consists of decay products of the original isotope. This period of 14 days is the half-life of this particular radioactive isotope of phosphorus. After another 14 days, half of the 3 grams, or 1.5 grams, of phosphorus-32 will remain. That is, after two half-life periods only $\frac{1}{4}$ of the mass of the original substance remains, $\frac{3}{4}$ having decayed. The formula for calculating the mass of material, m_f, that remains of the original mass, m_i, after a number, n, of half-life periods is

$$m_f = \frac{m_i}{2^n} \qquad (85)$$

Each isotope has a specific half-life, but the range of half-lives is enormous, from 10^{-22} sec to 10^{17} years. For example, Potassium-40, which is found in nature, has a half life of 10^9 years.

Atomic Mass Unit

The masses of single atoms are so small that to express them in terms of the kilogram is inconvenient. Physicists therefore use a unit called the *atomic mass unit* (amu) to express these minute magnitudes. One amu is defined as a mass equal to exactly 1/12 of the mass of the carbon-12 atom. Accordingly, the amu is equal to 1.66×10^{-27} kg. Using equation 84 for the equivalence of mass and energy, it is possible to express mass in terms of energy units. In equation 84, if $m = 1$ amu $= 1.66 \times 10^{-27}$ kg, and $c^2 = (3.0 \times 10^8 \text{ m/sec})^2$, the energy equivalent of 1 amu is 1.5×10^{-10} joules. In terms of electron-volts, 1 amu is equal to

$$1.5 \times 10^{-10} \text{ joules} \times \frac{1 \text{ ev}}{1.6 \times 10^{-19} \text{ joule}} = 9.3 \times 10^6 \text{ ev}$$

The energy equivalent of the mass of 1 amu is therefore 930 million electron volts (more exactly, 931 Mev).

Induced Transmutation

Since the beginning of science, men have attempted to change one element into another, a process named *transmutation*. This attempt had been given up as impossible until the discovery of radioactivity indicated that such changes are constantly occurring in nature. The first man-made transmutation of one element into another was accomplished by Rutherford when he bombarded $^{14}_{7}\text{N}$ with alpha particles. He produced nuclei of $^{17}_{8}\text{O}$ and protons. Rutherford had converted nitrogen into oxygen and hydrogen. The equation for the reaction is

$$^{14}_{7}\text{N} + ^{4}_{2}\text{He} \rightarrow ^{17}_{8}\text{O} + ^{1}_{1}\text{H}$$

Today many other such changes can be produced by bombarding nuclei with particles in the various accelerators.

The new isotopes produced by artificial transmutation are often radioactive themselves. The first artificially radioactive material was produced in 1934 by Irene Joliot-Curie in France. She bombarded $^{27}_{13}\text{Al}$ with alpha particles, producing phosphorus-30 and a neutron:

$$^{27}_{13}\text{Al} + ^{4}_{2}\text{He} \rightarrow ^{30}_{15}\text{P} + ^{1}_{0}n$$

Phosphorus-30 was found to be radioactive, decaying to $^{30}_{14}\text{Si}$ with the emission of a positive electron $(^{0}_{+1}e)$, which has been named the *positron*. The existence of such a particle (the anti-particle of the electron) had been predicted by theory only a few years previously and had been discovered by C. Anderson shortly before the Joliot-Curie experiment.

Beta-Positive Decay. The emission of either an electron or a positron is called beta decay. The loss of a positron, however, *decreases* the atomic number of the nucleus by 1 unit, whereas the loss of an electron *increases* it by 1. For example, the beta decay of copper-64 produces nickel-64 and a positron:

$$^{64}_{29}\text{Cu} \rightarrow ^{64}_{28}\text{Ni} + ^{0}_{+1}e$$

whereas the beta decay of sodium-24 produces magnesium-24 and an electron,

$$^{24}_{11}\text{Na} \rightarrow ^{24}_{12}\text{Mg} + ^{0}_{-1}e$$

Beta Decay of the Neutron. The neutron must be included among the radioactive particles because, although it is stable inside the nucleus, it has a half-life of about 15 minutes outside the nucleus. It decays according to the equation $^{1}_{0}n \rightarrow ^{1}_{1}\text{H} + ^{0}_{-1}e$. In effect, its decay produces the components of a hydrogen atom.

Because they have no charge, neutrons are not repelled by the nucleus, and therefore relatively little energy is needed to enable them to enter nuclear reactions. This makes them useful in nuclear experiments.

Nuclear Fission

Some massive radioactive nuclei undergo an additional type of radioactive decay in which they break into roughly equal fragments, called daughter nuclei, after absorption of an additional neutron. This process is called *fission*. The tremendous release of energy in the fission of $^{235}_{92}\text{U}$ led to its use in the atomic bomb during World War II, and later in atomic power reactors for peacetime use.

Thermal Neutrons. The fission of $^{235}_{92}U$ is initiated by the capture of relatively slow-moving or *thermal* neutrons. These move at about the speed of air molecules at ordinary temperatures. Since the neutrons produced in the fission process have a high speed, they must be slowed down in order to be useful in such applications as power reactors.

Moderators. All modern reactors using uranium and certain other elements make use of *moderators,* which are substances of low nuclear mass with which neutrons do not combine. Collisions with these nuclei slow down fast-moving neutrons. Moderator materials include such substances as carbon, water, and boron. A typical fission reaction initiated by such a slow neutron is expressed as

$$^{235}_{92}U + ^{1}_{0}n \rightarrow ^{140}X + ^{94}Y + 2\left(^{1}_{0}n\right) + \text{energy}$$

The nuclei X and Y are shown with average masses of daughter nuclei.

Fusion

The production of more massive nuclei from the combination of lighter ones is called *fusion*. This process goes on continually in the sun and is the source of its energy. On earth, the process has been duplicated in the form of a bomb, but attempts to produce energy by controlled fusion have thus far had only limited success. A typical fusion reaction that is believed to occur in the sun is the fusion of two isotopes of hydrogen to produce helium:

$$^{3}_{1}H + ^{1}_{1}H \rightarrow ^{4}_{2}He + \text{energy}$$

QUESTIONS

1. A neutral atom has 24 neutrons and 20 protons. The number of electrons in the atom is (1) 24 (2) 20 (3) 44 (4) 4
2. Which nucleus has the largest number of neutrons? (1) $^{3}_{1}A$ (2) $^{5}_{2}B$ (3) $^{7}_{3}C$ (4) $^{8}_{5}D$
3. Which could not be accelerated by a synchroton? (1) a proton (2) an electron (3) a neutron (4) an alpha particle
4. Which device is used normally to accelerate charged particles? (1) synchrotron (2) electroscope (3) cloud chamber (4) Geiger counter
5. The atoms of a certain element contain 12 protons and 13 neutrons. An atom of an isotope of this element must contain (1) 12 neutrons (2) 13 neutrons (3) 12 protons (4) 13 electrons
6. If all of the following particles were travelling at the same velocity, which would have the greatest energy? (1) alpha particle (2) beta particle (3) neutron (4) proton
7. Which device can be used to detect nuclear radiation? (1) synchroton (2) photographic plate (3) linear accelerator (4) Van de Graaff generator

8. The rest mass of a proton is approximately the same as the rest mass of (1) an electron (2) a neutron (3) an alpha particle (4) a deuteron

9. Nuclei of isotopes of the same element contain different numbers of (1) electrons (2) neutrons (3) protons (4) positrons

10. A tritium nucleus contains 1 proton and 2 neutrons. What is the mass number of the nucleus? (1) 1 (2) 2 (3) 3 (4) 0

11. Electromagnetic radiation may be produced by (1) an accelerating electron (2) an accelerating neutron (3) an electron moving at constant velocity (4) a neutron moving at constant velocity

12. Isotopes of the same element have the same number of (1) neutrons (2) neutrons and electrons, only (3) protons and electrons, only (4) electrons, protons, and neutrons

13. What is the relationship between the atomic number Z, the mass number A, and the number of neutrons N in a nucleus? (1) $A = Z + N$ (2) $A = Z - N$ (3) $A = N/Z$ (4) $A = NZ$

14. One amu is equal to (1) $\frac{1}{931}$Mev (2) $931/c^2$ Mev (3) 931 Mev (4) $931c^2$ Mev

15. If the half-life of $^{234}_{90}$Th is 24 days, the amount of a 12-g sample remaining after 96 days is (1) 1 g (2) 0.75 g (3) 6 g (4) 1.5 g

16. Given the equation $^{27}_{13}$Al $+ \, ^4_2$He $\rightarrow \, ^{30}_{15}$P $+$ X. The correct symbol for X is (1) $^0_{+1}e$ (2) $^0_{-1}e$ (3) $^4_2$He (3) ^1_0n

17. When lead $^{214}_{82}$Pb emits a beta particle, the resultant nucleus will be (1) $^{214}_{81}$Tl (2) $^{213}_{82}$Pb (3) $^{214}_{83}$Bi (4) $^{214}_{84}$Po

18. A particle accelerator can accelerate a (1) neutron (2) gamma photon (3) proton (4) hydrogen atom

19. For a given applied voltage, which particle will have the greatest acceleration? (1) an electron (2) a proton (3) a neutron (4) an alpha particle

20. It is difficult for a proton to approach the nucleus of an atom because of the (1) gravitational field (2) electrostatic field (3) magnetic field (4) nuclear force

21. In the equation $^{239}_{92}$U $\rightarrow \, ^{239}_{93}$Np $+$ X, particle X is (1) a proton (2) a neutron (3) an alpha particle (4) a beta particle

22. If each particle below were moving with the same speed, which particle could transfer the greatest amount of energy when colliding with a stationary helium nucleus? (1) an electron (2) a proton (3) a neutron (4) an alpha particle

23. In the equation $E = mc^2$, E may be expressed in (1) watts (2) coulombs (3) electron-volts (4) joules per second

24. When uranium, $^{238}_{92}$U, emits an alpha particle, the resulting nucleus will be (1) $^{230}_{90}$Th (2) $^{234}_{90}$Th (3) $^{234}_{91}$Pa (4) $^{234}_{92}$U

25. A platinum atom consists of 78 protons, 78 electrons, and 116 neutrons. Its mass number is (1) 78 (2) 116 (3) 194 (4) 272

26. The isotopes $^{235}_{92}$U and $^{238}_{92}$U both have the same (1) atomic mass (2) atomic number (3) binding energy (4) number of neutrons

27. As the mass of the isotopes of an element increases, the number of protons in their nuclei (1) decreases (2) increases (3) remains the same

28. As the mass number of nucleons in an atom increases, the mass number of the atom (1) decreases (2) increases (3) remains the same

29. As the number of neutrons in the nucleus of an atom increases, the atomic number of the atom (1) decreases (2) increases (3) remains the same

30. As the original mass of a radioactive substance decreases, its half-life (1) decreases (2) increases (3) remains the same

31. When a gamma ray is emitted by a nucleus, the atomic number of the nucleus (1) decreases (2) increases (3) remains the same

32-36. Base your answers to Questions 32 through 36 on the following information.

A sample of pure radon gas ($^{222}_{86}$Rn) is sealed in a glass ampule. The half life of radon is 4 days.

32. Which is an isotope of radon? (1) $^{222}_{88}$X (2) $^{220}_{84}$X (3) $^{220}_{86}$X (4) $^{222}_{89}$X

33. If the pressure inside the glass ampule were doubled, the half life of radon would (1) be halved (2) remain the same (3) be doubled (4) be quadrupled

34. Twelve days after the radon gas is sealed in the glass ampule, the fraction of radon gas remaining will be (1) ½ (2) ¼ (3) ⅛ (4) 1/16

35. The number of neutrons in the nucleus of $^{222}_{86}$Rn is (1) 86 (2) 136 (3) 222 (4) 308

36. Several days later, an analysis shows that there is a second gas in the sealed ampule. This second gas is most likely (1) hydrogen (2) helium (3) oxygen (4) nitrogen

37-41. Base your answers to Questions 37 through 41 on the Uranium Disintegration Series in the Physics Reference Tables.

37. An example of alpha decay is the change of
(1) $^{238}_{92}$U into $^{234}_{90}$Th   (3) $^{234}_{91}$Pa into $^{234}_{92}$U
(2) $^{234}_{90}$Th into $^{234}_{91}$Pa   (4) $^{214}_{82}$Pb into $^{214}_{83}$Bi

38. Which isotope below is not formed during the decay of $^{238}_{92}$U?
(1) $^{234}_{90}$Th (2) $^{230}_{90}$Th (3) $^{226}_{84}$Po (4) $^{218}_{84}$Po

39. Which will be emitted when $^{210}_{83}$Bi changes to $^{206}_{82}$Pb? (1) 1 alpha particle, only (2) 1 beta particle, only (3) 2 alpha particles, only (4) 1 alpha particle and 1 beta particle

40. Which stable isotope is formed when $^{238}_{92}$U decays?
(1) $^{214}_{83}$Bi (2) $^{214}_{84}$Po (3) $^{214}_{82}$Pb (4) $^{206}_{82}$Pb

41. What is the total number of alpha particles emitted as an atom of $^{238}_{92}$U decays to $^{206}_{82}$Pb? (1) 6 (2) 7 (3) 8 (4) 13

42-46. Base your answers to Questions 42 through 46 on the following information, the Physics Reference Tables, and your knowledge of physics.

When aluminum is bombarded with alpha particles, the following reaction occurs:

$$^{27}_{13}\text{Al} + ^{4}_{2}\text{He} \rightarrow ^{30}_{15}\text{P} + X$$

42. The atomic number of particle X is (1) 1 (2) 11 (3) 23 (4) 0
43. The mass number of particle X is (1) 1 (2) 0 (3) 11 (4) 23
44. The number of electrons in a neutral atom of $^{27}_{13}\text{Al}$ is (1) 0 (2) 13 (3) 14 (4) 27
45. The number of neutrons in $^{27}_{13}\text{Al}$ is (1) 13 (2) 14 (3) 27 (4) 40
46. The energy of a gamma-ray photon is 9.16×10^{-14} joule. The frequency of this photon is (1) 8.2×10^{15} Hz (2) 7.2×10^{19} Hz (3) 1.4×10^{20} Hz (4) 2.5×10^{23} Hz
47. The uranium atom $^{238}_{92}\text{U}$ decays at $^{234}_{90}\text{Th}$ by emitting (1) an alpha particle (2) a beta particle (3) a neutron (4) a proton
48. The radium (Ra) isotope in this series has (1) an atomic number of 88 and is a beta emitter (2) an atomic number of 88 and is a neutron emitter (3) a mass number of 226 and is an alpha emitter (4) an atomic number of 226 and a mass number of 88
49. All isotopes of polonium in this series are (1) alpha emitters (2) negative beta emitters (3) alpha and positive beta emitters (4) alpha and negative beta emitters
50. When radon (Rn) decays, it loses (1) 1 unit of charge only (2) 1 unit of mass only (3) 2 units of mass and 2 units of charge (4) 4 units of mass and 2 units of charge
51. Which equation represents a step in this series?
    (1) $^{231}_{90}\text{Th} \rightarrow ^{0}_{-1}e + ^{231}_{91}\text{Pa}$
    (2) $^{232}_{90}\text{Th} \rightarrow ^{228}_{88}\text{Ra} + ^{4}_{2}\text{He}$
    (3) $^{218}_{84}\text{Po} \rightarrow ^{214}_{82}\text{Pb} + ^{4}_{2}\text{He}$
    (4) $^{220}_{86}\text{Rn} \rightarrow ^{4}_{2}\text{He} + ^{216}_{84}\text{Po}$
52. During the process of radioactive decay, which of the following occurs? (1) Mass only is conserved. (2) Energy only is conserved. (3) Charge only is conserved. (4) Mass, energy, and charge are conserved.
53. The number of neutrons in the nucleus $^{17}_{8}\text{O}$ is (1) 8 (2) 9 (3) 17 (4) 25
54. One atomic mass unit is defined as (1) the mass of an electron (2) the mass of a proton (3) the mass of an atom of $^{12}_{6}\text{C}$ (4) 1/12 the mass of an atom of $^{12}_{6}\text{C}$
55. When a nucleus in an excited state changes to a more stable state, the nucleus normally emits (1) visible light (2) infrared waves (3) gamma radiation (4) long radio waves
56. Silver-108 has a half life of 2.4 minutes. If the initial mass is M, the mass remaining after 7.2 minutes is (1) $M/2$ (2) $M/4$ (3) $M/6$ (4) $M/8$
57. Materials for slowing neutrons commonly contain (1) lead (2) graphite (3) silver (4) tungsten
58. In the reaction $^{24}_{11}\text{N} \rightarrow ^{24}_{12}\text{Mg} + X$, the letter X represents (1) a neutron (2) a proton (3) an electron (4) a positron

59. In the reaction $^{30}_{15}P \rightarrow ^{30}_{14}Si + ^{0}_{+1}e$, the atoms $^{30}_{15}P$ and $^{30}_{14}Si$ have the same (1) mass number (2) atomic number (3) number of neutrons (4) number of electrons

60. In nuclear fusion, the total mass-energy of the system before fusion, compared to the total mass-energy of the system after fusion, is (1) smaller (2) larger (3) the same

61. When fast neutrons are slowed down, their effectiveness in producing fission is (1) decreased (2) increased (3) not changed

62. Which will be emitted when $^{238}_{92}U$ changes to $^{234}_{91}Pa$? (1) 1 alpha particle, only (2) 1 alpha particle and 1 beta particle (3) 1 alpha particle and 2 beta particles (4) 4 protons

63. What is the total number of beta particles emitted as the atom of $^{238}_{92}U$ decays to $^{206}_{92}Pb$? (1) 10 (2) 8 (3) 6 (4) 4

64. The mass of a radium nucleus is 226.024368 amu.
The mass of a radon nucleus is 222.016538 amu.
The mass of an alpha particle is 4.002605 amu.
In the reaction of $^{226}_{88}Ra \rightarrow ^{222}_{86}Rn + ^{4}_{2}He$ + energy, the energy emitted is equivalent to a loss of mass of (1) 0 amu (2) 0.005225 amu (3) 4.002605 amu (4) 4.007830 amu

65. During the decay of a radioactive atom, a gamma ray photon of frequency 4.5×10^{19} Hz is emitted. The energy of this photon is (1) 2.0×10^{-14} joule (2) 3.0×10^{-14} joule (3) 3.0×10^{14} joules (4) 2.0×10^{19} joules

66. The half life of thorium-234 is 24.1 days. If 8.0×10^{-3} kg of this isotope is present initially, what is the number of kilograms of the isotope remaining after 96.4 days? (1) 4.0×10^{-3} (2) 2.0×10^{-3} (3) 1.0×10^{-3} (4) 5.0×10^{-4}

APPENDIX I. BASIC MATHEMATICAL SKILLS

Several mathematical skills and related concepts are continually used throughout the physics course. A careful study of these basic skills and concepts is recommended.

1. MEASUREMENT

Measurement is a comparison of an unknown quantity with a known quantity. All physical measurements are subject to errors. Errors may be due to the method used, environmental changes, instrumental limitations, and personal error. Systematic errors tend to be in one direction. Random errors tend to occur in both directions. The random error may be reduced by increasing the number of observations.

2. SIGNIFICANT FIGURES

Significant figures are the reasonably certain digits in a measured quantity. In mathematical operations involving significant figures, the answer should not contain more significant figures than the *least* number of significant figures in the original quantities.

A significant figure is one which is known to be reasonably reliable, In expressing the results of a measurement, one estimated figure is considered significant; for example, in measuring temperature, if the thermometer is calibrated in degrees, the reading may be *estimated* to the tenth of a degree. In this case, in the reading 20.3°, the figure "3" is considered significant.

Zeros which appear in *front* of a number are not significant figures. The number 0.083 contains two significant figures.

Zeros which appear *between* numbers are always significant. The number 803 contains three significant figures.

Zeros which appear *after* a number are significant *only* (1) if followed by a decimal point, or (2) if they are to the right of a decimal point. For example, the number 1800 contains two significant figures, but the numbers 1800. and 18.00 contain four significant figures.

For whole numbers ending in two or more zeros, there is no way of indicating that some, but not all, of the zeros are significant; for example, the number 186,000 would indicate three significant figures if no decimal point is expressed, and six significant figures if the decimal point is expressed. There is no way of indicating its accuracy to four or five significant figures except by the use of *standard notation.*

Use the following rules in rounding off a number:

1. When the number dropped is less than 5, the preceding number remains unchanged; for example, 5.3634 to three significant figures becomes 5.36.

2. When the number dropped is 5 or more, the preceding number is increased by 1; for example, 2.4179 to three significant figures becomes 2.42.

3. In addition or subtraction, the answer should be rounded off so that the least accurately known figure is the final one; for example,

$$
\begin{array}{r}
32.6 \\
431.33 \\
+6144.212 \\
\hline
6608.142 = 6608.1
\end{array}
\qquad
\begin{array}{r}
531.46 \\
-86.3 \\
\hline
445.16 \ = \ 445.2
\end{array}
$$

4. In multiplication or division, the answer should be rounded off to contain only as many significant figures as are contained in the *least* accurate number; for example,

$$
\begin{array}{r}
1.36 \\
\times 4.2 \\
\hline
272 \\
544 \\
\hline
5.712 = 5.7
\end{array}
\qquad
\begin{array}{r}
2.39 \qquad = 2.4 \\
2.13 / \overline{\ 5.1000} \\
4.26 \\
\hline
840 \\
639 \\
\hline
2010
\end{array}
$$

5. In addition, subtraction, multiplication, or division, numbers may be rounded off to one more than the number of significant figures to be carried in the answer *before* the manipulation is carried out; for example, $2.7468 \times 3.2 = 2.75 \times 3.2 = 8.8$

3. STANDARD NOTATION (SCIENTIFIC OR EXPONENTIAL NOTATION)

Standard notation should be used to indicate the number of significant figures and to facilitate mathematical operations with large and small numbers.

Any number can be expressed in the form $A \times 10^n$ where A is any number with one digit to the left of the decimal point and n is an integer. All of the digits in A are significant. The value of n is determined by counting the number of places the decimal was moved. If the decimal was moved to the left, n is positive. If it was moved to the right, n is negative. For example 186,000 becomes 1.86×10^5, and 0.0000520 becomes 5.20×10^{-5}. In standard notation it is possible to indicate any desired number of significant figures. For example, if the figure 186,000 were known to four significant figures, it would be written 1.860×10^5.

Multiplication and Division in Standard Notation

To multiply or divide numbers in standard notation, multiply or divide the significant figure factors to obtain the new value of A, retaining the correct number of significant figures, and add or subtract the powers of 10 to obtain the new value of n. Adjust the decimal point if the new A has more or less than one non-zero digit to the left of the decimal point. Examples:

$2.2 \times 10^4 \times 3.01 \times 10^2 = 6.6 \times 10^6$

$2.2 \times 10^{-4} \times 3.01 \times 10^2 = 6.6 \times 10^{-2}$

$6.0 \times 10^3 \times 3.01 \times 10^4 = 18 \times 10^7 = 1.8 \times 10^8$

$6.0 \times 10^5 \div 3.0 \times 10^2 = 2.0 \times 10^3$

$6.0 \times 10^5 \div 3.0 \times 10^{-2} = 2.0 \times 10^7$

$3.0 \times 10^2 \div 6.0 \times 10^5 = 0.50 \times 10^{-3} = 5.0 \times 10^{-4}$

Addition and Subtraction in Standard Notation

Numbers expressed in standard notation can be added or subtracted *only* if the powers of 10 are the same; for example, $5 \times 10^3 + 2 \times 10^3 = (5 + 2) \times 10^3 = 7 \times 10^3$. If the numbers to be added or subtracted have different powers of 10, then the powers must be equalized. For example, $2 \times 10^2 + 3 \times 10^3 = 2 \times 10^2 + 30 \times 10^2 = 32 \times 10^2 = 3.2 \times 10^3$

4. MANIPULATION OF UNITS

In mathematical manipulations, units behave like algebraic quantities. In any physical equation the units on each side must be equivalent. For example, the electric potential difference between two points can be expressed in volts per meter. This is numerically equal to the force per unit charge in newtons per coulomb, as shown for a potential difference of 10V/m:

$$10V/m = \frac{10V}{m} \times \frac{J/coul}{V} \times \frac{nt\text{-}m}{J} = \frac{10V \times J \times nt \times m}{m \times V \times coul \times J}$$

$$= 10 \text{ nt/coul}$$

5. MATHEMATICAL FUNCTIONS

Graphs may be used to illustrate mathematical functions. Students should be able to recognize, interpret, and use mathematical expressions and graphs representing: (1) direct linear relations, $y = kx$; (2) direct second degree relations, $y = kx^2$; (3) inverse first degree relations, $y = \frac{k}{x}$; and (4) inverse square relations, $y = \frac{k}{x^2}$

A proportionality represents a ratio, and can be written as an equation by inserting the proper proportionality constant. Care should be taken to associate the proper units with the proportionality constant.

6. GRAPHS

Graphs should be used to illustrate physical relationships. A line representing the relationship should be smooth and probably will not pass through all measured points. Points should be circled to indicate their uncertainty.

APPENDIX II. PHYSICS REFERENCE TABLES

LIST OF PHYSICAL CONSTANTS

Gravitational Constant (G) . . . . 6.67×10^{-11} newton-meter^2/kg^2

Acceleration of gravity (g)
(near earth's surface) . . . . 9.81 meters/second^2

Speed of light (c) . . . . 3.00×10^8 meters/second

Speed of sound at S.T.P. . . . . 3.31×10^2 meters/second

Mechanical equivalent of heat . . . . . . $J = 4.19 \times 10^3$ joules/kilocalorie

$$\frac{1}{J} = 2.39 \times 10^{-4} \text{ kilocalorie/joule}$$

Mass energy relationship . . . . 1 amu $= 9.31 \times 10^2$ Mev

Electrostatic constant . . . . $k = 9.00 \times 10^9$ newton-meters^2/coul^2

Charge of the electron $= 1$
elementary charge . . . . 1.60×10^{-19} coulomb

One coulomb . . . . 6.25×10^{18} electrons

6.25×10^{18} elementary charges

Electron-volt (ev) . . . . 1.60×10^{-19} joule

Planck's Constant (h) . . . . 6.63×10^{-34} joule-second

Rest mass of the electron (m_e) . . . . . . 9.11×10^{-31} kilogram

Rest mass of the proton (m_p) . . . . . . 1.67×10^{-27} kilogram

Rest mass of the neutron (m_n) . . . . . . 1.67×10^{-27} kilogram

TRIGONOMETRIC FUNCTIONS

sine $0° = .000$
sine $30° = .500$
sine $45° = .707$
sine $60° = .866$
sine $90° = 1.000$

WAVELENGTHS OF LIGHT IN A VACUUM

VIOLET	$<4.5 \times 10^{-7}$ meters
BLUE	$4.5 - 5.0 \times 10^{-7}$ meters
GREEN	$5.0 - 5.7 \times 10^{-7}$ meters
YELLOW	$5.7 - 5.9 \times 10^{-7}$ meters
ORANGE	$5.9 - 6.1 \times 10^{-7}$ meters
RED	$>6.1 \times 10^{-7}$ meters

HEAT CONSTANTS

	Specific Heat (average)	Melting Point °C.	Boiling Point °C.	Heat of Fusion kcal/kg	Heat of Vaporization kcal/kg
Alcohol, ethyl	0.58 (liq.)	—115	78	25	204
Aluminum	0.21 (sol.)	660	2057	77	2520
Ammonia	1.13 (liq.)	—78	—33	84	327
Copper	0.09 (sol.)	1083	2336	49	1150
Ice	0.50 (sol.)	0	—	80	—
Iron	0.11 (sol.)	1535	3000	7.9	1600
Lead	0.03 (sol.)	327	1620	5.9	207
Mercury	0.03 (liq.)	—39	357	2.8	71
Platinum	0.03 (sol.)	1774	4300	27	—
Silver	0.06 (sol.)	961	1950	26	565
Steam	0.48 (gas)	—	—	—	—
Water	1.00 (liq.)	—	100	—	540
Tungsten	0.04 (sol.)	3370	5900	43	—
Zinc	0.09 (sol.)	419	907	23	420

ABSOLUTE INDICES OF REFRACTION
($\lambda = 5.9 \times 10^{-7}$ m.)

Air 1.00	Carbon Tetra-chloride 1.46	Glycerol 1.47
Alcohol 1.36	Diamond 2.42	Lucite 1.50
Benzene 1.50	Glass, Crown .. 1.52	Quartz, Fused .. 1.46
Canada Balsam . 1.53	Glass, Flint ... 1.61	Water 1.33

[OVER]

Atomic number and chemical symbol

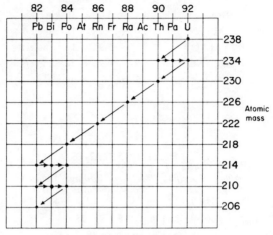

Uranium Disintegration Series

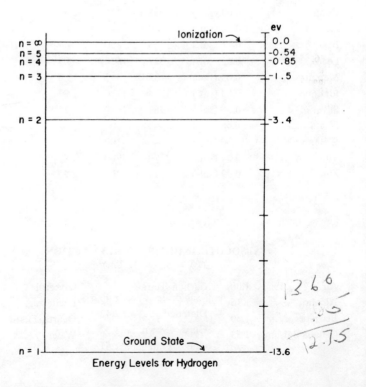

Energy Levels for Hydrogen

PHYSICS

Wednesday, June 19, 1968—1:15 to 4:15 p.m., only

Part I

Directions (1-70): In the space provided on the line at the right, write the *number* preceding the word or expression that, of those given, best completes the statement or answers the question. [70]

1. Which is a scalar quantity? (1) speed (2) displacement (3) force (4) momentum

2. How much work is needed to lift a 15-newton block 3.0 meters vertically? (1) 5.0 newton-meters (2) 12 newton-meters (3) 45 newton-meters (4) 150 newton-meters)

3. The force required to accelerate a 2.0-kilogram mass at 4.0 meters per second² is (1) 6.0 newtons (2) 2.0 newtons (3) 8.0 newtons (4) 16 newtons

4. Concurrent forces of 10. newtons east and 10. newtons south act on an object. The resultant force is (1) 0 newtons (2) 5.0 newtons southeast (3) 14 newtons southeast (4) 20. newtons southeast

5. Which is a unit of power? (1) joule (2) $\dfrac{\text{joule}}{\text{second}}$ (3) $\dfrac{\text{kilogram-meter}}{\text{second}}$ (4) $\dfrac{\text{newton-meter}^2}{\text{second}}$

6. A mass with a momentum of 40. kilogram meters/sec. receives an impulse of 30. newton-seconds in the direction of its motion. The final momentum of the mass is (1) 1.3 kilogram meter/sec. (2) 10. kilogram meter/sec. (3) 70. kilogram meter/sec. (4) 1,200 kilogram meter/sec.

7. An object originally at rest is uniformly accelerated along a straight-line path to a speed of 8.0 meters per second in 2.0 seconds. What was the acceleration of the object? (1) 0.25 m./sec.² (2) 10. m./sec.² (3) 16 m./sec.² (4) 4.0 m./sec.²

8. Which pair of concurrent forces may have a resultant of 20. newtons? (1) 5.0 newtons and 10. newtons (2) 20. newtons and 20. newtons (3) 20. newtons and 50. newtons (4) 30. newtons and 5.0 newtons

9. At a height of 10 meters above the earth's surface, the potential energy of a 2-kilogram mass is 196 joules. After the mass which starts at rest falls 5 meters, its kinetic energy will be (1) 196 joules (2) 147 joules (3) 98 joules (4) 49 joules

10. If the kinetic energy of an object is 16 joules when its speed is 4.0 meters per second, then the mass of the object is (1) 0.5 kg. (2) 2.0 kg. (3) 8.0 kg. (4) 19.6 kg.

11. A 30-kilogram boy exerts a force of 100 newtons on a 50-kilogram object. The force that the object exerts on the boy is (1) 0 newtons (2) 100 newtons (3) 980 newtons (4) 1,500 newtons

11....2....

12. A 10-kilogram mass rests on a horizontal frictionless table. How much energy is needed to accelerate the mass from rest to a speed of 5 meters per second? (1) 25 joules (2) 125 joules (3) 3,125 joules (4) 6,250 joules

12....2....

13. A force of 10 newtons is required to move an object at a constant speed of 5 meters per second. The power used is (1) 0.5 watt (2) 2 watts (3) 5 watts (4) 50 watts

13....4....

14. At what temperature is the internal energy of a body at a minimum? (1) 0° C. (2) —273° C. (3) 273° C. (4) 373° C.

14....2....

15. Which two temperatures are equivalent? (1) 0° C. and —273° A. (2) 100° C. and 273° A. (3) 0° A. and 273° C. (4) 0° A. and —273° C.

15....4....

16. What is the number of Kelvin (Absolute) degrees between the freezing point and the boiling point of pure water at standard pressure? (1) 0 (2) 100 (3) 180 (4) 273

16....2....

17. A beam of parallel rays of light is reflected from a plane mirror. After reflection, the rays will be (1) converging (2) diverging (3) parallel (4) diffused

17....3....

18. The direction of a light ray in air will change most when the light ray obliquely strikes and then enters (1) lucite (2) glycerol (3) alcohol (4) water

18....1....

19. Two wave trains will produce a standing wave in a medium if they have (1) the same frequency, different amplitudes, and the same direction (2) the same frequency, the same amplitude, and same direction (3) the same frequency, the same amplitude, and opposite directions (4) different frequencies, the same amplitude, and the same direction

19....3....

20. Longitudinal waves can *not* be (1) reflected (2) refracted (3) diffracted (4) polarized

20....4....

21. The moon is 4.0×10^8 meters from the earth. A radar signal transmitted from the earth will reach the moon in (1) 0.75 sec. (2) 1.3 sec. (3) 2.6 sec. (4) 12 sec.

21....2....

22. A glass rod having an index of refration of 1.50 is inserted into a colorless liquid. If no light is reflected from the glass rod, then the colorless liquid must be (1) carbon tetrachloride (2) water (3) alcohol (4) benzene

22.........

23. In a vacuum, radio waves and visible light waves must have the same (1) amplitude (2) frequency (3) speed (4) wavelength

23.........

24. What is the wavelength of the standing wave shown?

(1) 1.0 meter
(2) 0.5 meter
(3) 3.0 meters
(4) 1.5 meters

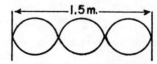

24.........

25. Which diagram corectly shows light rays passing through the lens?

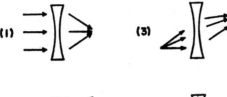

26. The focal length of a converging lens is longest for (1) green light (2) yellow light (3) red light (4) blue light   26........

27. Two pulses approach each other in a spring, as shown.

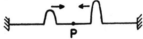

Which diagram below best illustrates the appearance of the spring after the two pulses pass each other at point *P*?   27........

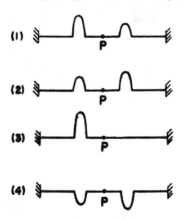

28. When a light wave enters a medium of greater optical density, there will be a decrease in the wave's (1) speed, only (2) frequency, only (3) speed and wavelength (4) frequency and wavelength   28........

29. An arrow is drawn in front of the plane mirror MM^1, as shown.

The orientation of the image formed by the mirror is best represented by   29........

(1)

(2)

(3)

(4)

30. The diagram shows light waves passing through slit S in barrier B. This is an example of

(1) reflection

(2) refraction

(3) polarization

(4) diffraction   30........

31. Maximum destructive interference of two waves occurs at points where the phase difference between the two waves is (1) 0° (2) 45° (3) 90° (4) 180°   31....4...

32. To which part of the electromagnetic spectrum will a photon belong if its wavelength in a vacuum is 5.6×10^{-7} meter? (1) X-ray (2) ultraviolet (3) visible light (4) infrared   32....3...

33. Which diagram best represents the electric field surrounding two positively charged spheres?   33....2...

(1) 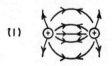   (3)

(2)   (4)

34. Which voltage would cause a curent of 0.5 ampere in a circuit that has a resistance of 24 ohms? (1) 6.0 volts (2) 12 volts (3) 24 volts (4) 48 volts

34.....

35. What is the current in a circuit if 15 coulombs of electric charge move past a given point in 3 seconds? (1) 5 amperes (2) 12 amperes (3) 18 amperes (4) 45 amperes

35.....

36. An electron moves through a potential difference of 3.00 volts. The energy acquired by the charge is
   (1) 5.33×10^{-19} joule
   (2) 1.60×10^{-19} joule
   (3) 4.80×10^{-19} joule
   (4) 3.00 joules

36.....

37. Three ammeters are located near junction P in a direct current electric circuit as shown.

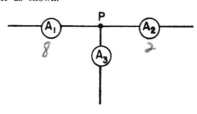

If A_1 reads 8 amperes and A_2 reads 2 amperes, then the reading of ammeter A_3 could be (1) 16 amp. (2) 6 amp. (3) 5 amp. (4) 4 amp.

37.....

38. A and B are two points in an electric field. If 6.0 joules of work are done in transferring 2.0 coulombs of electric charge from point A to point B, then the potential difference between points A and B is (1) 0.0 volts (2) 1.5 volts (3) 3.0 volts (4) 12 volts

38.....

39. A small, soft iron bar is placed between a north and a south pole. Which diagram represents the resulting magnetic field between these two poles?

39.....

(1)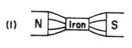

(3)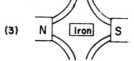

(2)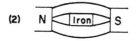

(4)

40. How is a positive charge usually given to a neutral object? (1) Neutrons are added to the object. (2) Electrons are removed from the object. (3) Protons are added to the object. (4) Protons are removed from the object.

40.....

41. Four electric charges, *A, B, C,* and *D,* are arranged as shown.

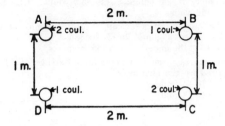

The electric force will be *least* between charges (1)*A* and *B* (2)*A* and *C* (3)*A* and *D* (4)*B* and *D*   41........

42. What information must be known to calculate the magnetic force on a charge as it moves perpendicularly through a magnetic field? (1) the speed of the charge, only (2) the speed and the magnetic field intensity, only (3) the magnetic field intensity and the magnitude of the charge, only (4) the speed, the magnetic field intensity, and the magnitude of the charge   42........

43. Which diagram best represents the magnetic field around a wire conductor in which electrons are moving as shown? [The *x* indicates that the field is into the page; the • indicates that the field is out of the page.]   43........

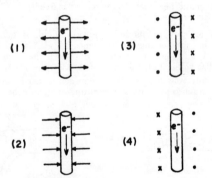

44. Assuming total conversion of electrical energy to heat energy, how many joules of heat energy are produced by a 20-watt heating unit in 5 seconds? (1) 100 (2) 25 (3) 24 (4) 4   44........

45. What is the energy of the photon emitted as a hydrogen atom changes from the *n* = 3 energy level to the *n* = 2 energy level? (1) .65 e.v. (2) 1.9 e.v. (3) 5.2 e.v. (4) 10.2 e.v.   45........

46. A series circuit contains a 4-Ω and a 2-Ω resistor connected to a 110-volt source. Compared to the energy dissipated in the 2-Ω

resistor, the energy dissipated in the 4-U resistor during the same time is (1) one-half as great (2) the same (3) twice as great (4) four times as great   46........

47. The relationship of the force between two point charges and the distance between them is best shown by graph   47........

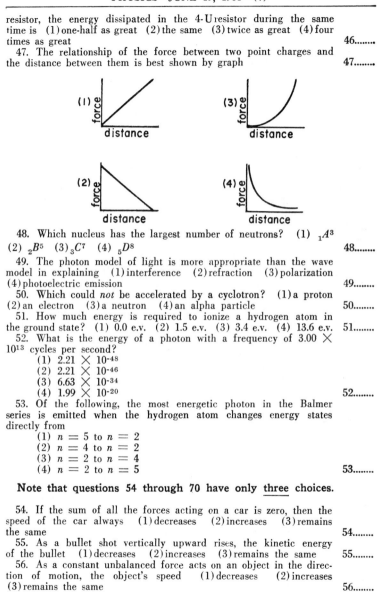

48. Which nucleus has the largest number of neutrons? (1) $_1A^3$ (2) $_2B^5$ (3) $_3C^7$ (4) $_5D^8$ 48........

49. The photon model of light is more appropriate than the wave model in explaining (1) interference (2) refraction (3) polarization (4) photoelectric emission   49........

50. Which could *not* be accelerated by a cyclotron? (1) a proton (2) an electron (3) a neutron (4) an alpha particle   50........

51. How much energy is required to ionize a hydrogen atom in the ground state? (1) 0.0 e.v. (2) 1.5 e.v. (3) 3.4 e.v. (4) 13.6 e.v.   51........

52. What is the energy of a photon with a frequency of 3.00×10^{13} cycles per second?
    (1) 2.21×10^{-48}
    (2) 2.21×10^{-46}
    (3) 6.63×10^{-34}
    (4) 1.99×10^{-20} 52........

53. Of the following, the most energetic photon in the Balmer series is emitted when the hydrogen atom changes energy states directly from
    (1) $n = 5$ to $n = 2$
    (2) $n = 4$ to $n = 2$
    (3) $n = 2$ to $n = 4$
    (4) $n = 2$ to $n = 5$ 53........

Note that questions 54 through 70 have only three choices.

54. If the sum of all the forces acting on a car is zero, then the speed of the car always (1) decreases (2) increases (3) remains the same   54........

55. As a bullet shot vertically upward rises, the kinetic energy of the bullet (1) decreases (2) increases (3) remains the same   55........

56. As a constant unbalanced force acts on an object in the direction of motion, the object's speed (1) decreases (2) increases (3) remains the same   56........

57. As the time required to lift a 60-kg. object 6 meters increases, the work required to lift the body (1) decreases (2) increases (3) remains the same   57........

58. A ball is thrown vertically upward. As the ball rises, its total energy (neglecting friction) (1) decreases (2) increases (3) remains the same   58........

59. As the angle between two concurrent forces is increased from 10° to 75°, the magnitude of the resultant force (1) decreases (2) increases (3) remains the same   59........

60. When two stationary objects are suddenly pushed apart by a compressed spring between them, the total momentum of the system (1) decreases (2) increases (3) remains the same   60........

61. As the average kinetic energy of the molecules of an ideal gas increases, its absolute temperature (1) decreases (2) increases (3) remains the same   61........

62. As the index of refraction of a material increases, the apparent speed of light in that material (1) decreases (2) increases (3) remains the same   62........

63. A light ray traveling through glass strikes a glass-air surface. As the angle of incidence increases, the critical angle (1) decreases (2) increases (3) remains the same   63........

64. A light bulb is in series with a rheostat (variable resistor) and a fixed voltage is applied across the total circuit. As the resistance of the rheostat decreases, the brightness of the bulb (1) decreases (2) increases (3) remains the same   64........

65. As the kinetic energy of an electron increases, its momentum (1) decreases (2) increases (3) remains the same   65........

66. As the current in a circular loop of wire increases, the magnetic field strength at the center of the loop (1) decreases (2) increases (3) remains the same   66........

67. As a charged object is moved parallel to the central region of a long uniformly charged rod, the electrical force on the object (1) decreases (2) increases (3) remains the same   67........

68. Given the diagram below, with switch S_1 open.

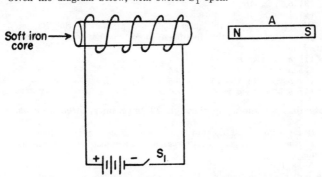

When switch S_1 is closed, the force of magnet A on the soft iron core (1) decreases (2) increases (3) remains the same   68........

69. As the electric charge on the surface of a hollow metal sphere increases, the electric field intensity inside the sphere (1) decreases (2) increases (3) remains the same

69........

70. As the mass of the isotopes of an element increases, the number of protons in their nuclei (1) decreases (2) increases (3) remains the same

70........

Part II

This part consists of four groups, each group testing a major area in the course. Choose two of these four groups. Write your answers in the spaces provided on the lines at the right.

Group 1—Mechanics

Answer any three of the four questions, 71 through 74, in this group. Each question counts 5 credits. For each part of the three questions chosen, write the number of the word or expression that best completes that statement or answers that question.

71. Base your answers to questions *a* through *e* on the information and diagram below:

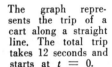

The graph represents the trip of a cart along a straight line. The total trip takes 12 seconds and starts at $t = 0$.

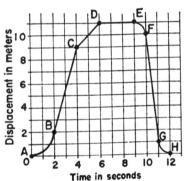

a. The part of the trip during which the cart was at rest is represented by line (1) *AB* (2) *BC* (3) *DE* (4) *GH*   a.........

b. What was the total *distance* covered by the cart during the trip (*AH*)? (1) 6 m. (2) 11 m. (3) 12 m. (4) 22 m.   b.........

c. What is the average speed of the cart during the part of the trip labeled *CD*? (1) 1 m./sec. (2) 2 m./sec. (3) 10 m./sec. (4) 11 m./sec.   c.........

d. Of the following, the part of the trip during which the cart was moving with a constant speed is represented by line (1) *AB* (2) *BC* (3) *EF* (4) *GH*   d.........

e. Of the following, the part of the trip during which acceleration was *not* 0 is represented by line (1) *AB* (2) *BC* (3) *DE* (4) *FG*   e.........

72. Base your answers to questions *a* through *e* on the information and diagram below:

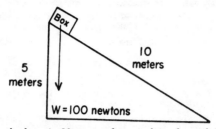

An inclined plane is 10 meters long and is elevated 5 meters on one end as shown. Starting from rest at the top of the incline, a box weighing 100 newtons accelerates at a rate of 2.5 meters per second.[2]

a. The potential energy of the box at the top of the incline was approximately (1) 1,000 joules (2) 500 joules (3) 50 joules (4) 0 joules   *a*........

b. How many seconds will it take the box to reach the bottom of the incline? (1) 2.8 (2) 2.0 (3) 4.6 (4) 4.0   *b*........

c. What is the approximate mass of the box? (1) 400 kg. (2) 100 kg. (3) 40 kg. (4) 10 kg.   *c*........

Note that questions d and e have only three choices.

d. If there is no friction as the box slides down the incline, the sum of its potential and kinetic energies will (1) decrease (2) increase (3) remain the same   *d*........

e. As the box slides down the incline, its momentum will (1) decrease (2) increase (3) remain the same   *e*........

73. Base your answers to questions *a* through *e* on the information and diagram below:

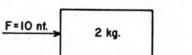

A horizontal force of 10 newtons accelerates a 2-kilogram block from rest along a level table at a rate of 4 meters per second.[2]

a. The work done in moving the block 8 meters is (1) 8 joules (2) 20 joules (3) 80 joules (4) 800 joules   *a*.........

b. When the speed of the block is 8 meters per second, its kinetic energy is (1) 8 joules (2) 16 joules (3) 64 joules (4) 80 joules   *b*.........

c. The number of seconds required for the block to attain a speed of 20 meters per second is (1) 1 (2) 2 (3) 5 (4) 4   *c*.........

d. What is the frictional force that is retarding the forward

     motion of the block? (1) 8 newtons   (2) 2 newtons
(3) 10 newtons (4) 19.6 newtons   *d*.........

   e. If there were no friction between the block and the table,
then the acceleration of the block would be (1) 20 m./sec.^{2}
(2) 9.8 m./sec.^{2} (3) 5 m./sec.^{2} (4) 4 m./sec.^{2} *e*.........

74. Base your answers to questions *a* through *e* on the information
below:

     Two kilograms of aluminum at a temperature of 300° C. are
placed on a block of ice whose temperature is 0° C. The ice
melts until the system achieves equilibrium at 0° C.

   a. What is the equilibrium temperature on the Kelvin scale?
(1) 0° (2) 100° (3) 273° (4) 573°   *a*.........

   b. How many kilocalories are lost by the block of aluminum?
(1) 63 (2) 126 (3) 154 (4) 600   *b*.........

Note that questions c̲ through e̲ have only three choices.

   c. Compared to the specific heat of ice, the specific heat of
water (liquid) is (1) greater (2) less (3) the same   *c*.........

   d. As the ice melts, the potential energy of its molecules
(1) decreases (2) increases (3) remains the same   *d*.........

   e. As the aluminum cools, the average kinetic energy of its
molecules (1) decreases (2) increases (3) remains the
same   *e*.........

Group 2—Wave Phenomena

**Answer any three of the four questions, 75 through 78, in this group.
Each question counts 5 credits. For each part of the three questions
chosen, write the number of the word or expression that best completes
that statement or answers that question.**

75. Base your answers to questions *a* through *e* on the diagram
below, which shows a ray of monochromatic light as it passes through
three transparent media.

   a. What happens to the light incident upon medium 2 from
medium 1? (1) All of the light is refrated. (2) Part of
the light is refracted and part is reflected. (3) Part of the
light is refracted and part is dispersed. (4) Part of the light
is diffracted and part is reflected.   *a*.........

   b. If medium 2 is carbon tetrachloride, then medium 3 could
be (1) crown glass (2) flint glass (3) lucite (4) fused
quartz   *b*.........

Note that questions c through e have only three choices.

   c. *As* the light enters medium 2, its frequency (1) decreases (2) increases (3) remains the same   c.........

   d. As angle *A* is increased, angle *B* will (1) decrease (2) increase (3) remain the same   d.........

   e. If the frequency of the light is increased, its wave-length in medium 1 will (1) decrease (2) increase (3) remain the same   e.........

76. Base your answers to questions *a* through *e* on diagrams *A* through *D* below, which represent four interference patterns. The dark bars indicate areas of minimum light intensity.

Central Maximum

   a. Which phenomenon was primarily responsible for producing all four interference patterns? (1) polarization (2) dispersion (3) refraction (4) diffraction   a.........

   b. If the distance from the slits to the screen upon which pattern *B* is displayed is increased, then the most likely pattern to appear would be (1) *A* (2) *B* (3) *C* (4) *D*   b.........

   c. In pattern *C*, the distance between the central maximum and the first bright line is 2.0×10^{-2} meter. The separation of the double slit is 1.0×10^{-4} meter and the distance from the slits to the screen is 4.0 meters. The wavelength of the source is

      (1) 2.2×10^{-3} meter   (3) 5.0×10^{-7} meter

      (2) 8.0×10^{2} meters   (4) 1.5×10^{-6} meter   c.........

   d. Which pattern was produced by passing light through a single slit? (1) *A* (2) *B* (3) *C* (4) *D*   d.........

   e. If pattern *B* is produced by using monochromatic green light and the source is changed to monochromatic red light, then the new pattern would be best represented by   (1) *A* (2) *B* (3) *C* (4) *D*

e.........

77. Base your answers to questions *a* through *e* on the diagram and information below:

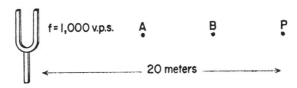

The speed in air of the sound waves emitted by the tuning fork above is 340 meters per second.

a. The time required for the waves to travel from the tuning fork to point *P* is (1) .020 sec. (2) .059 sec. (3) .59 sec. (4) 2.9 sec.

a........

b. The wavelength of the sound waves produced by the tuning fork is (1) .29 m. (2) .34 m. (3) .43 m. (4) 2.9 m.

b........

c. If the waves are in a phase at points *A* and *B*, then the minimum distance between points *A* and *B* is (1) 1 wavelength (2) 2 wavelengths (3) ¼ wavelength (4) ½ wavelength

c........

Note that questions d and e have only three choices.

d. If the tuning fork, vibrating with a constant amplitude, is moved toward *P*, the amplitude of the waves reaching point *P* will (1) decrease (2) increase (3) remain the same

d........

e. If the vibrating tuning fork is accelerated toward point *P*, the pitch observed at point *P* will (1) decrease (2) increase (3) remain the same

e........

78. Base your answers to questions *a* through *e* on the diagram below, which shows a lens whose focal length is 0.10 meter.

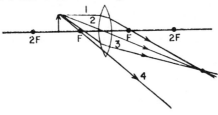

a. Which ray from the head of the arrow is *not* correctly drawn? (1) 1 (2) 2 (3) 3 (4) 4

a........

b. If the object is 0.15 meter from the lens, then the distance from the image to the lens is (1) 0.06 meter (2) 0.10 meter (3) 0.15 meter (4) 0.30 meter   b........

c. If an object 0.24 meter tall is placed at 2F, then the height of the image is (1) 0.06 meter (2) 0.12 meter (3) 0.24 meter (4) 0.48 meter   c.........

Note that questions d and e have only three choices.

d. As the object is moved from 2F toward F, the size of the image (1) decreases (2) increases (3) remains the same   d........

e. If the index of refraction of the lens increases, then the focal length of the lens (1) decreases (2) increases (3) remains the same   e........

Group 3—Electricity

Answer any three of the four questions, 79 through 82, in this group. Each question counts 5 credits. For each part of the three questions chosen, write the number of the word or expression that best completes that statement or answers that question.

79. Base your answers to questions a through e on the diagram and information below:

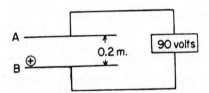

A proton (represented by +) is placed between the two parallel plates, A and B, as shown. The plates are 0.2 meter apart and connected to a 90-volt battery. The proton has a force exerted on it toward A.

a. The direction of the electric field between the two plates is from (1) positive plate A to negative plate B (2) negative plate A to positive plate B (3) positive plate B to negative plate A (4) negative plate B to positive plate A   a........

b. The magnitude of the electric field intensity between the two plates is (1) 18 nt./coul. (2) 45 nt./coul. (3) 180 nt./coul. (4) 450 nt./coul.   b........

c. The kinetic energy gained by the proton in moving from plate B to plate A is (1) 1.4×10^{-21} joule (2) 1.8×10^{-21} joule (3) 1.4×10^{-17} joule (4) 1.8×10^{-17} joule   c........

Note that questions d and e have only three choices.

    d. If the proton is now moved back toward plate *B*, its potential energy will   (1) decrease   (2) increase   (3) remain the same   *d.*........

    e. As the separation between plates *A* and *B* is increased, the electric field intensity between the plates will   (1) decrease increase   (3) remain the same   *e.*........

80. Base your answers to questions *a* through *e* on the diagram below, which shows a conducting loop in a uniform magnetic field of 5.6 $\times$ 10^{-2} weber/meter².

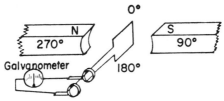

    a. As the loop is rotated clockwise through 360°, the galvanometer needle will   (1) deflect only to the left   (2) deflect only to the right   (3) deflect first in one direction and then in the other   (4) not deflect in either direction   *a.*........

    b. As the loop rotates, the induced voltage will be a maximum at   (1) 0° and 90°   (2) 0° and 180°   (3) 90° and 270°   (4) 180° and 270°   *b.*........

Note that questions c through e have only three choices.

    c. As the loop is made smaller, the maximum induced voltage will   (1) decrease   (2) increase   (3) remain the same   *c.*........

    d. As the speed of rotation of the coil increases, the flux density of the field due to the magnets   (1) decreases   (2) increases   (3) remains the same   *d.*........

    e. As the north and south poles are moved farther apart, the induced voltage   (1) decreases   (2) increases   (3) remains the same   *e.*........

81. Base your answers to questions *a* through *e* on the diagram below. This diagram shows a 0.5-ohm (Ω) resistor, *R*, and a light bulb, which are connected in series to a 6.0-volt battery. The current in resistor *R* is 4.0 amperes.

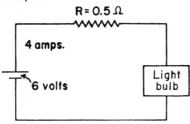

    a. The potential difference between the two ends of the
resistor is (1) 0.13 volt (2) 2.0 volts (3) 6.0 volts
(4) 8.0 volts   *a*........

    b. The electric curent through the light bulb is (1) .67 am-
pere (2) 2.0 amperes (3) 6.0 amperes (4) 4.0 amperes   *b*........

    c. How much chemical energy will the battery convert to
electrical energy in 10 seconds? (1) 24 joules (2) 240
joules (3) 360 joules (4) 600 joules   *c*........

    d. The resistance of the light bulb is (1) 1.0 ohm
(2) 0.5 ohm (3) .17 ohm (4) 23.5 ohms   *d*........

    e. What is the rate at which heat is being developed in
resistor *R*?   (1) 8 joules/sec.   (2) 2 joules/sec.
(3) 3 joules/sec. (4) 24 joules/sec.   *e*........

82. Base your answers to questions *a* through *e* on the accompanying diagram, in which circular lines are drawn at 60 volts, 30 volts,
and 20 volts about electric charge q^+. Positions *A* through *D* on the
equipotential lines are indicated.

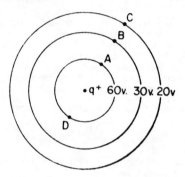

    a. The total work done in moving 1 coulomb of charge
from *A* to *D* is (1) 0 joules (2) 40 joules (3) 80 joules
(4) 4π joules   *a*........

    b. The total work done in moving 2 coulombs of positive
charge from position *C* to position *A* is (1) 0 joules
(2) 40 joules (3) 60 joules (4) 80 joules   *b*........

    c. If 5 coulombs of charge move from position *A* to position
B in 1 second, the current will be (1) .25 amp. (2) 5
amp. (3) 30 amp. (4) 100 amp.   *c*........

Note that questions d and e have only three choices.

    d. As compared with *A*, the magnitude of the electric field
intensity at *B* is (1) greater (2) less (3) the same   *d*........

    e. If q^+ is increased to $2q^+$, the potential at *B* (1) de-
creases (2) increases (3) remains the same   *e*........

Group 4—Atomic and Nuclear Physics

Answer any three of the four questions, 83 through 86, in this group. Each question counts 5 credits. For each part of the three questions chosen, write the number of the word or expression that best completes that statement or answers that question.

83. Base your answers to questions *a* through *e* on the graph below, which shows the maximum kinetic energy of photoelectrons when photons of various frequencies strike a metal plate.

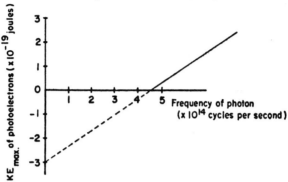

a. The slope of the line on the graph represents (1) Planck's constant (2) the gravitational constant (3) the electrostatic constant (4) Rydberg's constant

a.........

b. The work function of the metal is (1) -2×10^{-19} joule (2) -2 e.v. (3) 4.5 e.v. (4) 3×10^{-19} joule

b.........

c. If the intensity of the illumination on the metal plate is reduced to one-fourth its original value, then the maximum kinetic energy of the photoelectrons will be (1) one-sixteenth the original value (2) unchanged (3) twice the original value (4) four times the original value

c.........

Note that questions d and e have only three choices.

d. If a metal with a higher work function were used, the threshold frequency would (1) decrease (2) increase (3) remain the same

d.........

e. As the energy of a photon decreases, its wavelength (1) decreases (2) increases (3) remains the same

e.........

84. Base your answers to questions *a* through *e* on the information below:

A photon whose wavelength is 6.0×10^{-7} meter is emitted by a hydrogen atom.

a. Which color is associated with photons of this wavelength? 1. violet (2) blue (3) green (4) orange

a.........

b. The energy of this photon is approximately (7) 7.5×10^{47} joules (2) 3.3×10^{-19} joule (3) 2×10^{-25} joule (4) 4×10^{-40} joule

b.........

c. If the energy of this photon is equal to Ep joules and the photon strikes a photosensitive substance that has a work function of W joules, then the maximum energy of the ejected photoelectrons is equal to (1) $Ep + W$ (2) $Ep - W$ (3) $Ep \times W$ (4) $Ep \div W$ c........

Note that questions d and e have only three choices.

    d. As the photon is emitted, the energy state of the hydrogen atom (1) decreases (2) increases (3) remains the same d........

    e. As the photon is emitted, the mass of the atom's nucleus (1) decreases (2) increases (3) remains the same e........

85. Base your answers to questions a through e on the information below:

In the nuclear reaction

$$_1H^2 + {}_1H^3 \rightarrow {}_2He^4 + {}_0n^1 + Q,$$

Q represents energy released.

The masses of the nuclei are:

$_1H^2 = 2.01472$ amu

$_1H^3 = 3.01697$ amu

$_2He^4 = 4.00391$ amu

$_0n^1 = 1.00897$ amu

    a. The reaction shown is primarily an example of (1) alpha decay (2) ionization (3) fission (4) fusion a........

    b. The number of protons in $_1H^3$ is (1) 1 (2) 2 (3) 3 (4) 4 c........

    c. The number of neutrons in $_2He^4$ is (1) 1 (2) 2 (3) 3 (4) 4 c........

    d. The value of Q is nearest to (1) 5.01288 amu (2) 5.03169 amu (3) .01881 amu (4) 2.01472 amu d........

    e. The number of electrons in the neutral He atom is (1) 1 (2) 2 (3) 3 (4) 4 e........

86. Base your answers to questions a through e on the *Physics Reference Tables.*

    a. Which disintegration is the result of the emission of a negative beta particle? (1) Bi to Po (2) Po to Pb (3) Rn to Po (4) U to Th a........

    b. Which is the equation for the disintegration of Th into Ra?
(1) $_{90}Th^{230} \rightarrow {}_{88}Ra^{226} + {}_2He^4$
(2) $_{90}Th^{230} \rightarrow {}_{88}Ra^{226} + {}_{-1}e^0$
(3) $_{90}Th^{234} \rightarrow {}_{88}Ra^{226} + {}_2He^4$
(4) $_{90}Th^{234} \rightarrow {}_{88}Ra^{222} + {}_2He^4$ b........

    c. Which pair of isotopes is found in the Uranium Disintegration Series? (1) $_{90}Th^{234}$, $_{90}Th^{235}$ (2) $_{84}Po^{214}$, $_{84}Po^{218}$ (3) $_{82}Pb^{214}$, $_{82}Pb^{218}$ (4) $_{88}Ra^{226}$, $_{88}Ra^{225}$ c........

    d. Which particle is emitted as $_{92}U^{238}$ changes to $_{90}Th^{234}$? (1) a neutron (2) an alpha particle (3) a positive beta particle (4) a negative beta particle d........

    e. The half-life of Po^{218} is 3 minutes. What fraction of a 10-gram sample of Po^{218} will remain after 15 minutes?
(1) $\dfrac{1}{5}$ (2) $\dfrac{1}{25}$ (3) $\dfrac{1}{32}$ (4) $\dfrac{1}{64}$

PHYSICS

Wednesday, June 18, 1969—1:15 to 4:15 p.m., only

Part I

Directions (1-60): In the space provided on the line to the right, write the *number* preceding the word or expression that, of those given, best completes the statement or answers the question. [70]

1. Four forces act on a point as shown. The resultant of the four forces is (1) 0 nt.   (2) 5 nt.   (3) 14 nt.   (4) 20 nt.   1...*1*...

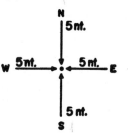

2. A 5-newton force directed north and a 5-newton force directed west both act on the same point. The resultant of these two forces is approximately   (1) 5 newtons northwest   (2) 7 newtons northwest   (3) 5 newtons southwest   (4) 7 newtons southwest

3. A force of 10. newtons applied to mass M accelerates it at 2.0 meters per second^2. The same force applied to a mass of $2M$ would produce an acceleration of   (1) 1.0 m./sec.^{2} (2) 2.0 m./sec.^{2} (3) 0.5 m./sec.^{2} (4) 4.0 m./sec.^{2}

4. Which graph represents the motion of an object that is moving with a constant velocity?   4......

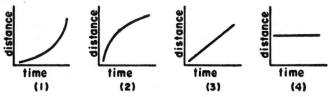

5. A temperature of 50° C. is the same as a Kelvin temperature of
(1) —223°
(2)   223°
(3) 273°
(4) 323°   5....*4*...

6. Object *A* with a mass of 2 kilograms and object *B* with a mass of 4 kilograms are dropped simultaneously from rest near the surface of the earth. At the end of 3 seconds, what is the ratio of the speed of object *A* to the speed of object *B*? [Neglect air resistance.] (1) 1:1 (2) 2:1 (3) 1:2 (4) 1:4   6...1....

7. A 20.-kilogram object is moved a distance of 6.0 meters by a net force of 50. newtons.. The total work done is (1) 120 joules (2) 300 joules (3) 420 joules (4) 1,000 joules   7...1....

8. An object weighing 20 newtons at the earth's surface is moved to a location where its weight is 10 newtons. The acceleration due to gravity at this location would be (1) 2.4 m./sec.² (2) 4.9 m./sec.² (3) 9.8 m./sec.² (4) 19.6 m./sec²   8...2....

9. A 2-kilogram mass is thrown vertically upward from the earth's surface with an initial kinetic energy of 400 newton-meters. The mass will rise to a height of approximately (1) 10 m. (2) 20 m. (3) 400 m. (4) 800 m.   9.......

10. Which is a scalar quantity? (1)acceleration (2)momentum (3)force (4)energy   10.......

11. Which is *not* a unit of power? (1)joules/second (2)newton-second (3)watts (4)calories/second   11........

12. The resultant of a 12-newton force and a 7-newton force is 5 newtons. The angle between the force is
(1) 0°   (3) 90°
(2) 45°   (4) 180°   12...4....

13. A box is sliding down an inclined plane as shown. The force of friction is directed toward point
    (1) *A*
    (2) *B*
    (3) *C*
    (4) *D*

13....B....

14. A 2.00-kilogram mass is at rest on a horizontal surface. The force exerted by the surface on the mass is approximately (1) (1) 0 nt. (2) 2.00 nt. (3) 9.80 nt. (4) 19.6 nt.   14...4....

15. A bullet fired from a rifle emerges with a kinetic energy of 2,400 joules. If the barrel of the rifle is 0.50 meter long, then the average force on the bullet in the barrel is approximately (1) 600 nt. (2) 1,200 nt. (3) 2,400 nt. (4) 4,800 nt.   15........

16. A rocket weighs 10,000 newtons at the earth's surface. If it rises to a height equal to the earth's radius, its weight will be (1) 2,500 nt. (2) 5,000 nt. (3) 10,000 nt. (4) 40.000 nt.   16........

17. In the diagram below, which point is in phase with point X?

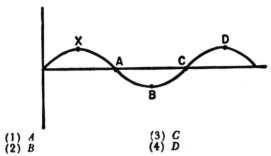

(1) A
(2) B

(3) C
(4) D

17........

18. The frequency of a water wave is 6.0 cycles per second. If its wavelength is 2.0 meters, then the speed of the wave is (1) .33 m./sec. (2) 2.0 m./sec. (3) 6.0 m./sec. (4) 12 m./sec.

18........

19. The diagram represents straight wave fronts passing through an opening in a barrier. The change in the shape of the wave fronts is an example of

(1) refraction
(2) polarization
(3) dispersion
(4) diffraction

19........

20. Which electromagnetic wave has the highest frequency? (1) radio (2) infrared (3) X-ray (4) visible

20........

21. A beam of light traveling in air is incident upon a glass block. If the angle of refraction is 30°, the angle of incidence is

(1) 0°
(2) between 0° and 30°
(3) between 30° and 90°
(4) 90°

21........

22. The critical angle is that angle of incidence which produces an angle of refraction of

(1) 0°
(2) 45°

(3) 60°
(4) 90°

22 ....

23. Which phenomenon is associated only with transverse waves? (1) interference (2) dispersion (3) refraction (4) polarization

23........

24. Which diagram shows the path that a monochromatic ray of light will travel as it passes through air, benzene, lucite, and back into air?

24........

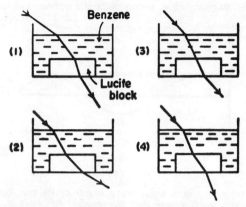

24........

25. A light beam from earth is reflected by an object in space. If the round trip takes 2.0 seconds, then the distance of the object from earth is (1) 6.7×10^7 meters (2) 1.5×10^8 meters (3) 3.0×10^8 meters (4) 6.0×10^8 meters   25........

26. A wave X meters long passes through a medium with a speed of Y meters per second. The frequency of the wave could be expressed as

(1) $\dfrac{Y}{X}$ cycles/sec.   (3) (XY cycles/sec.

(2) $\dfrac{X}{Y}$ cycles/sec.   (4) ($X + Y$) cycles/sec.   26........

27. Which will be produced when blue light with a wavelength of 4.7×10^{-7} meter passes through a double slit? (1) a continuous spectrum (2) two narrow bands of blue light (3) alternate blue and black bands (4) bands of blue light fringed with green and violet   27........

28. If the frequency of a train of waves is 25 cycles/second, then the period of waves is (1) 0.04 second (2) 0.25 second (3) 0.4 second (4) 25 seconds   28........

29. If three resistors of 9 ohms each are connected in series, their total resistance will be (1) 4.5 ohms (2) 27 ohms (3) 3 ohms (4) 9 ohms   29........

30. When a positively charged body touches a neutral body, the neutral body will (1) gain protons (2) lose protons (3) gain electrons (4) lose electrons   30........

31. Two parallel metal plates have a potential difference of 50 volts. How much work is done in moving a charge of 4.0×10^{-5} coulomb from one plate to the other? (1) 8.0×10^{-7} joule (2) 1.6×10^{-3} joule (3) 2.0×10^{-3} joule (4) 1.3×10^6 joules   31........

32. A 6.0-ohm resistor is connected in series with a 12-ohm resistor in an operating circuit. If the current in the 12-ohm resistor is 3.0 amperes, then the voltage drop across the 6.0-ohm resistor is   (1) 1.5 volts   (2) 18 volts   (3) 3.0 volts   (4) 36 volts   32........

33. The north pole of the solenoid shown would be located at point

    (1) A
    (2) B
    (3) C
    (4) D

33........

34. A resistor carries a current of 0.10 ampere when the potential difference across it is 5.0 volts. The resistance of the resistor is (1) 0.020 ohm   (2) 0.50 ohm   (3) 5.0 ohms   (4) 50 ohms   34........

35. Compared to the current in the 10 ohm resistor, the current in the 5-ohm resistor, in the circuit shown, will be

    (1) one-third as great
    (2) one-half as great
    (3) the same
    (4) twice as great

35........

36. A beam of electrons is moving from north to south as shown. The direction of the magnetic field above the beam is toward the   (1) north   (2) south   (3) east   (4) west   36........

37. Two point charges 1 meter apart repel each other with a force of 9 newtons. What is the force of repulsion when these two charges are 3 meters apart?   (1) 1 newton   (2) 27 newtons   (3) 3 newtons   (4) 81 newtons   37........

38. An electron gains 2 electron-volts of energy as it is transferred from point A to point B. The potential difference between points A and B is   (1) 3.2×10^{-19} volt   (2) 2 volts   (3) 32 volts   (4) 1.25×10^{19} volts   38........

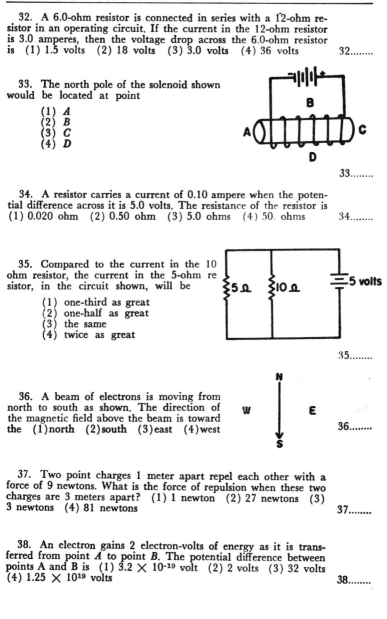

39. An electric motor lifts a 10-kilogram mass 100 meters in 10 seconds. The power developed by the motor is (1) 9.8 watts (2) 98 watts (3) 980 watts (4) 9,800 watts   39........

40. A neutral atom has 24 neutrons and 20 protons. The number of electrons in the atom is (1) 24 (2) 20 (3) 44 (4) 4   40........

41. Which diagram best represents the path of a positively charged particle as it passes near the nucleus of an atom?   41........

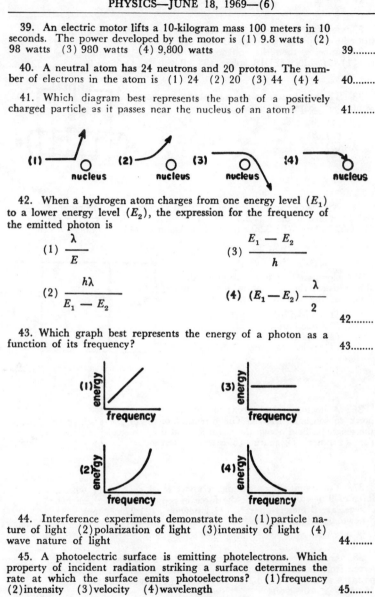

42. When a hydrogen atom charges from one energy level (E_1) to a lower energy level (E_2), the expression for the frequency of the emitted photon is

(1) $\dfrac{\lambda}{E}$

(3) $\dfrac{E_1 - E_2}{h}$

(2) $\dfrac{h\lambda}{E_1 - E_2}$

(4) $(E_1 - E_2)\dfrac{\lambda}{2}$

      42........

43. Which graph best represents the energy of a photon as a function of its frequency?   43........

44. Interference experiments demonstrate the (1) particle nature of light (2) polarization of light (3) intensity of light (4) wave nature of light   44........

45. A photoelectric surface is emitting photelectrons. Which property of incident radiation striking a surface determines the rate at which the surface emits photoelectrons? (1) frequency (2) intensity (3) velocity (4) wavelength   45........

Note that questions 46 through 60 have only three choices.

46. If the mass of an object is decreased, its inertia (1) decreases (2) increases (3) remains the same

46........

47. As the vector sum of all the forces acting on an object decreases, the acceleration of the object (1) decreases (2) increases (3) remains the same

47........

48. As a satellite in orbit moves from a distance of 300 kilometers to a distance of 160 kilometers above the earth, the kinetic energy of the satellite (1) decreases (2) increases (3) remains the same

48........

49. The graph below represents the velocity versus time relationship for a ball thrown vertically upward. Time zero represents the time of release.

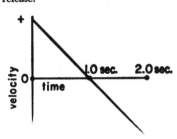

During the time interval between 1.0 second and 2.0 seconds, the displacement of the ball from the point where it was released (1) decreases (2) increases (3) remains the same

49........

50. As a ball falls freely toward the earth, the momentum of the earth-ball system (1) decreases (2) increases (3) remains the same

50........

51. As the amplitude of a wave increases, the energy transported by the wave (1) decreases (2) increases (3) remains the same

51........

52. As a wave travels into a medium in which its speed increases, its wavelength (1) decreases (2) increases (3) remains the same

52........

53. As the index of refraction of an alcohol and water mixture increases, the critical angle for the mixture (1) decreases (2) increases (3) remains the same

53........

54. As the current in a pair of parallel wires increases, the force between them (1) decreases (2) increases (3) remains the same

54........

55. When the current in a coil is halved and the number of coils is doubled, the magnetic field strength of the coil (1) decreases (2) increases (3) remains the same

55........

56. If the permeability of the core of a solenoid increases, its magnetic field strength (1)decreases (2)increases (3)remains the same

56........

57. A circuit is supplied with a constant voltage. As the resistance of the circuit decreases, the power dissipated by the circuit (1)decreases (2)increases (3)remains the same

57........

58. If the length and the cross-sectional area of a wire are both halved, the resistance of the wire will (1)decrease (2)increase (3)remain the same

58........

59. As additional resistors are connected in parallel to a source of constant voltage, the current in the circuit (1)decreases (2)increases (3)remains the same

59........

60. As the intensity of monochromatic light on a photo-sensitive surface increases, the maximum velocity of the ejected electrons (1)decreases (2)increases (3)remains the same

60........

Part II

This part consists of four groups, each group testing a major area in the course. Choose two of these four groups. Write your answers in the spaces provided on the line to the right.

Group 1 — Mechanics

Answer all three questions, 61 through 63, in this group. Each question counts 5 credits. For each part of the three questions, write the number of the word or expression that best completes that statement or answers that question.

61. Base your answers to questions *a* through *e* on the information below and on the *Physics Reference Tables*.

The temperature of 1 kilogram of mercury is changed from —73° C. to 727° C. by the addition of heat energy at the rate of 1 kilocalorie per minute. [Assume atmospheric pressure and no heat loss to the surroundings.]

a At which temperature can the mercury exist both as a liquid and as a gas? (1) 357° C. (2) 396° C. (3) 457° C. (4) 1,000° C.

a..........

b What is the total range of temperature in which mercury can exist as a liquid? (1)39 C.° (2)318 C.° (3)357 C.° (4)396 C.°

b..........

c What amount of heat is necessary to completely melt the mercury at its melting point? (1) 2.8 kcal. (2) 8.4 kcal. (3) 39 kcal. (4) 71 kcal.

c..........

d What amount of heat is necessary to raise the temperature of the mercury from —1° C. to 1° C.? (1)82 kcal. (2)2.0 kcal. (3).03 kcal. (4).06 kcal.

d..........

e How long will it take the mercury to change completely into a gas after it reaches its boiling point of 357°C.? (1)2.8 min. (2)39 min. (3)71 min. (4)357 min.

e..........

62. Base your answers to questions *a* through *e* on the graph below, which represents velocity versus time for an object in linear motion. The object has a velocity of 20 m./sec. at $T = 0$.

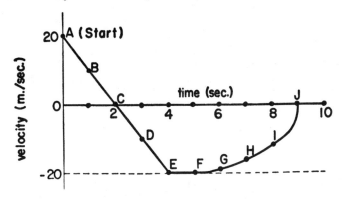

a During which interval is the magnitude of the acceleration greatest? (1)*EF* (2)*FG* (3)*GH* (4)*IJ*

a..........

b The acceleration of the object at point *D* on the curve is (1)0 m./sec.² (2)5 m.sec.² (3)—10m./sec.² (4)—20 m./sec.²

b..........

c During what interval does the object have a zero acceleration? (1)*BC* (2)*EF* (3)*GH* (4)*HI*

c..........

d At what point is the distance from start zero? (1)*C* (2)*E* (3)*F* (4)*J*

d..........

e At what point is the distance from start a maximum? (1)*C* (2)*E* (3)*G* (4)*J*

e..........

63. Base your answers to questions *a* through *e* on the diagram below, which represents a satellite orbiting the earth. The satellite's distance from the center of the earth equals 4 earth radii.

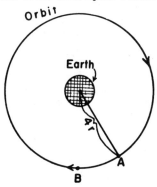

a Which vector best represents the velocity of the satellite at *B*?

(1) ↑

(3) ←

(2) ↓

(4) →

a...........

b The original satellite is replaced by one with twice the mass, and the orbit speed and radius are unchanged. Compared to the magnitude of the acceleration of the original satellite, the magnitude of the acceleration of the new satellite is (1) one-half as great (2) the same (3) twice as great (4) four times as great

b...........

c Which vector best represents the acceleration of the satellite at point *A* in its orbit?

(1) ↗

(3) ↘

(2) ↙

(4) ↖

c...........

Note that questions d and e have only three choices.

d As the satellite moves from point *A* to point *B*, its potential energy with respect to the earth will (1) decrease (2) increase (3) remain the same

d...........

e If the satellite's distance from the center of the earth were increased to 5 earth radii, the centripetal force on the satellite would (1) decrease (2) increase (3) remain the same

e...........

Group 2 — Wave Phenomena

Answer all three questions, 64 through 66, in this group. Each question counts 5 credits. For each part of the three questions, write the number of the word or expression that best completes that statement or answers that question.

64. Base your answers to questions *a* through *e* on the diagram and information below.

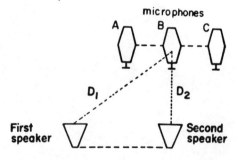

Two speakers are arranged as shown so that initially they will emit tones which are in phase, equal in volume, and equal in frequency. A microphone is placed at position A, which is equidistant from both speakers, and then is moved along a line parallel to the line joining the speakers until no sound is heard. [This is position B.] The microphone is then moved to position C where sound is again picked up by the microphone.

a Which phenomenon caused the sound to be louder at position C than at position B?   (1) reflection   (2) dispersion   (3) polarization   (4) interference

a..........

b Distance D_2 is shorter than distance D_1 by an amount equal to (1) the wavelength of the emitted sound   (2) one-half the wavelength of the emitted sound   (3) twice the wavelength of the emitted sound   (4) the distance between the two speakers

b..........

c If the sound waves emitted by D_1 and D_2 have a frequency of 660 v.p.s. and a speed of 330 meters per second, their wavelength is   (1) 1.0 meter   (2) 2.0 meters   (3) .25 meter   (4) .50 meter

c..........

Note that questions d and e have only three choices.

d As the first speaker is adjusted so that the sound which it emits is 180° out of phase with the sound emitted by the second speaker, the loudness of the sound received at A is   (1) greater   (2) less   (3) the same

d..........

e If speaker D_1 were removed and speaker D_2 were accelerated toward microphone B, the frequency of the waves detected at B would   (1) decrease   (2) increase   (3) remain the same

e..........

65. Base your answers to questions a through e on the information and diagram below.

The diagram represents a wave traveling from left to right along a horizontal elastic medium. The horizontal distance from b to f is 0.08 m. The vertical distance from x to y is 0.06 m.

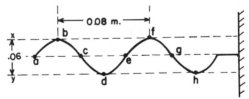

a If the crest at b takes 2.0 seconds to move from b to f, then what is the speed of the wave?   (1) 0.03 m./sec.   (2) 0.04 m./sec.   (3) 0.05 m./sec.   (4) 0.06 m./sec.

a..........

b If the period of the wave is 2.0 seconds, what is the frequency?   (1) 0.5 cycle/sec.   (2) 2.0 cycles/sec.   (3) 5.0 cycles/sec.   (4) 4.0 cycles/sec

b..........

c What is the amplitude of the wave? (1)0.03 m. (2)0.04 m. (3)0.05 m. (4)0.06 m.

c..........

d As the wave moves to the right from its present position, in which direction will the medium at point *e* first move? (1)down (2)up (3)to the right (4)to the left

d..........

e The frequency of the wave is now doubled. If the velocity remains constant, its wavelength is (1) quartered (2) halved (3) unchanged (4) doubled

e..........

66. Base your answers to questions *a* through *e* on the information and diagram below.

This diagram represents three transparent media arranged one on top of the other. A light ray in air is incident on the upper surface of layer *A*.

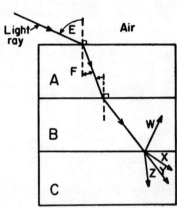

a If layers *B* and *C* both have the same index of refraction, in which direction will the light ray travel after reaching the boundary between layers *B* and *C*? (1)W (2)X (3)Y (4)Z

a..........

b If layer *A* were lucite, then layer **B** could be (1)water (2)diamond (3)benzene (4)flint glass

b..........

c If angle *E* is 60° and layer *A* has an index of refraction of 1.61, the sine of angle *F* will be closest to (1)1.00 (2)0.866 (3)0.538 (4)0.400

c..........

Note that questions d and e have only three choices.

d If angle *E* were increased, then angle *F* would (1)decrease (2)increase (3)remain the same

d..........

e Compared to the apparent speed of light in layer *A*, the apparent speed of light in layer *B* is (1)greater (2)the same (3)less

e..........

Group 3 — Electricity

Answer all three questions, 67 through 69, in this group. Each question counts 5 credits. For each part of the three questions, write the number of the word or expression that best completes that statement or answers that question.

67. Base your answers to questions *a* through *e* on the information and diagram below.

The diagram represents a rectangular wire loop, *ABCD*, rotating between two magnetic poles. Sides *AB* and *CD* move at a constant speed of 1.0 m./sec. The strength of the uniform magnetic field between the magnetic poles is 5.0 webers/m.². Side *AB* is 0.30 meter long.

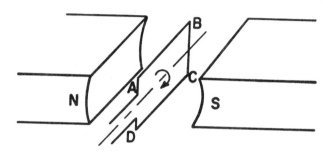

a The maximum e.m.f. induced in side *AB* is approximately (1) 1.5 volts (2) 2.0 volts (3) 3.0 volts (4) 6.0 volts   *a*..........

b The induced e.m.f. will be a maximum when the angle between the plane of the loop and the direction of the magnetic field is (1) 0° (2) 30° (3) 45° (4) 90°   *b*..........

Note that questions c through e have only three choices.

c If the number of loops in the coil is increased, the maximum e.m.f. induced in the coil will (1) decrease (2) increase (3) remain the same   *c*..........

d If the strength of the magnetic field is decreased and the rate at which the coil rotates remains constant, the maximum induced e.m.f. will (1) decrease (2) increase (3) remain the same   *d*..........

e If the speed at which the loop is rotating is increased, the maximum induced e.m.f. will (1) decrease (2) increase (3) remain the same   *e*..........

68. Base your answers to questions *a* through *e* on the information and diagram below.

This diagram represents two equal negative point charges, *A* and *B*, that are a distance *d* apart.

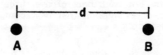

a Which diagram best represents the electrostatic lines of force between charge *A* and charge B?

a..........

b Where would the electric field intensity of the two charges be minimum?   (1) one quarter of the way between *A* and *B*   (2) midway between *A* and *B*   (3) on the surface of *B*   (4) on the surface of *A*

b..........

c Which graph expresses the relationship of the distance between the charges and the force between them?

c..........

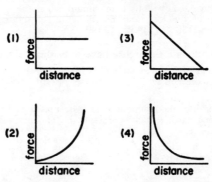

d If charge *A* is doubled, the force between *A* and *B* will be (1) quartered   (2) halved   (3) doubled   (4) quadrupled

d..........

e If *A* has an excess of 2.5 × 10¹⁹ electrons, its charge in coulombs is   (1)1.6   (2)2.5   (3)6.5   (4)4.0   *e*..........

69. Base your answers to questions *a* through *e* on the information and diagram below.

The diagram below represents a direct-current motor connected in series with a 12-volt battery, a resistance *R*, and an ammeter *A*. Mass *M* is suspended from a pulley that is attached to the shaft of the motor.

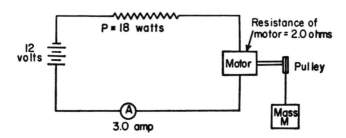

a What is the resistance of resistor *R*?   (1) 8.0 ohms (2) 2.0 ohms   (3) 3.0 ohms   (4) 6.0 ohms   *a*..........

b What is the potential difference across resistor *R*?   (1)0 volts (2)12 volts   (3)6.0 volts   (4)4.0 volts   *b*..........

c What is the rate at which the motor uses electrical energy? (1)0 watts   (2)18 watts   (3)36 watts   (4)4.0 watts   *c*..........

d What is the total charge that will pass through the motor in 5.0 seconds?   (1) 0.60 coulomb   (2) 15 coulombs   (3) 3.0 coulombs   (4) 4.0 coulombs   *d*..........

e If the motor is 100% efficient, how much will the gravitational potential energy of mass *M* change in 10 seconds? (1)9.8 joules   (2)12 joules   (3)18 joules   (4)180 joules   *e*..........

Group 4 — Atomic and Nuclear Physics

Answer all three questions, 70 through 72, in this group. Each question counts 5 credits. For each part of the three questions, write the number of the word or expression that best completes that statement or answers that question.

70. Base your answers to questions *a* through *e* on the information below.

A sample of pure radon gas ($_{86}Rn^{222}$) is sealed in a glass ampule. The half-life of radon is 4 days.

a Which is an isotope of radon? (1) $_{88}X^{222}$ (2) $_{84}X^{220}$ (3) $_{86}X^{220}$ (4) $_{89}X^{222}$ *a*..........

b If the pressure inside the glass ampule were doubled, the half-life of radon would   (1)be halved   (2)remain the same (3)be doubled   (4)be quadrupled   *b*..........

c Twelve days after the radon gas is sealed in the glass ampule, the fraction of radon gas remaining will be (1)1/2 (2)1/4 (3)1/8 (4)1/16   *c*...........

d The number of neutrons in the nucleus of $_{86}Rn^{222}$ is (1)86 (2)136 (3)222 (4)308   *d*...........

e Several days later, an analysis shows that there is a second gas in the sealed ampule. This second gas is most likely (1)hydrogen (2)helium (3)oxygen (4)nitrogen   *e*...........

71. Base your answers to question *a* through *e* on the Uranium Disintegration Series in the *Physics Reference Tables.*

a An example of alpha decay is the change of (1) $_{92}U^{238}$ into $_{90}Th^{234}$ (2) $_{90}Th^{234}$ into $_{91}Pa^{234}$ (3) $_{91}Pa^{234}$ into $_{92}U^{234}$ (4) $_{82}Pb^{214}$ into $_{83}Bi^{214}$ *a*...........

b Which isotope below is *not* formed during the decay of $_{92}U^{238}$? (1) $_{90}Th^{234}$ (2) $_{90}Th^{230}$ (3) $_{84}Po^{226}$ (4) $_{84}Po^{218}$ *b*...........

c Which will be emitted when $_{83}Bi^{210}$ changes to $_{82}Pb^{206}$? (1)1 alpha particle, only (2)1 beta particle, only (3)2 alpha particles, only (4)1 alpha particle and 1 beta particle   *c*...........

d Which stable isotope is formed when $_{92}U^{238}$ decays? (1) $_{83}Bi^{214}$ (2) $_{84}Po^{214}$ (3) $_{82}Pb^{214}$ (4) $_{82}Pb^{206}$ *d*...........

e What is the total number of alpha particles emitted as an atom of $_{92}U^{238}$ decays to $_{82}Pb^{206}$? (1)6 (2)7 (3)8 (4)13   *e*...........

72. Base your answers to questions *a* through *e* on the information below and the *Physics Reference Tables.*
A photon with 14.6 electron-volts of energy collides with a hydrogen atom in its ground state.

a What is the energy of the incident photon? (1)1.5 × 10⁻¹⁸ joule (2)2.3 × 10⁻¹⁸ joule (3)6.3 × 10⁻¹⁸ joule (4)9.1 × 10⁻¹⁸ joule   *a*...........

b What is the maximum potential energy that the hydrogen atom can gain in the collision without ionizing? (1)0 electron-volts (2)1.0 electron-volt (3)13.6 electron-volts (4)14.6 electron-volts   *b*...........

c What will be the energy of the photon emitted by a hydrogen atom as the hydrogen atom moves from $n = 3$ to $n = 2$? (1)1.0 electron-volt (2)1.5 electron-volts (3)1.9 electron-volts (4)12.1 electron-volts   *c*...........

d How many electron-volts of energy would be required to ionize a hydrogen atom in the $n = 3$ state? (1)1.5 (2)1.02 (3)1.21 (4)1.36   *d*...........

e Which transition results in the emission of a photon with the highest frequency? (1)$n = 5$ to $n = 4$ (2)$n = 5$ to $n = 3$ (3)$n = 3$ to $n = 2$ (4)$n = 2$ to $n = 1$ *e*...........

PHYSICS

JUNE 18, 1970

Part I

Directions (1-60): In the space provided on the separate answer sheet, write the *number* preceding the word or expression that, of those given, best completes the statement or answers the question.   [70]

1. An object is uniformly accelerated from rest to a speed of 25 meters per second in 10 seconds. The acceleration of the object is (1) 1.0 m./sec.² (2) 2.0 m./sec.² (3) 1.5 m./sec.² (4) 2.5 m./sec.²

2. What force is necessary to give a 2.0-kilogram mass initially at rest an acceleration of 5.0 meters per second²? (1) 0.4 nt. (2) 2.5 nt. (3) 10 nt. (4) 20 nt.

3. If the mass of an object were doubled, its weight would be (1) halved (2) doubled (3) quadrupled (4) unchanged

4. Which force could act concurrently with force *A* to produce force *B* as a resultant?

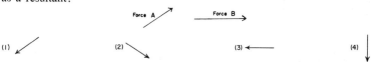

5. If the distance between two masses were tripled, the gravitational force between them would be (1) 1/9 as great (2) 1/3 as great (3) 3 times as great (4) 9 times as great

6. Two unequal masses falling freely from the same point above the earth's surface would experience the same (1) acceleration (2) decrease in potential energy (3) increase in kinetic energy (4) increase in momentum

7. A 1.0-kilogram object falls freely from rest. The magnitude of its momentum after one second of fall is (1) 1.0 kg.-m./sec. (2) 4.9 kg.-m./sec. (3) 9.8 kg.-m./sec. (4) 20. kg.-m./sec.

8. An increase in temperature of 54 Celsius degrees is equal to an increase of (1) 54 Kelvin degrees (2) 219 Kelvin degrees (3) 327 Kelvin degrees (4) 454 Kelvin degrees

9. An object is displaced 3 meters to the west and then 4 meters to the south. Which vector shown below best represents the resultant displacement of the block?

10. A 2-newton force acts on a 3-kilogram mass for 6 seconds. The change of velocity of the mass is (1) 18 m./sec. (2) 2 m./sec. (3) 36 m./sec. (4) 4 m./sec.

11. Which pair of units measures the same quantity? (1) kilogram and kilocalorie (2) kilocalorie and degree (3) joule and kilocalorie (4) degree and joule

12. The work done in accelerating an object along a frictionless horizontal surface is equal to the object's change in (1) momentum (2) velocity (3) potential energy (4) kinetic energy

13. A man weighing 800 newtons is standing in an elevator. If the elevator rises with an acceleration of 9.8 meters per second², the force exerted by the elevator on the man will be (1) 400 nt. (2) 800 nt. (3) 1,600 nt. (4) 2,000 nt.

14. What is the work required to raise a 10.-kilogram box from the surface of the earth to a height of 5.0 meters? (1) 50 joules (2) 100 joules (3) 200 joules (4) 490 joules

15. The graph shows the speed of an object plotted against the time. The total distance traveled by the object during the first 4 seconds is (1) 0.5 meter (2) 2 meters (3) 8 meters (4) 4 meters

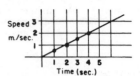

16. A wave which has a frequency of 20.0 cycles per second travels with a speed of 100 meters per second. What is the wavelength of this wave? (1) 0.200 meter (2) 5.00 meters (3) 20.0 meters (4) 2,000 meters

17. When a wave is reflected from a surface, there is a change in the wave's (1) frequency (2) direction (3) speed (4) wavelength

18. Which graph best represents the relationship between the Celsius temperature of an ideal gas and the average kinetic energy of its molecules?

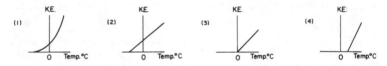

19. A pulse in a spring transmits (1) energy, only (2) mass, only (3) both energy and mass (4) neither energy nor mass

20. If the speed of light in a vacuum is C, then the speed of light in a medium with an index of refraction of 2 will be (1) $\frac{C}{2}$ (2) $2C$ (3) $\frac{C}{4}$ (4) $4C$

21. In a certain medium, waves of different frequencies travel with different speeds. Such a medium is (1) opaque (2) coherent (3) periodic (4) dispersive

22. The change in direction which occurs when a wave passes obliquely from one medium into another is called (1) diffraction (2) interference (3) refraction (4) superposition

23. Sources that produce waves with a constant phase relation are said to be (1) polarized (2) diffused (3) refracted (4) coherent

24. Which phenomenon indicates that light is a transverse wave? (1) diffraction (2) polarization (3) reflection (4) refraction

25. The frequency of ultraviolet radiation is less than that of (1) radio wave radiation (2) infrared radiation (3) violet radiation (4) gamma radiation

26. The critical angle when light passes from crown glass into air is 41 degrees. When the angle of incidence equals the critical angle, the angle of refraction will be (1) between 0° and 41° (2) 41° (3) between 41° and 90° (4) 90°

27. When two waves cross each other, maximum constructive interference will occur in places where the phase difference between the two waves is (1) 0° (2) 45° (3) 90° (4) 180°

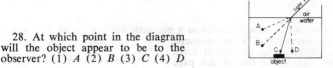

28. At which point in the diagram will the object appear to be to the observer? (1) A (2) B (3) C (4) D

29. The water wave shown is moving toward the right. In which directions are particles *A* and *B* moving? (1) Both *A* and *B* are moving upward. (2) Both *A* and *B* are moving downward. (3) *A* is moving upward, and *B* is moving downward. (4) *A* is moving downward, and *B* is moving upward.

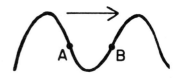

30. A metal sphere with +11 elementary charges touches an identical sphere with +15 elementary charges. After touching, the number of elementary charges on the first sphere is (1) +13 (2) +26 (3) −4 (4) +4

31. If three resistors of 3 ohms, 6 ohms, and 9 ohms are connected in parallel, the combined resistance will be (1) greater than 9 ohms (2) between 6 ohms and 9 ohms (3) between 3 ohms and 6 ohms (4) less than 3 ohms

32. How much electric energy is dissipated when a 120-volt appliance operates at 2 amperes for 1 second? (1) 60 joules (2) 240 joules (3) 480 joules (4) 28,800 joules

33. Two fixed parallel wires, each carrying a current of 1.0 ampere, attract each other with a force of 1.2×10^{-6} newton. If the current in one of the wires is doubled, the force of attraction between them will become
(1) 1.2×10^{-6} nt.   (3) 4.8×10^{-6} nt.
(2) 2.4×10^{-6} nt.   (4) 6.0×10^{-6} nt.

34. If the electrons in the wire shown are flowing eastward, in which direction will the needle of a compass held above the wire point? (1) north (2) south (3) east (4) west

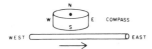

35. What amount of work is needed to transfer 10 coulombs of charge between two points having a potential difference of 120 volts? (1) 1/12 joule (2) 12 joules (3) 600 joules (4) 1,200 joules

36. Which is a unit of electric power? (1) watt (2) volt (3) ampere (4) kilowatt-hour

37. An electric potential difference will be induced between the ends of the conductor shown in the diagram when the conductor moves in direction (1) *A* (2) *B* (3) *C* (4) *D*

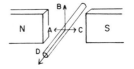

38. The diagram represents magnetic flux intersecting a plane at right angles. If the magnitude of the flux is 16 webers, the average flux density intersecting the plane is (1) 64 webers/m.^{2} (2) 16 webers/m.^{2} (3) 8 webers/m.^{2} (4) 4 webers/m.^{2}

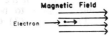

39. An electron moving parallel to a magnetic field as shown in the diagram will experience (1) no magnetic force (2) a magnetic downward force (3) a magnetic force out of the page (4) a magnetic force into the page

40. Which graph best represents the electric force between two point charges as a function of the distance between the charges?

41. As a positively charged rod is brought near to but not allowed to touch the knob of an uncharged electroscope, the leaves will diverge because (1) negative charges are transferred from the electroscope to the rod (2) negative charges are attracted to the knob of the electroscope (3) positive charges are repelled to the leaves of the electroscope (4) positive charges are transferred from the rod to the electroscope

42. An electron may be placed at positions A, B, or C between the two parallel charged metal plates shown below. The electric force on the electron will be (1) greatest at A (2) greatest at B (3) greatest at C (4) the same at all three positions

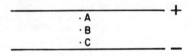

43. To reduce the resistance of a metal conductor one should (1). cool the conductor to a low temperature (2) heat the conductor to a high temperature (3) coat the conductor with an insulator (4) wire the conductor in series with another resistor

44. Two copper wires have the same length, but the cross-sectional area of wire A is twice that of wire B. Compared to the resistance of wire B, the resistance of wire A is (1) one-quarter as great (2) one-half as great (3) twice as great (4) four times as great

45. Which device is normally used to accelerate charged particles? (1) cyclotron (2) electroscope (3) cloud chamber (4) Geiger counter

46. The fact that most of the alpha particles directed at a thin metal foil pass through without being deflected indicates that the atom consists mostly of (1) electrons (2) neutrons (3) empty space (4) protons

47. If a hydrogen atom is in the n = 5 energy level, what is the minimum energy needed to ionize the atom? (1) 0.54 e.v. (2) 13.1 e.v. (3) 13.6 e.v. (4) 14.1 e.v.

48. What is the energy of the photon emitted by a hydrogen atom when the hydrogen atom changes directly from the n = 5 state to the n = 2 state? (1) 13.6 e.v. (2) 3.4 e.v. (3) 2.86 e.v. (4) 0.54 e.v.

49. The energy of a photon which has a frequency of 3.3×10^{14} cycles per second is approximately
(1) 2.0×10^{-48} joule   (3) 5.0×10^{-19} joule
(2) 2.0×10^{-19} joule   (4) 5.0×10^{48} joule

50. When photons with an energy of 3.0 electron-volts strike a photoelectric surface, the maximum kinetic energy of the emitted photoelectrons is 2.0 electron-volts. What is the work function of the surface? (1) 1.0 e.v. (2) .67 e.v. (3) 1.5 e.v. (4) 5.0 e.v.

51. The atoms of a certain element contain 12 protons and 13 neutrons. An atom of an isotope of this element must contain (1) 12 neutrons (2) 13 neutrons (3) 12 protons (4) 13 electrons

52. The mass number of an alpha particle is (1) 1 (2) 2 ((3) 3 (4) 4
Note that questions 53-60 have only three choices.

53. As a ball falls freely toward the earth, its kinetic energy (1) decreases (2) increases (3) remains the same

54. As the time required for a person to run up a flight of stairs increases, the power developed by the person (1) decreases (2) increases (3) remains the same

55. As an object moves away from the earth's surface, its inertia (1) decreases (2) increases (3) remains the same

56. As the frequency of a wave is increased, its period (1) decreases (2) increases (3) remains the same

57. As the difference in potential across the terminals of a solenoid increases, its magnetic flux density (1) decreases (2) increases (3) remains the same

58. A loop of wire rotating in a magnetic field is part of a closed circuit. As the current in this circuit increases, the force required to rotate the loop at a constant speed (1) decreases (2) increases (3) remains the same

59. As an electron in an atom moves in a circular path of constant radius around the nucleus, the total energy of the atom (1) decreases (2) increases (3) remains the same

60. As the frequency of a photon increases, its momentum (1) decreases (2) increases (3) remains the same

Part II

This part consists of four groups, each group testing a major area in the course. Choose two of these four groups. Write your answers in the spaces provided on the separate answer sheet.

Group 1 — Mechanics
Answer all fifteen questions, 61 through 75, in this group. Each question counts 1 credit. For each of the fifteen questions, write the number of the word or expression that best completes that statement or answers that question.

Base your answers to questions 61 through 64 on the graph, which shows the velocity of a 1,500-kilogram car during a 20-second time interval.

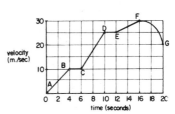

61. *No* unbalanced force is acting on the car during time interval (1) *BC* (2) *CD* (3) *EF* (4) *FG*

62. The acceleration of the car during time interval *AB* is (1) 0.40 m./sec.^{2} (2) 2.5 m./sec.^{2} (3) 10 m./sec.^{2} (4) 40 m./sec.^{2}

63. During time interval *CD*, the average velocity of the car is (1) 7.5 m./sec. (2) 17.5 m./sec. (3) 15 m./sec. (4) 35 m./sec.

64. The impulse applied to the car during time interval *AB* is (1) 9.0×10^2 nt.-sec. (2) 4.5×10^3 nt.-sec. (3) 6.0×10^3 nt.-sec. (4) 1.5×10^4 nt.-sec.

Base your answers to question 65 through 67 on the information and diagram at right.

A car is traveling around the track at a constant speed of 20 meters per second. *AG* and *CF* are the diameters of the semicircular ends of the track.

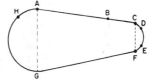

65. If the total length of the track is 700 meters, the time required for the car to make a complete trip is (1) 17.5 seconds (2) 35 seconds (3) 7,000 seconds (4) 14,000 seconds

66. The acceleration of the car is zero at point (1) *E* (2) *B* (3) *H* (4) *D*

67. As the car travels from point *C* to point *D*, the centripetal force on the car is (1) constant in magnitude but changing in direction (2) constant in both magnitude and direction (3) changing in magnitude but constant in direction (4) changing in both magnitude and direction

Base your answers to questions 68 through 71 on the information and diagram below.

Block *A* moves with a velocity of 2 meters per second to the right, as shown in the diagram, and then collides elastically with block *B*, which is at rest. Block *A* stops moving, and block *B* moves to the right after the collision.

A   B

| 10 kg. | 2 m./sec. → | | 10 kg. |

Frictionless Surface

68. What is the combined momentum of blocks *A* and *B* before the collision?

(1) 0 $\frac{\text{kg.-m.}}{\text{sec.}}$ (3) 20 $\frac{\text{kg.-m.}}{\text{sec.}}$

(2) 10 $\frac{\text{kg.-m.}}{\text{sec.}}$ (4) 40 $\frac{\text{kg.-m.}}{\text{sec.}}$

69. What is the total change in momentum of blocks *A* and *B*?

(1) 0 $\frac{\text{kg.-m.}}{\text{sec.}}$ (3) 40 $\frac{\text{kg.-m.}}{\text{sec.}}$

(2) 20 $\frac{\text{kg.-m.}}{\text{sec.}}$ (4) 200 $\frac{\text{kg.-m.}}{\text{sec.}}$

70. If block *A* is stopped in 0.1 second, the average force acting on block *A* is (1) 50 nt. (2) 100 nt. (3) 200 nt. (4) 400 nt.

71. If the blocks had remained together after collision, their velocity would have been (1) 1 m./sec. (2) 2 m./sec. (3) 0 m./sec. (4) .5 m./sec.

Base your answers to questions 72 through 75 on the graph at right. The graph shows the temperature for 10 kilograms of an unknown substance as heat is added at a constant rate of 15 kilocalories per minute. The substance is a solid at 0° Celsius.

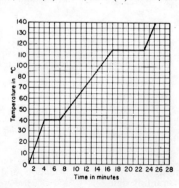

72. How much heat is added to the substance from the time that it stops melting to the time that it begins to boil? (1) 10 kcal. (2) 15 kcal. (3) 80 kcal. (4) 150 kcal.

73. What is the total heat necessary to change the substance at its melting point from a solid to a liquid? (1) 3 kcal. (2) 40 kcal. (3) 45 kcal. (4) 90 kcal.

Note that questions 74 and 75 have only three choices.

74. From the 17th minute to the 23rd minute, the average kinetic energy of the molecules of the substance (1) decreases (2) increases (3) remains the same

75. As the temperature of the solid increases from 0° C. to 40° C., its specific heat (1) decreases (2) increases (3) remains the same

Group 2 — Wave Phenomena

Answer all fifteen questions, 76 through 90, in this group. Each question counts 1 credit. For each of the fifteen questions, write the number of the word or expression that best completes that statement or answers that question.

Base your answers to questions 76 through 79 on the diagram, which shows four waves, all traveling in the same medium.

76. Which two waves will produce a resultant wave with the greatest amplitude? (1) *A* and *B* (2) *A* and *C* (3) *A* and *D* (4) *C* and *D*

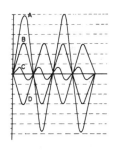

77. Which pair of waves has the same amplitude? (1) *A* and *C* (2) *B* and *C* (3) *B* and *D* (4) *D* and *A*

78. Compared to the wavelength of wave *C*, the wavelength of wave *A* is (1) one-half as great (2) the same (3) twice as great (4) three times as great

79. Which pair of waves would produce complete destructive interference? (1) *A* and *C* (2) *A* and *D* (3) *B* and *C* (4) *B* and *D*

Base your answers to questions 80 through 82 on the diagram below, which represents a thin converging lens and its principal axis. *F* represents the principal focus.

80. If the light rays are parallel when they leave the lens, the light source must be placed (1) between *F* and the lens (2) at *F* (3) between *F* and 2*F* (4) at 2*F*

81. As an object is moved from point *A* toward point *B*, its image will (1) become erect (2) move toward the lens (3) change from real to virtual (4) become enlarged

82. If the image is located at 2*F'* the object must be located (1) at *F* (2) between *F* and 2*F* (3) at 2*F* (4) beyond 2*F*

Base your answers to questions 83 through 86 on the diagrams below, which show the paths of beams of monochromatic light as they reach the boundary between two media. N is the normal to the surface.

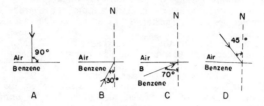

83. The direction of the beam of light will not change in diagram (1) A (2) B (3) C (4) D

84. The beam of light will undergo total internal reflection at the boundary in diagram (1) A (2) B (3) C (4) D

85. The angle of refraction of the beam of light will be greater than the angle of incidence in diagram (1) A (2) B (3) C (4) D

86. What is the sine of the angle of refraction for the beam of light in diagram D? (1) 1.00 (2) 0.707 (3) 0.47 (4) 0.30

Base your answers to questions 87 through 90 on the information and diagram below.

The diagram below represents the interference pattern produced by a source of monochromatic light with a wavelength of 6.0×10^{-7} meter. The light is incident upon two slits that are 2.0×10^{-5} meter apart and 2.0 meters from the screen.

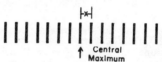

87. The color of the incident light is (1) green (2) yellow (3) red (4) orange

88. Distance x is equal to (1) 1.7×10^{-2} m. (2) 3.0×10^{-2} m. (3) 6.0×10^{-2} m. (4) 1.2×10^{-1} m.

Note that questions 89 and 90 have only three choices.

89. If the distance between the slits and the screen is increased, then distance x will (1) decrease (2) increase (3) remain the same

90. If the light source is made brighter, then distance x will (1) decrease (2) increase (3) remain the same

Group 3 — Electricity

Answer all fifteen questions, 91 through 105, in this group. Each question counts 1 credit. For each of the fifteen questions, write the number of the word or expression that best completes that statement or answers that question.

Base your answers to questions 91 through 94 on the information and diagram below.

Two conducting spheres, A and B, are separated by a distance of 2 meters between centers. Sphere A has a charge of $+2 \times 10^{-4}$ coulomb, and sphere B has a charge of $+6 \times 10^{-4}$ coulomb.

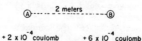

91. Which diagram best represents the electric lines of force around sphere *A* and sphere *B*?

92. The force that these two spheres exert upon each other is (1) 3.0 × 10^{-8} newton (2) +5.4 × 10^2 newtons (3) 9.0 × 10^9 newtons (4) 2.7 × 10^2 newtons

Note that questions 93 and 94 have only three choices.

93. As the distance between the two positively charged spheres increases, the force of repulsion between them (1) decreases (2) increases (3) remains the same

94. The spheres are brought together until they touch, and are then separated. As compared to the original total charge on the spheres, the net charge after separation is (1) less (2) greater (3) the same

Base your answers to questions 95 through 98 on the diagram.

95. What is the total resistance of the circuit? (1) 6.6 ohms (2) 10 ohms (3) 20 ohms (4) 30 ohms

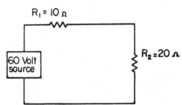

96. If the potential difference across R_1 is *V* volts, the potential difference across R_2 would equal (1) *V* volts (2) ½(60 − *V*) volts (3) (60 − *V*) volts (4) (60 + *V*) volts

Note that questions 97 and 98 have only three choices.

97. If the potential difference of the source were decreased, the total heat developed in the circuit would (1) decrease (2) increase (3) remain the same

98. Compared to the current in R_1, the current in R_2 is (1) less (2) greater (3) the same

Base your answers to questions 99 through 102 on the diagram and information below.

The diagram shows a unit positive charge moving at a constant speed perpendicular to the direction of a magnetic field in a vacuum.

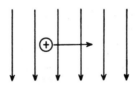

99. If the unit positive charge on the particle were replaced by a unit negative charge, the magnitude of the force exerted on the particle would be (1) quartered (2) halved (3) doubled (4) unaffected

100. If the magnetic field strength were doubled, the force exerted on the particle would be (1) halved (2) unaffected (3) doubled (4) quadrupled

101. If the charge on the particle were doubled, the force exerted on the particle would be (1) halved (2) unaffected (3) doubled (4) quadrupled

102. If the speed of the particle were doubled, the force exerted on the particle would be (1) halved (2) unaffected (3) doubled (4) quadrupled

Base your answers to questions 103 through 105 on the information and diagram.

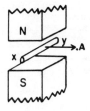

Conductor, *xy,* is moving through a uniform magnetic field toward point *A,* as indicated by the arrow. The length of the wire is 0.20 meter and the magnetic field strength is 0.50 newton per ampere-meter. The wire moves at a uniform velocity of 1.0 meter per second.

103. Which vector correctly represents the direction of the magnetic field between the north and south poles of the magnet?

104. What is the magnitude of the induced voltage in conductor *xy*? (1) 0.0 volts (2) 0.10 volt (3) 2.5 volts (4) 10. volts

105. If the conductor were moving from its position directly toward the north pole, then the magnitude of the induced voltage in the conductor would be (1) 0.0 volts (2) 0.1 volt (3) 2.5 volts (4) 10.0 volts

Group 4 — Atomic and Nuclear Physics

Answer all fifteen questions, 106 through 120, in this group. Each question counts 1 credit. For each of the fifteen questions, write the number of the word or expression that best completes that statement or answers that question.

106. Charged particles can be accelerated by (1) a gravitational field, only (2) an electric field, only (3) a magnetic field, only (4) both an electric field and a magnetic field

107. Isotopes of the same element have the same number of (1) neutrons and protons, only (2) neutrons and electrons, only (3) protons and electrons, only (4) electrons, protons, and neutrons

108. What is the relationship between the atomic number *Z,* the mass number *A,* and the number of neutrons *N* in a nucleus?

(1) $A = Z + N$ (3) $A = \dfrac{N}{Z}$

(2) $A = Z - N$ (4) $A = NZ$

109. One a.m.u. is equal to

(1) $\dfrac{1}{931}$ Mev.   (3) 931 Mev.

(2) $\dfrac{931}{c^2}$ Mev.   (4) $931c^2$ Mev.

110. If the half-life of $^{234}_{90}\text{Th}$ is 24 days, the amount of a 12-gram sample remaining after 96 days is (1) 1 gram (2) 0.75 gram (3) 6 grams (4) 1.5 grams

111. Given the equation $^{27}_{13}\text{Al} + ^{4}_{2}\text{He} \rightarrow ^{30}_{15}\text{P} + X$ The correct symbol for *X* is

(1) $^{0}_{+1}e$ (2) $^{0}_{-1}e$ (3) $^{4}_{2}\text{He}$ (4) $^{1}_{0}n$

112. When lead $^{214}_{82}\text{Pb}$ emits a beta particle, the resultant nucleus will be

(1) $^{214}_{81}\text{Tl}$ (2) $^{213}_{82}\text{Pb}$ (3) $^{214}_{83}\text{Bi}$ (4) $^{214}_{84}\text{Po}$

Base your answers to questions 113 and 114 on the information below.

Monochromatic light strikes a metal surface that has a work function of 6.7×10^{-19} joule. Each photon has an energy of 8.0×10^{-19} joule.

113. What is the maximum kinetic energy of the photoelectrons emitted by the metal?
(1) 1.3×10^{-19} joule (3) 6.7×10^{-19} joule
(2) 2.6×10^{-19} joule (4) 8.0×10^{-19} joule

114. What is the energy of each photon expressed in electron-volts?
(1) 5.4×10^{-37} electron-volt (3) 8.0×10^{-19} electron-volt
(2) 1.6×10^{-19} electron-volt (4) 5.0 electron-volts

115. Which determines the number of electrons emitted by a photoelectric material? (1) intensity (2) color (3) frequency (4) wavelength

Base your answers to questions 116 through 118 on the diagram below, which represents three visible lines in the hydrogen spectrum. Either the energy or the frequency for each of these lines appears below the diagram.

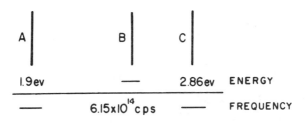

116. What is the energy of the photons that produced line *B*?
(1) 3.23×10^{-19} joule (3) 9.28×10^{-19} joule
(2) 4.07×10^{-19} joule (4) 9.85×10^{-19} joule

117. Which energy level transition produced line *A*?
(1) $n = 2$ to $n = 1$ (3) $n = 4$ to $n = 3$
(2) $n = 3$ to $n = 2$ (4) $n = 5$ to $n = 2$

118. If the diagram represented an *absorption* (dark line) spectrum, which energy level transition would have produced line *A*?
(1) $n = 2$ to $n = 3$ (3) $n = 3$ to $n = 2$
(2) $n = 2$ to $n = 4$ (4) $n = 4$ to $n = 2$

119. A particle accelerator can accelerate a (1) neutron (2) gamma photon (3) proton (4) hydrogen atom

120. For a given applied voltage, which particle will have the greatest acceleration? (1) an electron (2) a proton (3) a neutron (4) an alpha particle

PHYSICS
TUESDAY, JUNE 22, 1971
Part I

Directions (1-60): In the space provided on the separate answer sheet, write the *number* preceding the word or expression that, of those given, best completes the statement or answers the question.   [70]

1. Which is a vector quantity? (1) distance (2) speed (3) displacement (4) time

2. Forces *A* and *B* have a resultant *R*. Force *A* and resultant *R* are shown in the diagram below.

Which vector below best represents force *B*?

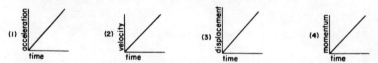

3. Which could be expressed in units of mass only? (1) force/acceleration (2) power × time (3) momentum/time (4) energy/force

4. A 40-newton object is released from rest at a height of 10 meters above the earth's surface. Just before it hits the ground, its kinetic energy will be closest to (1) 0 joules (2) 400 joules (3) 800 joules (4) 1,200 joules

5. An object is allowed to fall freely near the surface of a planet. The object has an acceleration due to gravity of 24 m./sec.^{2}. How far will the object fall during the first second? (1) 24 meters (2) 12 meters (3) 9.8 meters (4) 4.9 meters

6. Which graph best represents an object in equilibrium?

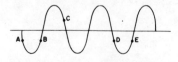

7. When an unbalanced force of 10. newtons is applied to an object whose mass is 4.0 kilograms, the acceleration of the object will be (1) 40. meters/sec.^{2} (2) 2.5 meters/sec.^{2} (3) 9.8 meters/sec.^{2} (4) 0.40 meters/sec.^{2}

8. A 1-kilogram object rests on a horizontal table top. The force that the table top exerts on the object is (1) 1 nt. (2) 2 nt. (3) 0 nt. (4) 9.8 nt.

9. An astronaut weighs 600 newtons at the earth's surface. If he doubles his distance from the earth's center, his weight will be (1) 100 nt. (2) 150 nt. (3) 300 nt. (4) 400 nt.

10. A 2-newton force acts on a mass. If the momentum of the mass changes by 120 kg.-meters/sec., the force acts for a time of (1) 8 sec. (2) 30 sec. (3) 60 sec. (4) 120 sec.

11. How much work is done by a force of 8 newtons acting through a distance of 6 meters? (1) 0 joules (2) 12 joules (3) 48 joules (4) 192 joules

12. The rate at which a force does work may be measured in (1) watts (2) newtons (3) joules (4) kilocalories

13. If the kinetic energy of a 10-kilogram object is 2,000 joules, its velocity is (1) 10 meters/sec. (2) 20 meters/sec. (3) 100 meters/sec. (4) 400 meters/sec.

14. Which point in the wave shown in the diagram is in phase with point *A*? (1) *E* (2) *B* (3) *C* (4) *D*

15. Which color of light has the greatest period? (1) violet (2) green (3) orange (4) red

16. Which wave phenomenon is *not* common to both light and sound waves? (1) reflection (2) refraction (3) polarization (4) diffraction

17. All electromagnetic waves in a vaccum have the same (1) frequency (2) wavelength (3) speed (4) energy

18. The speed of light in water is closest to the speed of light in (1) a vacuum (2) benzene (3) carbon tetrachloride (4) alcohol

19. The wave nature of light is best shown by the phenomenon of (1) diffraction (2) reflection (3) refraction (4) dispersion

20. As a wave enters a different medium with no change in velocity, the wave will be (1) reflected but not refracted (2) refracted but not reflected (3) both reflected and refracted (4) neither reflected nor refracted

21. The diagram at right shows light ray *R* entering air from water. Through which point is the ray most likely to pass? (1) *A* (2) *B* (3) *C* (4) *D*

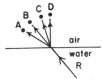

22. If the speed of light in a medium is approximately 2×10^8 meters per second, the medium could be (1) water (2) benzene (3) alcohol (4) diamond

23. Maximum constructive interference will occur at points where the phase difference between two waves is (1) 0° (2) 90° (3) 180° (4) 270°

24. Compared to the object, real images formed by a lens are always (1) larger (2) smaller (3) inverted (4) erect

25. When ray *I* emerges from the lens shown in the diagram, it will travel along a path toward point (1) *A* (2) *B* (3) *C* (4) *D*

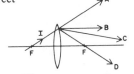

26. A positively charged body must have (1) an excess of neutrons (2) an excess of electrons (3) a deficiency of protons (4) a deficiency of electrons

27. Negatively charged rod *A* is used to charge rod *B* by induction. Object *C* is then charged by direct contact with rod *B*. The charge on object *C* is (1) neutral (2) positive (3) negative (4) not able to be determined

28. Two point charges attract each other with a force of 8.0×10^{-5} newton. If the distance between the charges is doubled, the force will become (1) 16×10^{-5} newton (2) 2.0×10^{-5} newton (3) $64. \times 10^{-5}$ newton (4) 4.0×10^{-5} newton

29. A volt is defined as a (1) joule/coulomb (2) joule/second (3) coulomb /second (4) joule-second/coulomb

30. The two large metal plates shown in the diagram are charged to a potential difference of 100 volts. How much work is needed to move 1 coulomb of negative charge from point *A* to point *B*? (1) 1 joule (2) 100 joules (3) 1 electron-volt (4) 100 electron-volts

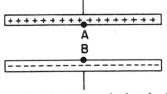

31. Which diagram best represents the relationship between the length of a metal conductor and its resistance?

32. If the potential difference across a 30.-ohm resistor is 10. volts, what is the current through the resistor? (1) 0.25 amp. (2) 0.33 amp. (3) 3.0 amp. (4) 0.50 amp.

33. The diagram at right represents an electric circuit. If the voltage between A and B is 10 volts, the voltage between B and C is (1) 5 volts (2) 10 volts (3) 15 volts (4) 20 volts

34. Three equal resistances are connected in parallel across a battery. Compared to the power dissipated in one resistance, the power supplied by the battery is (1) one-ninth as great (2) one-third as great (3) three times as great (4) nine times as great

35. The algebraic sum of all the potential drops and applied voltages around a complete circuit is equal to zero. This is an application of the law of conservation of (1) mass (2) energy (3) charge (4) momentum

36. A 120-volt toaster is rated at 600 watts. Under normal conditions, the current in the toaster is (1) 0.20 amp. (2) 5.0 amp. (3) 10. amp. (4) 25 amp.

37. In Rutherford's scattering experiments with thin metal foil, most of the alpha particles were deflected through very small angles. This indicated that the atomic nucleus is (1) very small in size (2) positively charged (3) negatively charged (4) neutral

38. Which phenomenon is evidence of the quantum nature of light? (1) interference (2) diffraction (3) polarization (4) photoelectric effect

39. Which color light has photons of the greatest energy? (1) red (2) yellow (3) green (4) blue

40. A lithium nucleus contains 3 protons and 4 neutrons. What is the atomic number of the nucleus? (1) 1 (2) 7 (3) 3 (4) 4

41. The energy needed to ionize a hydrogen atom in the ground state is (1) 2.9 e.v. (2) 3.2 e.v. (3) 13.06 e.v. (4) 13.6 e.v.

Note that questions 42 through 60 have only three choices.

42. Two forces are in equilibrium at an angle of 180 degrees. If one force increases in magnitude while the other force decreases, their resultant (1) decreases (2) increases (3) remains the same

43. A constant force is exerted on a box as shown in the diagram. As angle θ decreases to $0°$, the magnitude of the horizontal component of the force (1) decreases (2) increases (3) remains the same

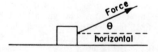

44. An object rests on an incline. As the angle between the incline and the horizontal increases, the force needed to prevent the object from sliding down the incline (1) decreases (2) increases (3) remains the same

45. As a space ship from earth goes toward the moon, the force it exerts on the earth (1) decreases (2) increases (3) remains the same

46. When water at $10°$ Celsius is heated to $20°$ Celsius, its internal energy (1) decreases (2) increases (3) remains the same

47. When a rising baseball encounters air resistance, its total mechanical energy (1) decreases (2) increases (3) remains the same

48. As a wave enters a medium of higher refractive index, its wavelength (1) decreases (2) increases (3) remains the same

49. As the frequency of a wave increases, its period (1) decreases (2) increases (3) remains the same

50. A pulse traveling along a stretched spring is reflected from the fixed end. Compared to the pulse's speed before reflection, its speed after reflection is (1) less (2) greater (3) the same

51. As the frequency of an electromagnetic wave increases, its speed in a vacuum (1) decreases (2) increases (3) remains the same

52. A rod is rubbed with wool. Immediately after the rod and wool have been separated, the net charge of the rod-wool system (1) decreases (2) increases (3) remains the same

53. As the electric field intensity at a point in space decreases, the electrostatic force on a unit charge at this point (1) decreases (2) increases (3) remains the same

54. As the temperature of a coil of copper wire increases, its electrical resistance (1) decreases (2) increases (3) remains the same

55. A resistor is connected to a source of constant voltage. If a lamp is connected in parallel with the resistor, the potential difference across the resistor will (1) decrease (2) increase (3) remain the same

56. A straight conductor in a magnetic field is perpendicular to the lines of force. If the current in the conductor increases, the magnetic force exerted on it (1) decreases (2) increases (3) remains the same

57. As the binding energy of a nucleus increases, the energy required to separate it into nucleons (1) decreases (2) increases (3) remains the same

58. As the mass number of an isotope increases, its atomic number (1) decreases (2) increases (3) remains the same

59. As the speed of an electron increases, its wavelength (1) decreases (2) increases (3) remains the same

60. As the intensity of monochromatic light on a photoemissive surface increases, the maximum kinetic energy of the photoelectrons emitted (1) decreases (2) increases (3) remains the same

Part II
This part consists of four groups, each group testing a major area of the course. Choose two of these four groups. Write your answers in the spaces provided on the separate answer sheet.

Group 1—Mechanics
Answer all fifteen questions, 61 through 75, in this group. Each question counts 1 credit. For each of the fifteen questions, write the number of the word or expression that best completes that statement or answers that question.

Base your answers to questions 61 through 63 on the graph and information at right.

Cars A and B both start from rest at the same location at the same time.

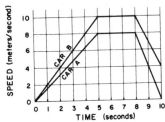

61. What is the magnitude of the acceleration of car A during the period between $t = 8$ seconds and $t = 10$ seconds? (1) 20 m./sec.^{2} (2) 16 m./sec.^{2} (3) 8 m./sec.^{2} (4) 4 m./sec.^{2}

Note that questions 62 and 63 have only three choices.

62. Compared to the speed of car B at 6 seconds, the speed of car A at 6 seconds is (1) less (2) greater (3) the same

63. Compared to the total distance traveled by car B during the 10 seconds, the total distance traveled by car A is (1) less (2) greater (3) the same

Base your answers to questions 64 through 66 on the information below and the diagram which represents the moon in circular orbit around the earth.

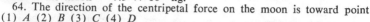

Mass of the earth = 6.0×10^{24} kg.
Mass of the moon = 7.3×10^{23} kg.

64. The direction of the centripetal force on the moon is toward point (1) A (2) B (3) C (4) D

65. If an astronaut has a mass of 91 kilograms on the earth, his mass on the moon would be (1) 11 kg. (2) 45 kg. (3) 70 kg. (4) 91 kg.

66. Compared to the force of the earth on the moon, the magnitude of the force of the moon on the earth is (1) 10^{-2} as great (2) the same (3) 10^1 as great (4) 10^2 as great

Base your answers to questions 67 through 69 on the information below.

A 2.0-kilogram mass is pushed along a horizontal frictionless surface by a 3.0-newton force which is parallel to the surface.

67. The weight of the mass is approximately (1) 9.8 nt. (2) 2.0 nt. (3) 20 nt. (4) 4.0 nt.

68. How much work is done in moving the mass 1.5 meters horizontally? (1) 4.5 joules (2) 2.0 joules (3) 3.0 joules (4) 30. joules

69. How much gravitational potential energy would be gained by the mass if it is moved 2 meters horizontally? (1) 0 joules (2) 6 joules (3) 40 joules (4) 4 joules

70. Which substance has the highest specific heat? (1) copper (sol.) (2) ammonia (liq.) (3) water (liq.) (4) steam (gas)

71. Equal amounts of heat energy are added to 1 kilogram of lead and 1 kilogram of metal X. If the increase in temperature for metal X is one-half the temperature increase for the lead, then metal X could be (1) iron (2) tungsten (3) zinc (4) silver

72. How many kilocalories of heat are needed to raise the temperature of one kilogram of platinum from 500° C. to 600° C.? (1) 3,000 (2) 100 (3) 3 (4) 30

73. If equal masses of the metals listed were at an initial temperature of 100° C., which metal would require the most heat to reach a temperature of 200° C.? (1) silver (2) lead (3) aluminum (4) iron

74. Which graph best represents the change of phase of a substance?

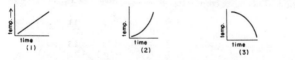

75. If the pressure on a gas is doubled and its absolute temperature is halved, the volume of the gas will be (1) quartered (2) doubled (3) unchanged (4) halved

Group 2—Wave Phenomena
Answer all fifteen questions, 76 through 90, in this group. Each question counts 1 credit. For each of the fifteen questions, write the number of the word or expression that best completes that statement or answers that question.

Base your answers to questions 76 through 78 on the diagram below, which represents periodic water waves in a ripple tank. The speed of a wave decreases as it moves from the deep to the shallow portion of the tank.

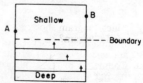

76. Which drawing best represents the waves after they enter the shallow section?

77. Which diagram best represents the pattern produced when the waves are reflected from the boundary between the deep and shallow sections of the ripple tank?

78. If a barrier is placed in the ripple tank connecting points *A* and *B*, which drawing best represents the waves after reflection from the barrier?

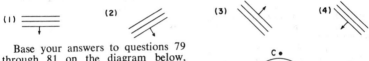

Base your answers to questions 79 through 81 on the diagram below, which shows a vibrating source moving at a constant speed, producing the wave pattern shown.

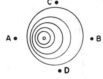

79. The above diagram illustrates (1) interference (2) diffraction (3) the Doppler effect (4) polarization

80. The source is moving toward point (1) *A* (2) *B* (3) *C* (4) *D*

81. If the source were to accelerate, the wavelength immediately in front of the source would (1) increase, only (2) decrease, only (3) increase and then decrease (4) remain the same

Base your answers to questions 82 through 87 on the information below.

A ray of monochromatic orange light passes into a glass tank containing a lucite block that is submerged in a liquid. The wavelength of the light in air is 6.0×10^{-7} meter.

82. Which diagram shows the path that the light could follow if the liquid were benzene?

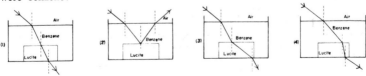

83. Which diagram shows the path that the light could follow if the liquid were Canada balsam?

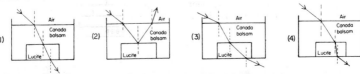

84. What is the frequency of the light? (1) 1.5×10^1 c.p.s. (2) 9.0×10^{14} c.p.s. (3) 2.0×10^{16} c.p.s. (4) 5.0×10^{14} c.p.s.
Note that questions 85 through 87 have only three choices.

85. If angle θ_1 in the diagram at the right were increased, angle θ_2 would (1) decrease (2) increase (3) remain the same

86. As the frequency of the incident light is increased in the diagram for question 85, angle θ_2 would (1) decrease (2) increase (3) remain the same

87. If the lucite block were removed from the tank at the right, angle θ_3 would (1) decrease (2) increase (3) remain the same

Base your answers to questions 88 through 90 on the diagram below, which shows a crown glass lens mounted on an axis. The focal length (f) of the lens is 0.30 meter.

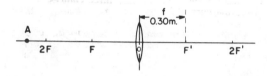

88. If the object is placed between the focal point and the lens, the image formed will be (1) virtual, enlarged, erect (2) virtual, smaller, erect (3) real, smaller, inverted (4) real, enlarged, erect
89. An object placed 0.40 meter from the lens produces an image located 1.20 meters from the lens. If the size of the object is 0.05 meter, the size of the image will be (1) 0.03 m. (2) 0.05 m. (3) 0.15 m. (4) 0.20 m.
90. If an object is placed at point A, an image will be formed (1) between O and F' (2) at F' (3) between F' and $2F'$ (4) beyond $2F'$

Group 3—Electricity
Answer all fifteen questions, 91 through 105, in this group. Each question counts 1 credit. For each of the fifteen questions, write the number of the word or expression that best completes that statement or answers that question.

Base your answers to questions 91 through 95 on the diagram at right which shows three small metal spheres with different charges.

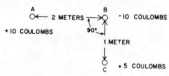

91. Which vector best represents the net force on sphere B?

92. Compared to the force between spheres A and B, the force between spheres B and C is (1) one-quarter as great (2) twice as great (3) one-half as great (4) four times as great

Note that questions 93 through 95 have only three choices.

93. If sphere A is moved further to the left, the magnitude of the net force on sphere B would (1) decrease (2) increase (3) remain the same

94. If the charge on sphere B were decreased, the magnitude of the net force on sphere B would (1) decrease (2) increase (3) remain the same

95. If sphere B were removed, the force of sphere C on sphere A would (1) decrease (2) increase (3) remain the same

Base your answers to questions 96 through 100 on the circuit diagram at right.

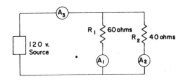

96. The effective resistance of the circuit is (1) 600 ohms (2) 100 ohms (3) 24 ohms (4) 20 ohms

97. The reading of ammeter A_1 is (1) 5 amp. (2) 2 amp. (3) 3 amp. (4) 8 amp.

Note that questions 98 and 99 have only three choices.

98. Compared to the current in ammeter A_3, the sum of the currents in A_1 and A_2 is (1) greater (2) less (3) the same

99. If a third resistor is connected in parallel to the circuit, the total resistance will (1) decrease (2) increase (3) remain the same

100. If a third resistor were connected in parallel to this circuit, the potential difference across the third resistor would be (1) 20 volts (2) 40 volts (3) 60 volts (4) 120 volts

Base your answers to questions 101 through 105 on the diagram below, which shows a circuit containing a solenoid with an iron core.

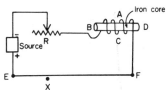

101. The north pole of the solenoid is nearest to point (1) A (2) B (3) C (4) D

102. The direction of the magnetic field caused by conductor EF at point X is (1) into the page (2) out of the page (3) to the left (4) to the right

Note that questions 103 through 105 have only three choices.

103. If the resistance of the variable resistor R is decreased, the magnetic field strength of the solenoid will (1) decrease (2) increase (3) remain the same

104. If the iron core is removed, the magnetic field strength in the solenoid will (1) decrease (2) increase (3) remain the same

105. If the number of turns in the coil is increased and the current kept constant, the magnetic field strength of the solenoid will (1) decrease (2) increase (3) remain the same

Group 4—Atomic and Nuclear Physics
Answer all fifteen questions, 106 through 120, in this group. Each question counts 1 credit. For each of the fifteen questions, write the number of the word or expression that best completes that statement or answers that question.

Base your answers to questions 106 through 108 on the graph below which shows the maximum kinetic energy of the photoelectrons ejected when photons of different frequencies strike a metal surface.

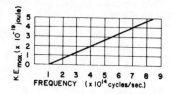

106. Which is the lowest frequency photon that will produce photoelectrons? (1) 0 c.p.s. (2) 1.0 c.p.s. (3) 1.0×10^{14} c.p.s. (4) 1.5×10^{14} c.p.s.

107. Photons with a frequency of 4×10^{14} c.p.s. will produce photoelectrons with a maximum kinetic energy of (1) 4.0×10^{14} joules (2) 1.3 joules (3) 1.3×10^{-19} joule (4) 2.0×10^{-19} joule

Note that question 108 has only three choices.

108. Compared to the energy of the bombarding photon, the energy of the emitted photoelectron is (1) less (2) greater (3) the same

109. The energy change is greatest for a hydrogen atom which changes state from (1) $n = 2$ to $n = 1$ (2) $n = 3$ to $n = 2$ (3) $n = 4$ to $n = 3$ (4) $n = 5$ to $n = 4$

110. What is the energy of the emitted photon when a hydrogen atom changes from an energy state of $n = 5$ to $n = 4$? (1) 13.06 electron-volts (2) 1.39 electron-volts (3) 0.54 electron-volt (4) 0.31 electron-volt

111. A 14-electron-volt photon ionizes a hydrogen atom in its ground state. What is the kinetic energy of the ejected electron? (1) 27.6 electron-volts (2) 14.0 electron-volts (3) 13.6 electron-volts (4) 0.4 electron-volt

112. Which device could be used to determine if a substance is radioactive? (1) Van de Graaff generator (2) Geiger counter (3) cyclotron (4) linear accelerator

113. How many neutrons are in the nucleus of ^{214}Pb? (1) 296 (2) 214 (3) 132 (4) 82

114. When a nucleus emits a gamma ray, its charge will (1) decrease by one (2) decrease by two (3) remain unchanged (4) increase by one

115. In the fusion reaction $^3_1H + ^2_1H \rightarrow ^4_2He + X +$ energy, X is (1) a proton (2) a neutron (3) an alpha particle (4) a beta particle

116. As one atom of U-238 changes to U-234, there is an emission of (1) one alpha particle, only (2) one beta particle, only (3) one alpha and two beta particles (4) three beta particles

117. Which atom has a stable nucleus? (1) ^{234}Th (2) ^{218}Po (3) ^{210}Pb (4) ^{206}Pb

118. ^{222}Rn decays directly into (1) ^{218}At (2) ^{218}Po (3) ^{222}Po (4) ^{218}Rn

119. A hydrogen atom emits blue light when it changes from the $n = 4$ energy level to the $n = 2$ energy level. Which color of light would the atom emit when it changes from the $n = 5$ level to the $n = 2$ level? (1) red (2) yellow (3) green (4) violet

120. When $^{226}_{88}$Ra emits an alpha particle, what will be the atomic number of the resulting nucleus? (1) 86 (2) 88 (3) 222 (4) 226

bg. 7   1-28

Pg. 136-7

Subject	Date	Time
English		
Physics	Wed June 20	1:00
Math 12	Fri. June 15	8:30